The
Eloquent Body

The
Eloquent Body

Dance and Humanist Culture in
Fifteenth-Century Italy

Jennifer Nevile

Indiana
University
Press

BLOOMINGTON AND INDIANAPOLIS

This book is a publication of

Indiana University Press
601 North Morton Street
Bloomington, IN 47404-3797 USA

http://iupress.indiana.edu

Telephone orders   800-842-6796
Fax orders   812-855-7931
Orders by e-mail   iuporder@indiana.edu

MANUFACTURED IN THE UNITED STATES OF AMERICA

Library of Congress Cataloging-in-Publication Data

Nevile, Jennifer.
The eloquent body : dance and humanist culture in fifteenth-century Italy / Jennifer
Nevile.
p.   cm.
Includes bibliographical references and index.
ISBN 0-253-34453-0 (cloth : alk. paper)
1. Dance—Social aspects—Italy—History—15th century.
2. Humanism—Italy—History—15th century.   3. Dance—Italy—History—15th
century.   I. Title.
GV1588.6.N48 2004
306.4'846'094509024—dc22
2004002131

1 2 3 4 5 09 08 07 06 05 04

To the two Tims—T. W. and T. M.

Contents

Acknowledgments

The idea for this book originated over a decade ago, and since then its scope has grown considerably. During these years I have been fortunate to receive assistance in various ways from friends and colleagues, to whom I owe a deep debt of gratitude. It is my pleasure to acknowledge their help and encouragement here, as a small recompense for their efforts.

The manuscript was read in its entirety in its various stages by Mary Chan, Timothy McGee, and John O. Ward. Their comments and suggestions greatly strengthened the structure and flow of the argument, and sharpened the focus of the study. Their varying fields of expertise meant that errors both large and small were eliminated, and any that remain are solely the responsibility of the author. All three were very generous with their time, and in their belief in and continuing support of the project. Their efforts in this regard are deeply appreciated.

While the community of dance history scholars worldwide is not large, it is a true community, and I would like to thank Katherine McGinnis, Barbara Sparti, and David Wilson in particular for their prompt replies to my many questions, e-mails, and letters over the years, asking their opinion on contentious issues. I have also been fortunate to have had the opportunity to spend time with Alessandro Arcangeli, the late Ingrid Brainard, Andrea Budgey, Diana Cruickshank, Yvonne Kendall, Barbara Ravelhofer, Randall Rosenfeld, Barbara Segal, Jennifer Thorp, and Bill Tuck, discussing problems in early dance research and reconstruction in general, and fifteenth-century Italian dance in particular.

Dance and music were inseparable in *quattrocento* Italy, and this study has benefited greatly from my dialogue with the musicologist John Caldwell, as well as from the advice of David Fallows.

Giovanni Carsaniga provided invaluable help with the translations of the fifteenth-century Italian sources, and his elegant and lucid translation of the description of the 1459 Florentine ball adds immeasurably to this book. I would also like to thank Roberto Pettini, a dear friend, who over many years has always been willing to advise on translation problems with Italian sources, and to enter into my enthusiasms for this period in Italian history. I would like to record my thanks to Deirdre Stone for her translation of the twelfth-century Latin passage in chapter 3.

Graham Pont, whom I first met twenty years ago when I was a young and inexperienced scholar, has been a continuing source of inspiration for his pushing the boundaries of traditional academic disciplines, and for his dragging me into a realization of the crucial importance of ancient Greek thought to the intellectual, and artistic, culture of fifteenth-century Italy.

The Inter-Library Loan staff and the Social Sciences and Humanities librarians at the University of New South Wales Library never complained at the volume of requests for manuscripts and obscure sources that they received, and it is partly due to their efforts that the UNSW Library now has such a good collection of pre-eighteenth-century dance history material. I would also like to thank Suzanne Meyers Sawa, Assistant Librarian at the Faculty of Music Library, University of Toronto, for her assistance in lending a microfilm copy of the MS Magl. VII 1121, and Edward Forgács for encoding the music in appendix 3 into the computer program Finale.

This book would never have happened without the love and support, both emotional and financial, of my husband, Tim Wooller. He read and reread the manuscript in every stage of its long evolution, and was forced to become an expert in topics such as the use of mensuration signs in the fifteenth century, topics remote from his day-to-day expertise and interests. His clarity of thought and ruthlessly logical criticisms contributed to what is, I hope, the lucidity of the final manuscript. Tim, this book is for you.

The
Eloquent Body

Introduction

[T]he courtier must acquire this grace from those who appear to possess it. . . .

However, having already thought a great deal about how this grace is acquired, and leaving aside those who are endowed with it by their stars, I have discovered a universal rule which seems to apply more than any other in all human actions or words: namely, to steer away from affectation at all costs, as if it were a rough and dangerous reef, and (to use perhaps a novel word for it) to practise in all things a certain nonchalance which conceals all artistry and makes whatever one says or does seem uncontrived and effortless. I am sure that grace springs especially from this. . . . Similarly in dancing, a single step, a single unforced and graceful movement of the body, at once demonstrates the skill of the dancer. . . . Our courtier, therefore, will be judged to be perfect and will show grace in everything, . . . if he shuns affectation.[1]

For Castiglione, author of *Il libro del cortegiano*, the necessity for a courtier to be skilled in the art of dance was without question. The ability to perform gracefully, seemingly without any effort, was one of the distinguishing marks of a courtier and the absence of this ability exposed a gentleman or lady to ridicule and derision from colleagues:

Who is there among you who doesn't laugh when our Pierpaolo dances in that way of his, with those little jumps and with his legs stretched on tiptoe, keeping his head motionless, as if he were made of wood, and all so laboured that he seems to be counting every step?[2]

Even though Castiglione was writing his book at the court of Urbino during the second decade of the sixteenth century, his depiction of life at one of the most renowned literary and artistic centers of his day was a retrospective one. The values he articulated in *The Book of the Courtier* reflected the values held by Italian elite society of the previous century. Correct bearing, carriage, and manner of moving, engendered by years of dance training, were important social skills, since the posture when dancing was a courtier's natural way of moving. It was not a posture adopted only while performing a dance and then cast aside when the performance was over. The rules according to which courtiers were expected to move on the dance floor applied to every other part of their lives: a noble and temperate bearing helped to distinguish them from those who did not belong to the elite. Thus the instruction the young children of the nobility received from the *maestri di ballo* was extremely important socially and ethically, as it not only allowed them to obtain approbation when they exhibited their skills in the dance, but also trained them in the patterns of behavior and deportment essential for membership in the social elite. If you moved ungracefully, you immediately demonstrated to others that you did not belong to the right class in society, as you could not perform properly the movement patterns appropriate to that class. As a consequence, you appeared foolish, and would certainly not obtain recognition or esteem in the best circles.

Clumsiness had other implications as well. Movements of the body were believed to be the outward manifestation of movements of the soul. Consequently, if the movements of the body were ungraceful, then the movements of the soul would be presumed to be similarly ugly and inharmonious. The movements of the body would be an outward manifestation of a soul that was full of vice, corrupt, ugly and bad. The belief that movements of the soul are manifest through movements of the body partly accounts for the strong attacks made on the dances of the peasants, and the efforts made by the dance masters to differentiate their noble art from the corrupt and ignoble dances of the poor. The dances of the peasants were condemned not only for their vulgar movements, but also because those performing such movements exposed to others the baser nature of their souls.

The dance practice of the elite section of *quattrocento* Italian society had an intellectual and philosophical framework: it was not just a set of physical skills. The dance masters were fully aware that for dance to be included (through its association with music) in the liberal arts, it had to be understood both on a physical level and at an intellectual level. If dance was a liberal art it could then lay claim to be a demonstration of eternal truths, a microcosm of the cosmos, as was its sister and progenitor music. Their argument, that it was essential to understand the art of dance through the intellect, was another way in which the dance masters separated their dance practice from the dances of the poorer sections of society. The latter were often condemned as excuses for riotous and lewd behavior, lacking any desirable moral effects. In order for dance to be a demonstration of eternal truths, mere physical movement was not sufficient. The movements had to be understandable at an intellectual level, and based on the appropriate framework. Only this could produce the necessary virtuous movements, rather than morally repugnant ones.

Dance was far more socially acceptable to those in the ruling elite as an intellectual activity than as only a set of physical skills. The intellectual framework moved dance closer to the humanist belief that an education in the *studia humanitatis* was essential for those entrusted with the governance of the state; that is, those in the ruling section of society had to have a sufficient intellectual understanding and knowledge of the human condition that their exercise of power was restrained by virtue and ideas of the common good. In order to govern wisely, the ruling elite had to have the appropriate intellectual training and skills.

In this book I will examine the place of dance in elite society in fifteenth-century Italy and in particular the development of dance as an art, that is, as a practice to be understood through the mind. I will demonstrate how dance interacted with contemporary intellectual concerns, in particular those generated by the humanist movement. Through the use of choreographic evidence—the dances themselves—and the ideas presented in the three dance treatises written during this period, I will show how the dance masters, like practitioners in other fields of artistic endeavor,[3] reacted to, used, and applied the knowledge generated by the humanist movement. The dance masters belonged to the same world as the humanists, and shared similar concerns. Both were concerned to use their special knowledge (the former in dance, the latter in classical scholarship) to bolster and preserve the existing power structures and modes of social organization. Both groups were also eager to use the authority of ancient Greek and Latin

authors to support their own position and intellectual standing in
the world of the Italian courts. Even though it may not always be
possible to show a direct influence, or a causal relationship between
the dance masters and their choreographic work and the work of
the humanists, the dance masters shared humanist ideas and attitudes because these ideas and attitudes were part of the common
currency and intellectual climate of the age.

Part of the picture I am describing here is not new. Many
scholars have written on the humanist movement in fifteenth-
century Italy and its effect on the intellectual culture in Italy and
elsewhere in Europe. But dance has never been a part of this picture. Even though dance has a long history in human societies,
often forming part of religious worship and serving as a means of
human communication with and understanding of the divine, it has
not enjoyed a similar status in the "artificial" society of academic
discourse. It is only in the last twenty years that scholarly research
into the dance practice of Western Europe prior to the twentieth
century has burgeoned. But dance in Western Europe, as in all
other cultures around the world, did not take place in a vacuum.
As a cultural phenomenon it participated in, and was influenced
by, other contemporary artistic practices, intellectual movements,
social conditions, and philosophical enquiries. Placing dance in its
wider socio-historical context is the second step in the maturation
of dance research as a scholarly discipline, and is only beginning
to be attempted by dance historians. Similarly, other academic discipline groups, such as social historians, are not yet entirely convinced that the study of dance is relevant to their concerns. The
late arrival of dance into the network of academic discourse has
meant that dance usually does not figure in histories of early modern Western societies. The Italian early Renaissance is no exception. For these reasons, when Paul Oskar Kristeller and other major scholars of Renaissance humanism asserted that humanism
influenced, either directly or indirectly, all areas of Renaissance
civilization, they did not mention dance. The following passage
from Kristeller is typical:

> [T]he classical humanism of the Italian Renaissance can be shown
> to be a very significant phenomenon in the history of Western
> civilization. . . . [A]lthough the movement was in its origin liter-
> ary and scholarly, it came to affect . . . all other areas of Renais-
> sance civilization, in Italy as well as elsewhere: its art and music,

its science and theology, and even its legal and political theory and practice.[4]

Even in more recent scholarship the result is the same. For example, the three-volume work *Renaissance Humanism: Foundations, Forms, and Legacy*, published in 1988, has chapters on humanism and art, humanism and music, humanism and science, humanism and rhetoric, grammar, poetics, and history, humanism and philosophy in all its manifestations, and humanism in the major centers of fifteenth-century Italy.[5] But dance is silently passed over, a ghostly or invisible part of society, an artistic practice of marginal interest and one which is so ephemeral that it can easily be forgotten or ignored. But dance in fifteenth-century Italy was much more than an ephemeral, insignificant practice. It was woven into the fabric of *quattrocento* Italian life in a way that is difficult for us to appreciate today. My aim in this book is to integrate discussions of the intellectual concerns of the humanists with information about the dance practice of the time in a manner that is accessible to readers from a range of scholarly disciplines.

The Italian peninsula in the fifteenth century included a number of different political systems: from republics like Venice and Florence, to ducal or princely courts such as Ferrara, Mantua, Milan, and Naples, to Rome, which was governed by the papal court and its ecclesiastical hierarchy. Whatever the system of government, the families at the top of the social pyramid were those who held political power. It is the dance practice of this group that was recorded in the treatises, and which will be dealt with in this book. The terms "noble" and "courtly" describe these families who enjoyed high social rank, regardless of whether their members held the title of king or prince, duke or count. It is these families who employed the dance masters and participated in the dance performances at important public and state festivities, and to whom were dedicated a number of the surviving dance treatises. The authors of these dance treatises were all *maestri di ballo*: men who taught dancing, choreographed dances for the important celebrations, and performed with the members of the upper strata of society in these same spectacles. The dances they recorded in their treatises, and which form the basis of this study, were for both men and women, and for more than one person. Single-sex dances were a part of the dance culture of the time, but they were not recorded in the treatises.[6] Improvised dances, another aspect of fifteenth-

century Italian practice, are also excluded from this study for the
simple reason that their choreographies were not written down.[7]

Dance teaching in Italy in the fifteenth century was not confined solely to the authors of the dance treatises. Evidence has
survived of other dance teachers, who worked both at the courts[8]
and in the cities, teaching the children of the middle-ranking merchant classes.[9] Fashions in dances changed, with the noble patrons
always demanding the newest and latest compositions. But dances
that had been performed at a court wedding could have been
taught, five to ten years later, to a merchant's daughter by a town
musician who also taught dance.[10] In the last few years more evidence has come to light that points to a wider spectrum of dance
activity than was thought one to two decades ago. Dance is now
seen to have been taught to members of society from a number of
levels, not just those in the positions of power, and the teachers
themselves came from a variety of social backgrounds. While
pointing readers to studies that discuss the wider scope of dance
activity in Italy at this time, this book does not concentrate on this
aspect of the topic.[11] The basis of this study is the written records
of the dance masters, both choreographic and theoretical. While
dance historians have unearthed the names of, and economic data
on, an increasing number of dance teachers, so far there is no
evidence of their having written dance treatises, as did the three
maestri di ballo discussed here: Domenico da Piacenza, Antonio
Cornazano, and Guglielmo Ebreo da Pesaro.[12]

Geographical Limits

In this work I concentrate on fifteenth-century Italy because it
is from this country and this period that the earliest choreographic
records have survived. These treatises contain not only a large
number of choreographic descriptions (and some music) but also
a theoretical section that provides the philosophical justification for
dancing, lists the principles necessary for a good dancer, and briefly
describes the steps used. Other parts of Europe at this time also
had flourishing dance cultures, with members of the nobility performing at important state occasions. But the theoretical and literary orientation of dance was nowhere near as strong in England,
Spain, Germany, France, and Burgundy as it was in Italy. The few
treatises that have survived from these countries are far closer to
simple compilations of choreographies than to the sophisticated

treatises produced by the Italians. Even the French *basse danse* treatises, the next most substantial body of choreographic material from the period, are much later, mainly coming from the late fifteenth or early sixteenth century,[13] although the dance material they represent was being performed from the middle of the fifteenth century at the French and Burgundian courts.[14] These works are far closer to practical "self-help" manuals than to the Italian treatises. The French works contain choreographies, instructions on how to perform the five steps of the *basse danse* and on how to arrange these five steps in different combinations or *mesures*. But these French sources do not name any dance masters, nor do they make any attempt to place the *basse danse* practice within the contemporary intellectual framework. They make no attempt to link this dance practice with other artistic practices, not even dance practices from other countries, nor does the text of the treatises show any consciousness of the milieu in which these dances were performed.

The sole surviving source for a specifically English dance practice in the fifteenth century is a similar collection of choreographies and tunes.[15] The dance material forms part of a small pocketbook obviously intended for personal use rather than for presentation, and it is perhaps unreasonable to expect a philosophical justification from such a work. Nevertheless, the names of English dance masters only start appearing in the official records in the sixteenth century, not in the fifteenth century as in Italy.[16] While it is impossible to know how much choreographic material was recorded in fifteenth-century England and how much was subsequently lost or destroyed, so far no substantial body of choreographic material with a large theoretical section in the Italian tradition has been discovered. Thus, this study concentrates on Italy, where humanist concerns first emerged as a subject for serious discussion among the intellectual and political elites, and where the first dance treatises with a substantial theoretical component were written.

Chronological Scope

The three dance masters who wrote treatises were active during the forty years from the 1430s onward, while their treatises were all written (in one version at least) by the mid-1460s. These decades saw a flowering of this art, with festivities, both private and

state, providing many opportunities for performances by members
of the elite. The intellectual climate that influenced these men,
therefore, was the world that was dominated by such men as Leonardo Bruni, Vittorino da Feltre, Lorenzo Valla, Guarino Guarini, and Leon Battista Alberti, public figures who were influential
in the literary, philosophical, artistic, and political affairs of the first
half of the fifteenth century. It was in a world dominated by the
concerns and preoccupations of men such as these that the dance
masters lived and worked, adapting their choreographies and professional activities to the intellectual agenda set out by Alberti and
his colleagues. The nobility's enjoyment of dance and its presence
at important state occasions were not sudden innovations in the
1430s with the activities of Domenico. It was present and significant much earlier, in the thirteenth and fourteenth centuries. The
material considered in this book, therefore, while concentrating on
the fifteenth century, will also include sources from the two previous centuries, in order to illustrate the omnipresent part dance
played in aristocratic life in both Italy and Northern Europe.[17]

Chapter 1 discusses the interaction between dance and the upper levels of society in fifteenth-century Italy, exploring both the
personal links between the dance masters and the humanists and
the part dance played in the humanists' education curriculum.
Chapter 1 also sets out the characteristics both of the dances recorded in the treatises, the *ballo* and the *bassadanza*, and of the
moresca, which was also performed on important state occasions.
Following this discussion of the choreographic characteristics of
the dance genres is an outline of the social context of the dance
practice, that is, a discussion of where and on what occasions the
choreographies were performed, and who performed them. The
final section of the chapter examines the significance dance had in
elite society in fifteenth-century Italy. The *moresca*, a "theatrical"
genre whose performers were often masked and wearing exotic costumes while representing mythological or allegorical figures, was
used as a sign of communal identity by the various states, while
certain other specific dances, performed at weddings, affirmed fa-
milial ties. Because the dance practice I am discussing in this book
belonged to the elite, it was also part of that section of society's
expression of power. Dance was one of the mechanisms by which,
the elite believed, their superiority was demonstrated to the rest of
society: it was one way their group defined itself and excluded others. Finally, the dance practice at this time also functioned as rit-

ualized courtship. Since the dances recorded in the treatises were for both men and women, their performance provided a rare opportunity for and encouragement of social interaction between aristocratic women and their male peers.

Chapter 2 focuses on the humanist influences on the structure and content of the dance treatises. The most obvious influence on the dance masters was the impulse to write a treatise on dance in the first place. While dance had been part of the aristocratic lifestyle for several centuries, it was not until the text-based approach of the humanists began to permeate society in general that any attempt was made to describe in writing the theoretical foundation of the dance practice, as well as record individual choreographies. Parallels between the dance treatises and humanist treatises on other subjects can be seen in the way both sets of works appealed to ancient authorities to support their arguments, and embraced the dialogue form as a method to structure their work. Furthermore, in an effort to establish a mode of discourse for their dance practice, the dance masters discussed dance using the same concepts as did the humanists in their discussions of painting and sculpture. These concepts, first established by Petrarch, were expressed as contrasting pairs: informed and uninformed viewers, matter and form, sensuous pleasure and useful pleasure, and finally nature and art.

Chapter 3 returns to the theme of language: the spoken and written texts of the humanists, and the kinetic language of the dance masters. Spoken and written expression were passionate concerns of the humanists, since they believed that excellence in language was necessary for the good running of the state. Just as the humanists were concerned with eloquence in their texts, so too were the dance masters concerned to promote eloquence in movements of the human body. The dance masters responded to this preoccupation of the humanists by writing their own treatises on dance, a major part of which was the development of a technical vocabulary with which to better discuss their art. A large part of the new technical vocabulary developed by the dance masters described the nuances of these eloquent movements. In developing this vocabulary the dance masters both used existing everyday terms in new and specialized ways and borrowed and adapted terms from other arts, such as rhetoric and painting.

Moderation in movement was a central component of the dance masters' understanding of eloquent movement. The humanists also stressed such moderation, since it originated in the teachings of Aristotle and in Latin rhetorical texts. In the writings of humanists such as Matteo Palmieri, who discussed the appropriate gestures and movements of a person while walking and standing, moderation in movement was seen as natural, while excessive movement, or lack of movement, was regarded as unnatural, ugly, and a sign of the vices or defects in a person's character. Palmieri, like the dance masters, believed that the nature of a person's soul was revealed by bodily movements and facial expressions. Moderation in movement signified a virtuous soul, a person who was neither dominated by an excess of vice nor skewed by an excessive amount of one particular virtue. Excessive movement, or lack of any movement, was a sign of a soul full of moral defects. Thus, for the fifteenth-century intellectual, dance had the ability to teach ethical behavior. A person watching a dance performance could learn to recognize virtues by observing their physical manifestations. Chapter 3 concludes with a discussion of what constituted virtuous movements in fifteenth-century Italy, as identified by the three dance masters in their treatises and by Leon Battista Alberti in his treatise on painting.

Chapter 4 revolves around the importance of intelligence, or the intellect, to both the dance masters and the humanists. In their treatises the former stressed the importance of intellectually understanding the dance practice, in addition to mastering the required physical skills. The dance masters, especially Domenico, devoted a great deal of attention to setting out the intellectual basis of the art of dance, which had the same numerical basis as music and the other mathematical arts of the quadrivium. According to the dance masters, dance was a path to understanding the nature of God. Since dance shared the numerical basis of the cosmos, it also fostered contemplation of the divine realm. Thus chapter 4 is an extended analysis of how this numerical basis, or proportion (*misura*), manifested itself in the art of dance.

The belief that geometric order led to moral virtue was commonplace in fifteenth-century Italy, and it was shared by the dance masters, as well as by humanists like Leonardo Bruni and Leon Battista Alberti. The implications of this belief for dance, architecture, and garden design are explored in chapter 5, through analyses of Alberti's treatise on architecture, the choreographies created by the dance masters, and the descriptions of the grand gardens of the nobility. Through the use of geometric shapes in their choreographies, the dance masters were constructing a representation of the cosmos, just as the architects were using the geometric forms and proportions found in nature in designing buildings or laying out cities. It was this ordered, geometrical movement in dance that would encourage men and women to imitate the divine order in their own lives through noble and virtuous behavior.

1

Dance and Society

> The harmony in the sweet music of Guglielmo Ebreo is as sweet and heavenly as his fair dancing is elegant. It would make Maccabeus sheathe his sword. His dance comes not from human skill but from heavenly wit and divine knowledge. . . . Eagles on the wing are not so agile as Guglielmo, whose skills may be deemed to have been willed by Fate. Hector was never so outstanding in military prowess as this man is in his art, outstripping all others.[1]

The poem, part of which is quoted above, was written by a humanist in praise of a dance master: not a prince or duke, a political statesman or powerful government bureaucrat, but a dance master. In his ode in praise of Guglielmo Ebreo, Mario Filelfo favorably compares Guglielmo with heroes like Hector, and asserts that Guglielmo is so gifted in the art of dance that his skills must be divinely inspired.[2] The effect of his dancing, which is beautiful in itself, is so powerful that it can influence warriors and philosophers—Maccabeus, Solomon, Socrates, Aristotle, and Plato—and even goddesses such as Diana. Guglielmo indeed excels all others in the practice of his art. The claims that Filelfo makes concerning Guglielmo and the art of dance are bold ones, and echo the stance Guglielmo himself takes in his treatise. Guglielmo was more than a craftsman, a practitioner of the mechanical arts. He was worthy to be compared with respected figures of authority from the ancient world. Filelfo's praise of Guglielmo and his association with the heroes of antiquity is testimony to the latter's fame among the intellectual and courtly world of fifteenth-century Italy. This poem is one of the first examples of the glorification of a living artist, and is comparable to the praise of the virtuoso lutenist and improviser Pietrobono, who was equated with the mythical figure of Orpheus.[3]

Filelfo claimed that Guglielmo's dancing skill came from a source other than human talent, which could be learnt through the passing on of skills from a master to an apprentice. Guglielmo possessed *ingenio*, a creative power that was inborn (given by God) and through which the artist had the vision and intellectual capacity to conceive of the work, as opposed to just carrying it out. *Ingenio* was closely associated with the inventiveness, as opposed to the skill or workmanship (*ars*), of an artist or work of art. By crediting Guglielmo with the gift of *ingenio*, Filelfo was admitting him into an intellectual circle, and claiming that the practice of the art of dance was a way of expressing one's intellectual qualities.

The humanists praised not only each other for possessing both *ars* and *ingenio* but also painters, and so by 1450 the term had become part of the discussion of the arts in Italian writings.[4] For example, Ghiberti in his *Commentari* states that for a work of art to be perfect it must have both *ars* and *ingenio*.[5] It should not be surprising, therefore, that a humanist used the same term to praise Guglielmo, and that the term also became an important part of the theoretical writings on the art of dance.

It is not clear when Guglielmo and Filelfo knew each other, and how close was the association. From the ode we learn that Guglielmo had taught dancing to Filelfo's daughter, Theodora. "He makes many women appear noble and eminent like Diana, even though they are only human. My daughter Theodora is the most recent."[6] The lessons may have taken place while Filelfo was in Milan (from April 1458), as Guglielmo was present in Milan for many of the festivities held there during Francesco Sforza's reign as duke from 1450 to 1466, including a visit in 1459.[7] But whenever the teaching took place, it is clear that the two men knew each other, and that Filelfo saw nothing socially degrading in using his intellectual and literary abilities as a humanist to write a poem in praise of a dance master, nor in associating himself and his work with a treatise on dance. In writing this ode, Filelfo believed that dancing was an accepted part of life at the elite level of society.

For it was the elite level of society that constituted the social world of the dance masters and the humanists in fifteenth-century Italy. Cornazano was born into one of the families of the minor nobility at Piacenza, and his whole life was centered on the courts of northern Italy as a poet, humanist, ambassador, military advisor, and courtier, as well as a skilled dancer and author of a dance treatise. Throughout his life he was involved in literary activities, often modeling his works on classical models.[8] He corresponded with other humanists, in 1471 exchanging Latin and Italian verses with Francesco Filelfo, the father of Mario Filelfo and the leading figure in humanist circles in Milan for forty years.[9] Cornazano's role as courtier and diplomat is illustrated by his inclusion in the ambassadorial party sent to Paris by the duke of Milan, Francesco Sforza, to congratulate Louis XI on his succession to the throne of France. A few years later, in 1465, Cornazano accompanied Ippolita Sforza on her wedding journey to Naples, and in 1479, near the end of his life, he was one of Piacenza's ambassadors to Milan. Domenico spent most of his working life at the d'Este court at Ferrara, where he is referred to in court records by the titles "spectabilis eques" and "spectabilis miles." He was a Knight of the Golden Spur,[10] as was Guglielmo, who was knighted by the Holy Roman Emperor in Venice in 1469. A further indication of Domenico's social standing is the fact that he married into the Trotto family, one of the leading Ferrarese families. Marriage in fifteenth-century Italy was a serious affair that imposed a number of important obligations and duties upon individuals, such as the duty to marry well, which could mean contracting an alliance with a family with a great deal of money or an established lineage. Marriage was looked upon as a means of social advancement for the whole family, and an old family like the Trottos would not wish to step backward by virtue of their marriage alliances. Therefore Domenico could not have been too far below the rank of the Trotto daughter he married.

The humanist movement in fifteenth-century Italy was a movement among the upper levels of Italian society. Whatever the origins of individual humanists, whether they were members of the patriciate like Donato Acciaiuoli or were from more humble social origins like Leonardo Bruni, they undertook their working lives, their ambitions, their marriages, and their social contacts and friendships among the upper levels of society as courtiers, diplomats, or bureaucrats. The humanists did not wish their affiliation with the center of power in society to be questioned. Therefore, they actively identified with the ruling elite, consciously seeking to identity themselves with the philosophers and decision makers of the ancient world. A constant refrain in humanist writings was the fact that Aristotle was the tutor to Alexander the Great, that Plato was involved in teaching the kings of Sicily, and that Cicero played an important and influential role in the public affairs of imperial Rome.[11]

Any discussion of the social position of the dance masters cannot ignore the fact that these men not only taught dancing to the children of the nobility (a private activity) but also performed in public with their patrons' wives, sisters, daughters, and other female relatives. In his working life Domenico not only choreographed dances for weddings and important state functions at the d'Este court and other leading centers in Italy, but he also performed in public as a partner with women from the leading families. In 1455 Francesco Sforza asked Domenico to come to Milan to organize the dances for the wedding of Tristano Sforza, Francesco's illegitimate son, and Beatrice d'Este, the illegitimate daughter of Niccolo III d'Este. On this occasion Domenico not only choreographed and directed several large "ballets," but also participated in the dancing himself.[12] In one of the dances Domenico danced with Bianca Maria Sforza, while the other performers were Galeazzo Maria and Ippolita Sforza (the children of Bianca Maria and Duke Francesco Sforza), the Marchioness Barbara of Mantua and the Marquess Guglielmo of Monferrato, and Beatrice d'Este, who danced with Alessandro Sforza. Ippolita Sforza, daughter of the duke and duchess of Milan, appeared in public on many occasions with her dance teacher Cornazano,[13] and a letter of 1481, when Isabella d'Este was only six, records the fact that she had twice danced with Guglielmo.[14] No members of the patriciate would be prepared to jeopardize their social status by dancing in public with a person from a totally inferior social class. Aristocratic women especially were normally not permitted to dance with men from a lower level in the social hierarchy. Dancers often joined hands, so not only would Bianca Maria or Ippolita Sforza have to appear in public close to her dance master, she would have to have physical contact with him, something that was not an insignificant matter.[15] The physical contact between dance partners would magnify the relationship, however temporary, between them. In an age increasingly conscious of rank and social status, which were indicated by a host of subtle signals, no one would be able to ignore such an obvious sign as physical contact between dance partners. Unlike other participants in festive celebrations, such as musicians, dance masters could not be confined to a box or gallery separate from the courtiers. The very act of exercising their art brought them into physical proximity, if not contact, with members of the leading families in very public situations. Therefore, Domenico and Guglielmo cannot have been vastly inferior in social status to their patrons and pupils, as the Sforza, d'Este, and other ruling families did have a choice in this matter. They could have allowed Domenico or Guglielmo to choreograph the dances that would be performed for a celebratory occasion, learned the dances from them, and performed without the dance masters' participation. The fact that they did not do so points to the higher—rather than lower—social standing of these men.

Dance as an Aristocratic Pastime

Dance did not suddenly become a part of elite behavior with Domenico in the 1430s; it had been part of aristocratic life and civilized behavior in previous centuries. At the beginning of the fourteenth century Siena already had a flourishing dance tradition among the elite. In 1310, on the occasion of the visit of the king of Naples, the official state celebrations included balls held in honor of the royal visitors.[16] The Burgundian knight Geoffroi de Charny, who lived in the first half of the fourteenth century, wrote in his treatise on chivalry that dancing was one of the pastimes that men of knightly rank should pursue if they wished to safeguard their reputation and honor.

> Yet it should be apparent that the finest games and pastimes that people who seek such honor should never tire of engaging in would be in the pastimes of jousting, conversation, dancing, and singing in the company of ladies and damsels as honorably as is possible and fitting, while maintaining in word and deed and in all places their honor and status. All good men-at-arms ought rightly to behave thus. . . . Such pastimes are finer and more honorable and can bring more benefits than can games of dice, through which one can lose one's possessions and one's honor and all good company.[17]

Charny was overwhelmingly concerned with living honorably in one's profession as a knight, and he saw no conflict between participating in dancing and maintaining one's honor. Dancing, as well as conversation and singing in the company of ladies, was a practice entirely appropriate to the status of aristocratic males who had accepted the obligations and duties of the knightly code. This was in direct contrast to such diversions as playing dice for money, which was only fit for "rakes, bawds, and tavern rogues."[18] Dancing was one of the diversions that had a positive effect on the knight, as it stimulated the cultivation of the proper mental attitude for the achieving of great and honorable deeds of chivalry.[19] Dance was seen as civilizing behavior, and was naturally associated with elite groups in society, not the poor and powerless.

The natural alliance between dancing and a patrician lifestyle is found throughout the literature of the fourteenth century. Giovanni Boccaccio's ladies and gentlemen, fleeing plague-stricken Florence in mid-century, arrive at their first country estate: a noble residence set in the middle of gracious gardens. In such an aristocratic setting the company spends a great deal of the mornings and evenings in dancing and singing.

> The sun was already trailing the new day in his wake of light, . . . when with one accord all the ladies and the three young men arose, and entered the gardens. . . . The day passed like its predecessor; they breakfasted in the shade, and danced and slept until noon.[20]

> [T]hen supper-time being come, they supped with all gay and festal cheer. When they were risen from the table, Emilia, at the queen's command, led the dance. . . . Some other songs and dances followed, to the accompaniment of divers sorts of music.[21]

Even such a moralist as Christine de Pisan judged it acceptable that young ladies at court participate in dancing, although always in a courteous, seemly, and modest manner.

> [The wise princess] will want [the ladies of her court] to amuse themselves with decent games. . . . The women should restrain themselves with seemly conduct among knights and squires and all men. They should speak demurely and sweetly and, whether in dances or other amusements, divert and enjoy themselves decorously and without wantonness.[22]

Christine de Pisan wrote *The Treasure of the City of Ladies* in 1405, and it was above all a practical book, a guide for women—mostly those with power and authority—in their everyday life. Thus as far as Christine was concerned dancing was a normal part of court life, and an activity that was entirely suitable for aristocratic women. From the large number of references in thirteenth-century French literature to dancing in courtly settings by aristocratic performers, it is clear that dancing was a normal part of court life even in the century before Christine de Pisan wrote this work.[23] Thus by the time Domenico, Guglielmo, and Cornazano had begun writing their dance treatises, patrician dancing had been a tradition for over two centuries.

In Dante's (1265–1321) *Divine Comedy* dancing nearly always is associated with moments of religious revelation. The souls of the damned in hell are depicted as dancing without ceasing,[24] but that is the one reference to dance, apart from David's dancing before the Ark of the Covenant,[25] until the climax of the journey through Purgatory.[26] From this point on dancing is part of the continuing revelation of God's love and wisdom. In the journey through Paradise dance is encountered with increasing frequency, with all the souls of the blessed and all the angelic host revolving, circling, and praising their creator.[27]

The diaries of the Florentine merchant class also reveal that dancing was a normal part of aristocratic life in the fourteenth century. In 1380 the Florentine Buonaccorso Pitti, international merchant and professional gambler, found himself in France. After a short sojourn in Paris he moved to Brussels in order to gamble with the duke of Brabant, who, with many other great gentlemen, was diverting himself with "tournaments, jousting, dancing and the gaming tables."[28] Pitti describes how one evening

> [t]he Duke and a group of gentlemen rose and went into another room where many ladies and gentlemen were dancing and, as I stood enjoying the spectacle, a young unmarried beauty, the daughter of a great baron, came over to me and said: "Come and dance, Lombard, don't fret over your losses for God will surely help you." Then she led me onto the floor.[29]

Therefore, by the 1430s when Domenico began his career as choreographer and dancing master, there was an established tradition of dance within the elite level of society. Dance had its critics (many of whom were from the clergy) who condemned dance as a path to sexual license,[30] while other writers saw it as a "worldly vanity" and a form of madness.[31] The differing attitudes toward dance that existed at the time among different groups in society can also be seen in individuals.[32] Alfonso, king of Naples, regarded dancing as having an intoxicating effect, and therefore it was something to be avoided. Yet he greatly enjoyed watching others dance; he appreciated their skills, and when protocol demanded it, Alfonso would even participate in the dancing himself.[33] In spite of the disapproval, or even condemnation, of dance by some sections of society, by the mid-fifteenth century dance composition, not just performance, was an accepted part of the accomplishments of the educated upper classes. Ippolita Sforza was praised for her composition of two *balli* by her father-in-law, Ferrante d'Aragona, king of Naples.[34] Lorenzo de' Medici, who today is favorably regarded as a poet, musician, and composer, also composed dances.[35] Two of his choreographies survive, the *bassadanze Lauro* and *Venus*, in three redactions of Guglielmo's treatise.[36] Both Lorenzo and Ippolita were regarded by their contemporaries as educated, cultured, and intelligent, and it is a measure of the place dance held in courtly society, and the length of time it had held it, that it was considered perfectly acceptable for them to choreograph dances. Just as it enhanced the reputation of a member of the elite to be able to write poetry, engage in philosophical discussions, read Latin, or compose music, so too was the creation of dances an intellectual accomplishment.

Upper-class women especially were able to gain respect and admiration for their ability in dancing. This is illustrated by Cornazano's praise of Beatrice d'Este (the wife of Tristano Sforza). In his treatise he upholds her as a model for Ippolita Sforza, and urges Ippolita to copy Beatrice's dexterity in dancing.[37] Cornazano then quotes a Ferrarese proverb that ends by comparing the sight of Beatrice at a *festa* (presumably dancing) to a vision of Paradise on earth.

> He who wishes to pass to the next world let him hear Pietrobono play. He who wishes to be admitted to Paradise, let him experience the bounty of Duke Borso. He who wishes to see Paradise on earth should see Madonna Beatrice at a *festa*.[38]

Cornazano is saying that the sight of Beatrice d'Este is something so splendid, so graceful, and so beautiful that it can only be compared with a vision of heaven; she is beyond comparison with anything in the earthly realm, and it is through her dancing that this angelic vision is created.

Dance and the Humanists' Education Curriculum

The dance masters and humanists inhabited the same social sphere, they taught the same group in society—the sons and daughters of those in power—and they were employed by the same men: Francesco and Alessandro Sforza; Leonello, Borso, and Ercole d'Este; Federico da Montefeltro. The dance masters and humanists also both influenced the education of their employers' children. Two of the most famous schools in the first half of the fifteenth century were run by Vittorino da Feltre at Mantua and Guarino Guarini at Ferrara. Even though these schools emphasized training the mind rather than the body, the latter was not totally ignored.[39] From a list of specialist teachers employed at Vittorino da Feltre's school we know that the pupils received instruction from dancing masters (*saltatores*), as well as music instructors.[40] At Guarino's school dancing was also considered one of the acceptable forms of physical activity, along with ball games, hunting, walking, and riding.[41] Furthermore, in humanist writings on education in fifteenth-century Italy physical education is given a place of respect.[42] Physical education was promoted partly because of its place in ancient Greek and Latin educational practices,[43] and partly because it helped the young develop the graceful bearing and ease of movement that was essential for anyone in the upper levels of society. Aeneas Silvius Piccolomini (1405–64), who in later life became Pope Pius II, was another of the humanist educational writers active in Italy at this time. While Piccolomini does not specifically mention dance in his educational program for Prince Ladislaus, he devotes half his treatise *De liberorum educatione* to the care of the student's body, with particular attention on how to hold one's body, how to control the movement of one's head and eyes, neck, arms, and hands.[44] The important point to emphasize is that control over the movements of one's body, with which Piccolomini was so concerned, was also one of the primary objectives of dance training. While Piccolomini may not have expressed his arguments in terms of learning to dance, he was still covering the same territory as were the dance masters in their treatises. Leon Battista Alberti was also very clear as to the value of exercise, especially in the education of the young.

> Body and mind should be exercised. Indeed it is not easy to give enough praise to the value and necessity of all sorts of exercise.

. . . The only person who should not engage in exercise is one who does not wish to lead a happy, joyous, healthy life. Socrates . . . often used to dance and jump, both at home and in company. . . . In this way he kept fit, and so he even favored for exercise activities which certainly would otherwise have been lascivious and improper.[45]

Thus for Alberti exercise was so important and beneficial that dancing as exercise was acceptable, since exercise could "make a bad and vice-ridden human being into an honorable and disciplined one."[46]

One example of a humanist's opinion on the value of dance in the education of a young prince comes from the court of Urbino. In 1437 Duke Federico married Gentile Brancaleoni (and Guglielmo Ebreo performed at the ceremony), but he did not beget the heir he was hoping for. Federico, therefore, trained his illegitimate son, Buonconte, to be his heir, and gave him a humanistic education. Buonconte spoke Greek and Latin, and he also studied dance and music.[47] Unfortunately, he did not live to succeed his father, as he died in 1458. But just before he died Porcellio Pandoni wrote verses praising Buonconte's physical appearance and intellectual achievements.[48] In this poem Buonconte's ability in the dance is seen as distinctive evidence of the classical, Greek-inspired education that he had received.[49] Thus for Pandoni, and for the court circle at Urbino, dancing was part of the classical education that was promoted so strongly by the humanists. Skill in dancing was regarded as an accomplishment for which its practitioners could be praised, along with their abilities in music, knowledge of Latin and Greek, and skills in the military and gymnastic arts.

Federico da Montefeltro was one of the noble pupils who studied under Vittorino da Feltro at Mantua. During his reign as duke of Urbino, Federico was revered as the perfect prince, a humanist and scholar, as well as a successful soldier, living out in his own life the humanistic precepts he was taught at Vittorino's school. Federico was renowned for his interest in music, poetry, architecture, theology and philosophy, and dance. As is illustrated by Buonconte's education, dance was an important part of life at the court of Urbino. The importance of dance at the Italian courts is also illustrated by its presence at the major festive events in Urbino. Guglielmo participated in the dancing at Federico's first marriage (in 1437)[50] as well as his second (in 1460), when he married Battista

Sforza, the daughter of Alessandro Sforza, Guglielmo's patron.[51] The year 1460 also saw Guglielmo at Urbino for the *feste* in honor of Alfonso d'Avalos. On this occasion Guglielmo reports that there were two days of carnival festivities, which included *moresche* and many other dances.[52] Eleven years later he was back in Urbino choreographing *moresche* for the betrothal of Isabetta da Monte-feltro (Federico's daughter) to Roberto Malatesta.[53] After the death of Alessandro Sforza in 1473, Guglielmo entered the service of the duke of Urbino, where both he and his son Pierpaolo served as dancing masters to the court. Guglielmo even dedicated a copy of his treatise to Federico, but unfortunately the manuscript has not survived.

Who Were the Dance Performers?

> [From] the sweet melodies and the elegant dancing of
> the beautiful ladies and young visitors, it seemed that
> everyone was in paradise.[54]

From the picture of the dancing at the 1460 wedding of Federico da Montefeltro written by the court poet, Gaugello Gaugelli, we are presented with an image of paradise: the dancing of the ladies and gentlemen was so beautiful that it could only be compared to that heavenly place. It is an image that recurs in poems describing dancing at fifteenth-century Italian festivities, and one could assume it had become standard in the description of such events. If this is true, one of the reasons for the common appearance of the image could be that the persons performing the dancing were the author's employers, that is, members of the ruling family. (It would always be in the interests of a court poet to describe his patron and his family in the most flattering manner.) The dance practice described in the treatises of Domenico, Guglielmo, and Cornazano was that of the elite in society: whether a ball was being held outside in the main piazza, or inside in the *sale grande* of the duke's *palazzo*, members of the ruling family and the court were the performers. The list of dancers at the 1455 wedding of Tristano Sforza and Beatrice d'Este reads like a "who's who" of the surrounding ruling families. Eighteen years later, in 1473 in Naples, a magnificent series of *feste* was held in honor of Eleonora d'Aragona's engagement to Ercole d'Este. On 16 May Sigismondo d'Este (Ercole's brother) entered Naples with his retinue of five hundred. The procession was met by the king of Naples, and then continued on to the Piazza dell'Incoronata. A stage had been erected in the center of the piazza for the king, his court, and his guests, and around the sides of the piazza stands had been built in order to accommodate the thousands of spectators. On the stage, in full public view of all these spectators, Eleonora herself opened the dancing: not a dancing master or a "professional" dancer, but the member of the ruling family in whose honor the celebrations were being held.

The dances of the elite in fifteenth-century Italy were participatory events. Unlike today, when visiting dignitaries, presidents, and monarchs are entertained by passively sitting still in a theater and watching a performance by professionals, in *quattrocento* Italy it was the visiting dignitaries themselves and their hosts who had to perform and who had to possess the necessary skill and ability in dance to be able to do so in a creditable manner. At the ball held at the ducal palace in Ferrara on 17 October 1476 in honor of Beatrice d'Aragona, who was about to be married to the king of Hungary, Matthias Corvinus, it was a group of gentlemen from the Hungarian delegation who danced for the entertainment of the court.[55]

In order for members of the elite to be able to dance in a graceful and elegant manner at important public events, it was necessary that their education in dance begin at an early age. The children of the ruler often performed in public well before they had reached adolescence. This is illustrated by an event at the Schifanoia Palace in Ferrara in 1486, where on 2 February the duke's children dined with the legal and canonical scholars. After the meal the d'Este children, all under twelve, along with the ladies from the leading families, joined the scholars in the dancing.[56] Isabella d'Este, who was nearly twelve at this time, had certainly been dancing in public since at least the age of six, while Ippolita Sforza was only ten when she danced at Tristano Sforza's wedding *feste* in Milan in 1455. Galeazzo Maria Sforza's second son, Ermes, is recorded as having danced a *moresca* when not yet five years old in order to entertain his father's honored guest, Antoine, the illegitimate half-brother of the duke of Burgundy.[57] Ermes's dance was a more private affair than those performed by Isabella d'Este and Ippolita Sforza, as it took place in Antoine's chambers. The less formal nature of the event may be one reason why Ermes was permitted to perform at such a young age.

The style of dancing practiced and taught by Domenico and

his colleagues and successors was not easy. A potential dancer had to master many skills before he or she would be able to perform in public, gracefully and without error. All these skills, including correct carriage of the body and mastery of changes in speed and meter, needed years of regular practice if any performance was to be carried out with an air of ease and self-assurance. The way of moving on the dance floor had to become completely natural, as members of the elite had to move in the same way whether walking, standing in repose, or dancing. The difficulty of learning these skills as an adult is illustrated by a story from the life of Albrecht Dürer, who, while on a visit to Venice in 1506, wished to improve his social standing. Apart from buying some new and luxurious clothes, Dürer also enrolled in a dancing class. He found this part of the process of social ascension much more difficult than just purchasing expensive clothes, as the somewhat complaining tone of his letter reveals.

> I set to work to learn dancing and twice went to the school. There I had to pay the master a ducat. Nobody could make me go there again. I would have to pay out all that I have earned, and at the end I still wouldn't know how to dance![58]

Skill in and knowledge of dance were seen as assets by the upwardly mobile in fifteenth-century Italy, and so dance masters catered to the demand from this section of society as well as to their courtly pupils. We know that dance was taught outside the environs of the court, as there are records of schools, or some form of dance teaching, in Florence, Siena, Perugia, and Venice at this time. Giuseppe Ebreo, Guglielmo's brother, ran a school in Florence with a Christian partner for several years from 1467, teaching both music and dancing.[59] In 1460 the shawm player Bernardo di Santi was hired by Francesco di Matteo Castellani to teach dancing to his two eldest daughters, aged ten and seven.[60] In this case the family was a wealthy one, part of the elite of the city.[61] Whether this was the section of society the harp player Mariotto di Bastiano di Francesco was aiming to attract when he rented a room in Florence in order to teach dance cannot be stated with any certainty, as his tax record for 1446 is the only evidence we have of his activities as a dance teacher.[62] More evidence is still needed before we can make definitive statements as to the extent of dance teaching in Florence and the other Italian cities, in terms of both the numbers of pupils and the social position of those pupils.

In Perugia both Deodato and Mariotto Marchetto were work-ing as dance teachers,[63] while the latter is also mentioned in the Sienese records. Mariotto was in Siena from 1470 onward, where he remained to work and raise a family, with his son, grandson, and great-grandson continuing the family tradition of teaching dance in Siena.[64] On 22 October 1493 three dance masters drew up a contract to teach dance and the playing of instruments in Siena for a period of ten years. They would share equally in both expenses and profits, but only if they remained in Siena. An ab-sence from the city for more than twenty days would cause the absentee's earnings to be forfeit.[65] Committing to a partnership for ten years indicates a healthy interest in dancing and dance instruc-tion among the Sienese population, as does the fact that dance schools continued to operate in Siena well into the sixteenth cen-tury, teaching dances such as the new and fashionable *gagliarda*, the *moresca*, and the *calata*.[66]

Types of Dances Performed

The choreographies recorded in the dance treatises of Domen-ico, Guglielmo, and Cornazano were either *balli* or *bassadanze*. The dances in these two genres were all individually choreographed, each with its unique sequence of steps and floor patterns and its individual name. And it is from the listing of the names of these *balli* and *bassadanze* in contemporary descriptions of dancing at im-portant state events that we know that these two genres of dances were among those regularly performed at festivities, official cere-monies, and spectacles throughout Italy. Many of the names of the dances were associated with the families for whom the dance mas-ters worked. In 1448 Guglielmo's patron Alessandro Sforza married Sveva Colonna da Montefeltro, the half-sister of the duke of Ur-bino. The festivities took place in Pesaro and Guglielmo was pres-ent.[67] The Siena redaction of his treatise dedicates a *ballo* called *Colonnese* to Madonna Sveva, and it is most likely that Guglielmo prepared the choreography for these festivities.[68] The dance itself involves a great deal of interaction between the three couples, who take it in turn to weave around the other two couples and also around each other, with each man circling his partner and each lady responding in the same way. One can imagine Alessandro and Sveva as one of the couples enjoying the opportunity provided by the choreography to pay attention to and interact with each other

during the course of the dance. Other dance titles are not so specific, but still point to courtly recipients; for example, the *balli Du-
chessa* (duchess) and *Marchesana* (marchioness) and the *bassadanza
Principessa* (princess) by Guglielmo.

Domenico also wrote dances that can be identified with the
d'Este family and their life at Ferrara. Two of his *balli* are named
after Estenese country villas: *Belfiore* and *Belriguardo*. Belfiore is the
name of the villa built by Alberto d'Este as a hunting retreat
around 1390–92, and by 1435, when work began on the country
villa Belriguardo, Belfiore was already famous for its frescoes,
which included a scene of Alberto's court dancing beside a foun-
tain.[69] Belriguardo was the largest and most luxurious of all of the
d'Este palaces, and Borso and Ercole d'Este spent a large amount
of time there. It too was decorated with a series of frescoes, this
time honoring Eleonora d'Aragona, the wife of Ercole. These
scenes include one of the ladies and gentlemen of the court dancing.[70] Given the time spent by the d'Este family at these villas, and
their importance as centers of courtly activity, it is perhaps not
surprising that they should also be commemorated in dance.

Domenico also honored Leonello d'Este by naming two of his
balli Leonçello. With this title he was also associating Leonello with
the image of a lion, a symbol of courage and wisdom. Whether
Domenico wrote these *balli* for either of Leonello's two marriages
is not known,[71] but it does not seem too implausible. There were
certainly plenty of opportunities for dancing at the celebration of
Leonello's second marriage in 1444, as the festivities continued for
a month with many "great jousts and great balls."[72] Furthermore,
other court artists also associated Leonello with a lion in their
commemoration of this event. For instance, on the reverse side of
the portrait medal Pisanello made for Leonello's wedding was the
figure of a lion.

Each *ballo* had its own music that was especially composed, or
adapted from an existing chanson, to fit the choreography. The
music for a *ballo* is dependent upon the choreography, since each
ballo is constructed of a number of short, irregular sections of steps
in the four different *misure*, that is, in the four different combinations of tempi and meters. These sections do not follow any
regular pattern, and are unique to each *ballo*. Thus the music has
to be different for every choreography, and is often provided in
the dance treatises themselves.[73] The *bassadanze* were normally in
only one combination of speed and meter, *bassadanza misura*, with

only a few bars of *saltarello misura* occurring occasionally. Thus any music with the right time signatures and with the same number of breves as steps in the dance would fit a *bassadanza* choreography. The dance masters do not provide music for the *bassadanze* in their treatises. The only exception is Cornazano, who records three tenor lines that were often used in performances of *bassadanze*.[74]

The music was an integral part of a *ballo,* and just as important as any other aspect of the dance. It was much more than a passive aural blanket to cover the swish of the dancers' feet on the floor, and to mask the murmur of the watching courtiers. The sections of differing meters and speeds were not randomly arranged, changing only for the sake of variety. There was a purpose in that variety, and this purpose was the intimate connection the music had with the choreography. One example of how the dance masters manipulated the music so that it added to the dramatic effect of the dance is the way they used the repetitions of musical material. In the *ballo Pizochara* (see appendix 3) the sixth musical section (bars 35–44) is a repeat of the fourth musical section (bars 26–33), and the choreography for these two sections is almost identical. In bars 26 to 33 the men are weaving around the stationary line of women, parading themselves and their mastery of the dance technique with a sequence of eleven *bassadanza doppi*.[75] Such an extended sequence of a single step required each *doppio* to be subtly varied in performance, and the slow tempo of the *bassadanza misura* would give the men time to add improvised variations to each step. The men arrive back beside their partners, taking hands with them while doing a *ripresa,* a step to the side. Instead of remaining beside their partners, the women suddenly depart, weaving around the line of men, but with a series of far more lively *saltarello doppi*. In its first appearance the tenor line is in the slow *bassadanza misura*, and in a clear compound duple ($\frac{6}{8}$) rhythm. When the melody returns in the sixth musical section, Domenico has increased the speed of the music by calling for *saltarello misura,* and the unambiguous $\frac{6}{8}$ rhythm has been changed to a mixture of $\frac{3}{4}$ and $\frac{6}{8}$. The rhythmic syncopation of the sixth musical section, and its faster tempo, reflect the men's surprise and confusion at the unexpected departure and teasing parade of the women at this point.

The connection between the music and the choreography is brought into sharp relief when one considers the relationship between the floor shapes and the musical sections. In this context the term "floor shape" is defined as the smallest unit of shape: it is the portion of the floor track that is contained between the words "and then" in the written choreographic descriptions. The combination of several floor shapes is called a "floor pattern," while the term "floor track" refers to the path of the entire dance from start to finish, that is, a sequence of several floor patterns.[76] When the points at which the musical sections begin and end are compared with the floor shapes of each *ballo*, one finds that musical sections change at the beginning of a new floor shape, not in the middle of one.[77] *Ingrata* (see appendix 3) is one *ballo* in which the musical and choreographic boundaries can be clearly seen, as the pauses in the choreographic sequence occur at the end of the musical sections. The first musical section is entirely taken up with the opening floor shape: the *saltarello doppi* in *saltarello misura*. The second floor shape, four *sempi* forward by the woman, is performed to the second musical section, with the musical repeat matching the repetition of the choreographic material by the two men. The start of the third musical section introduces a new phase in the choreography, that is, the separation of the woman and the two men to form a triangle, a shape that is maintained throughout the third and fourth musical sections. The short fifth musical section accompanies the *meza volta* by the men and the women, as they turn to face one another again, preparatory to their final advance in order to meet again. The advance of two *sempi* and two *riprese*, repeated twice, is performed to the sixth musical section, which is also heard three times. The final musical section accompanies the woman's performance of a figure-of-eight, turning as she does so to first one man and then the other, in order that the three dancers finish as they began, standing beside each other in a line.

The total dramatic effect of the dance was created by the fusion of the music and the choreography, and the manipulation of the tensions between movement and stillness within the stylistic framework of the time. The contrast between movement and stillness in the choreographies is seen most dramatically in *Sobria*, a dance for one woman and five men. The one woman departs from her partner to move behind her starting position and into the middle of the square created by the four unattached men. Two by two the men approach her with a slow *bassadanza doppio* and a *riverenza*[78] in *bassadanza misura*. The woman, rejecting the advances of the first two men, disdainfully steps backward away from them, turns her back on them, and pauses. Spurned, the two men immediately retreat to their places somewhat hurriedly, with a *salteto*, turning

180 degrees, and a *saltarello doppio*. Up until the men's *salteto* the tenor line has been proceeding slowly in semibreves. For the jumped turn the music also explodes into movement with six semiminima. When the men arrive back at their places, they turn a little to face inward and pause (*posada*) while looking directly at each other.[79] This whole sequence is then repeated by the fourth and fifth men, to the accompaniment of a repeat of the same music—the fourth musical section. The third playing of the fourth musical section accompanies the advance of the woman and her partner toward each other with two *sempi* and one *doppio*. This time the six semiminima signal a quick touching of their hands and the beginning of their circling movement around each other in two *doppi*. This turn must have been made tightly, with the partners close to one another, since one cannot turn in a large circle in only two *doppi*. The tightness of the turn emphasizes the bonds between the couple and the woman's fidelity to her partner. Thus the *maestri di ballo* were just that—masters of their art. Not only were they skillful at creating subtle and varied choreographies, they were equally as competent in handling the musical side of their compositions, and in fashioning the latter to support the choreographic content of each dance.

Before each dance could be performed the courtiers had to memorize its individual sequence of steps and the places where the *misura* changed, as well as its floor patterns. A lapse in memory or other error by one dancer would cause the whole structure to disintegrate. These dances were complicated, and needed rehearsing before they were performed in public. Thus Clarice Orsini began to learn and practice new dances for her wedding to Lorenzo de' Medici several months before the actual event in June 1469.[80] Lorenzo himself received a letter from the dance master Filippus Bussus, who offered to teach Lorenzo and his siblings "some elegant, beautiful and dignified *balli* and *bassadanze*"[81] that he had brought from Lombardy.

> And if you would like to learn two or three of these *balli* and a few *bassadanze* from me, I would come eight or ten days before the *festa* to teach them to you with my humble diligence and ability; and in that way it will also be possible to teach your brother Giuliano and your sisters so that you will be able to acquire honour and fame in this *festa* of yours by showing that not everyone has them [i.e., the dances], since they are so little known and rare.[82]

From Bussus's letter it is clear that the choreographies he was pro-
posing to bring to Florence needed to be learnt and memorized,
and that this could not be done in a couple of hours. Furthermore,
social esteem was obtained by performing new, original dances that
no one had ever seen before. Whether or not Lorenzo availed
himself of Bussus's offer is not known, but the practice of engaging
a dance master as part of the preparations for a major *festa* continued. In 1505 Isabella d'Este wrote to her brother Cardinal Ippolito
d'Este asking if she could borrow his dancer, Ricciardetto, as she
wished to practice before the forthcoming marriage of their
brother Alfonso d'Este to Lucrezia Borgia. The bride had the reputation of being a skilled dancer, and presumably Isabella did not
wish to be overshadowed in performance by Lucrezia at the wedding celebrations.

The *balli* and the *bassadanze* were for both men and women,
with the number of participants ranging from one couple up to
four couples, or two men and one woman, or, more rarely, two
women and one man, or differing numbers of men and women,
such as *Tesara* (with six men and four women) and *Sobria* (with five
men and one woman). The dance masters utilized the interaction
between the two sexes in their choreographies. Often the dances
include a section where one partner circles or weaves around the
other, or where a line of men and women face each other at a
distance, and then advance and retreat. In some of the *balli* the
relationship between the sexes lies at the heart of the choreography,
as in *Merçantia*, *Sobria*, and *Verçeppe*. Cornazano begins his description of *Merçantia* (merchandise) with the words

> *Merçantia* is a dance appropriately named, as one woman dances
> with three men and gives audience to each and every one, just
> exactly like the woman whose trade is in lovers.[83]

This is indeed the theme of this *ballo*, as the sole woman in *Merçantia* very early on ignores her partner and encourages the over-
tures of each of the other two men, who take it in turn to approach
her while her partner's back is turned. *Sobria*, on the other hand,
is the opposite of *Merçantia*, as in this dance the woman remains
steadfast to her partner, always rejecting the importuning of the
other four men. *Verçeppe*, for three men and two women, is performed in a line, with men and women alternating. Cornazano
describes this dance as "like a skirmish,"[84] and that is what it is, a

skirmish between the men on one side and the women on the other. The agonistic nature of this *ballo* is emphasized by the large number of changes in *misura:* eight.[85] The dance starts in *bassadanza misura*, the slowest *misura*, and increases in speed as the dance (and the skirmish) progresses, with sections in *saltarello* and *piva misura* near the end of the dance. *Piva misura* is very fast, being twice the speed of *bassadanza misura*. The dance itself revolves around patterns in which the men and women advance, circle around each other—scouting or harassing the enemy—before retreating to their own place, or territory, again.

Thus the dances that were recorded in the dance manuals of fifteenth-century Italy were above all social dances.[86] The dances were not just combinations of steps and music, put together for an intellectual exercise, nor were they allegorical enactments of mythological scenes, designed solely for the further aggrandizement of the prince or duke: they were enactments of the daily life of the court. The movements of the performers, the floor patterns created by those movements, every part of the choreographies went into building up a moving depiction of the relationships between men and women of the social elite.

The patterns created by the dancers while performing a *ballo* or *bassadanza* were geometric, usually rectilinear rather than circular. By this I mean that the overall movement of the dances was in straight lines. Even though many of the dances contain sections where one partner circles around the other, or where two people change places while circling around a third, in the majority of the dances the overall effect was linear, with movement forward and backward along one axis. One example of this is the *bassadanza Lauro*, by Lorenzo de' Medici. Figure 1 shows the floor track of this couple dance. The path traced by the two dancers is predominantly forward. There are movements to the side (the *riprese*) and a section in the middle of the dance where the couple take right hands and circle around each other, changing places, and then return to their places while taking left hands, but at the end of the dance the couple are standing a distance of nine *doppi* steps in front of their starting position.

One of the reasons for this predominance of linear movement in the floor track of the dances is the shape of the rooms in which they were performed. While many of the fifteenth-century palaces no longer exist in their original form, contemporary descriptions have survived. In his description of the d'Este palace, Belriguardo,

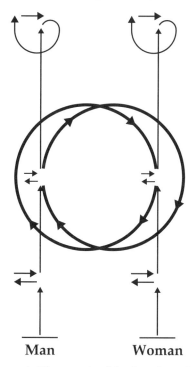

Man   **Woman**

Figure 1. Floor track of the *bassadanza Lauro*

Giovanni Sabadino degli Arienti notes that the biggest room, which was used for the large ceremonial functions of the court, was eighty-three *passi* long and twenty-one *passi* wide.[87] Since this room was used for the *feste* and other grand occasions, of which dancing would normally be a part, many of the court dances would have been performed in it. The patterns which best fit this space are those whose length is far greater than their width, that is, rectangular patterns rather than circular ones. These are the patterns we find in the choreographies.

The characteristic linear movement of the *balli* and *bassadanze* is reinforced by the starting positions of the dancers. In all but two *balli* the performers start and end in either a horizontal or a vertical line. No *ballo* begins or ends with the dancers in a circle, and only three *balli* contain passages in which the dancers progress in a circle.[88] Circular patterns are also rarely found within the *balli*, with only ten to fifteen percent of the dances containing hays, or hay-like figures, or circular, spiral, or weaving patterns.

The *moresca* is one dance genre that is often mentioned in chronicles and accounts of fifteenth-century *feste*, as well as by Guglielmo in the autobiographical section of his treatise, but it is not found in any collection of choreographies. Since the genre was such an important part of the dance culture of the elite, it cannot be excluded from any discussion of the dance practice of fifteenth-century Italy. Details of the choreographic structure, step vocabulary, and floor patterns of the *moresca* are difficult to determine with any accuracy. It is possible, however, to discuss the general characteristics of this genre. *Moresche* were frequently performed during formal state occasions, such as banquets, triumphal entries, jousts and tournaments, marriage celebrations, and theatrical performances, and were danced by courtiers as well as by "professional" dancers. Thus *moresche* were more than private entertainments.[89] They were elaborate stage shows with sumptuous costumes and opportunities for display. The *moresche* were all part of public spectacles, spectacles in which this dance form was used to help establish the identity of a city—or state—and also to perpetuate or unify the city. The public events were part of the way a city or state negotiated its relationship with other states, and, in the process, realized its own identity. The spectacles in which the *moresche* occurred were public rituals in which every action, no matter how small, had enormous implications. Every aspect of a visit by foreign dignitaries was carefully planned and controlled by the host city. Richard Trexler has argued that every step in a foreign prince's or ambassador's visit to Florence was very carefully choreographed. What would be the number and social standing of the citizens who would meet the foreign visitor? At which point would the visiting party be met? If outside the city, how far outside the city, or, if inside the city, at the entry gate or at the main piazza? At which spot would the visitor dismount from his horse as he approached the *Signoria?* All these questions, and many more, were carefully debated, as all nuances had meaning for the Florentine citizens and the visiting party.[90] It was expected that a visitor would dismount from his horse precisely as the *Signoria* rose from their seats, so that neither party had to stand and wait for the other.[91] Dance, a major component of the public spectacles, would not be ignored by the festival planners.

Dances labeled *moresca*, *morisco*, or *morris* were found throughout Europe from the thirteenth century onward, and therefore this dance type encompassed a wide variety of elements.[92] The characteristics of *moresche* in fifteenth-century Italy included danced combat and other pantomimic dancing, including the depiction of agricultural work, exotic characters such as wild men, allegorical figures such as vices and virtues, and mythological figures such as Hercules and centaurs.[93] The performers were often masked or had their faces blackened, and their costumes were usually made of silk or other precious fabrics.[94] It is worth noting that whether the dancers engaged in combat with swords and shields or mimed agricultural activities such as sowing or harvesting, their actions were always in time with the music.

The *moresca* also often depicted rural activities, particularly in the later fifteenth century when the *moresca* became almost synonymous with the *intermedio*. For example, in the marriage festivities of Costanzo Sforza and Camilla d'Aragona, held in Pesaro in 1475, beautifully dressed and adorned young men, carrying diverse agricultural implements of gold and silver, enacted the pursuits of sowing (by scattering flowers from gilded baskets) and harvesting the grain in time with the music.[95] In all the descriptions of rural *moresche* the costumes of the dancers are sumptuous, and the agricultural implements they carry are made of (or gilded with) gold or silver.

Social Context of the Dance Performances

Dance was ubiquitous in the life of the *quattrocento* elite. Dance performances occurred during celebrations of official state events such as betrothals, weddings, baptisms, and visits from neighboring rulers or foreign ambassadors. Dancing was also a part of the *feste* for the carnival season or the patron saint of a city, military victories,[96] and jousts and tournaments, as well as the banquets held in the houses of the leading citizens, where it often continued for three, four, or five hours. The balls and dance performances took place both indoors, in the large halls of the *palazzi*, and outside in the major piazzas, as well as in the gardens of the elite. Dancing as a part of state festivities was so ingrained into the patrician psyche that it even continued during times of civic disruption and war. The Sienese, for example, hastily arranged a grand ball for Charles VIII of France on his return to the city on 13 June 1495, after his devastating military campaign in Naples. The French king had expressed a wish to see the ladies of Siena, and so around fifty were quickly invited to a ball, where Charles danced between two noble ladies until very late in the evening.[97]

The indoor dance spaces were not places especially set aside for dancing. The great halls in which dances were usually held were also the places in which banquets and receptions were conducted. When *gran balli* were held the dancing itself took place in the middle of the room, which was left empty, while tiers of seats were erected along the sides of the space on which the ladies and gentlemen sat. The description of the hall in which the dancing for the wedding festivities of Elizabetta Gonzaga and Guidobaldo da Montefeltro took place is typical:

> By the right-hand side of the entrance is the dresser covered with a large amount of silver plate and vessels. By the other side is the dais, decorated with crimson velvet and pieces of cloth of gold. Along one side of the hall, from the top of the pillars of the vault as far as the benches, pieces of crimson and green velvet are stretched onto square frames with columns of painted wood. And the ladies stay along this side of the hall. Along the other side are scaffolds with steps, where the men remain to watch, [and] from these scaffolds to the top of the pillars are also pieces of green and sky-blue velvet stretched around the columns as is done on the other side. And the body of the hall is left free for the dancing. At the dresser end of the hall there is a pit for the musicians, and also the ladies who are not part of the dancing.[98]

Normally, as here, the seats or benches reserved for the dancing men and women were separated, and the women who were not involved in the dancing were seated in a third area that was not so easily accessible from the dance space. The benches or seats, and the walls of the hall, were often covered with precious fabrics or tapestries, in order to increase the aura of luxuriousness and magnificence. If the dancing took place outdoors, then the stage itself and the seats for the honored guests were covered with carpets, with expensive fabrics forming a covering above the stage. Sometimes wooden architectural structures that resembled the indoor spaces were constructed, and were decorated with tapestries, precious fabrics, leaves and flowers, and gauze veils that formed a temporary ceiling. Fountains that poured forth red and white wine, or scented water, were common, while in Rome in June 1473 three large bellows were erected in an effort to create a cooling breeze for the guests as they sat in the hot and humid summer air.[99]

Betrothal and wedding festivities were frequently celebrated with dancing, either by itself or as part of a banquet. Many of the occasions Guglielmo mentions being present at in his autobiog-

raphy were celebrations of weddings in his patron's family, or of
other leading figures in *quattrocento* Italy.

> First I found myself at the marriage of the Marchese Leonello
> [d'Este], who married the daughter of the king [of Aragon], Al-
> fonso. The festivities lasted a month, and impressive jousts and
> grand balls were made.[100]

The wedding of Costanzo Sforza and Camilla d'Aragona in 1475
was one of the most celebrated of its time. A description of the
festivities was published at Vicenza in 1475, and consequently
much more information is available to us on the dancing that took
place, in comparison with the condensed references in Guglielmo's
treatise and in many of the chronicles. There were three days of
feste: an elaborate banquet on Sunday and jousting on Tuesday,
while Monday saw theatrical and social dancing both before and
after another grand banquet, along with fireworks in the piazza.
Monday's *spettacoli* started with a series of pantomimic dances and
moresche. A mountain entered the hall, and from it emerged a lion
(that is, a man dressed in the skin of a lion) and a wild man "all
hairy and horrid."[101] The wild man then fought the lion, after
which two young men emerged from the mountain. Both were
richly dressed and masked, one with the head of an eagle, the other
with a lion's head. Both descended from the mountain dancing *a
tempo* and with a good *maniera.*[102] After all four performers had fled
back into the mountain, ten young men emerged, five dressed in
a deep, rich, sky-blue silk, the other five in green silk, exactly like
the two previous dancers, and each held in his hand a *cassata* (a
ricotta-based cake), all decorated and painted. These ten young
men danced a beautiful *moresca* to many *misure,* with dignified leaps
and gestures.[103] Still dancing, the group then advanced to the dais
and gave the *cassate* to Costanzo Sforza and his bride, and to all
the other noble lords and ladies seated on the dais with them. Then
each of the young men took a lady as his partner, and they danced
together, before the men returned to the mountain.[104]

Thus in this first interlude of dancing on Monday there was
both rehearsed pantomimic, theatrical dancing (as the two young
men danced in time with each other [*a tempo*]) and more social
dancing between couples formed by the ten young men and ten of
the ladies who were watching the spectacle. It is interesting to note
that the description of the dancing by the two groups of young

men is similar to the dance masters' descriptions of the art of dance in their treatises. It is stressed that the two young men danced *a tempo*, in time with each other and with the music, and the dance masters also stressed such coordination. The men were also described as dancing with a good *maniera*. *Maniera* was one of the fundamental principles of the art of dance as discussed in the dance treatises, without which any performance would be imperfect and lacking in grace.[105] Furthermore, the ten young men who danced a *moresca* did so to "*molti mesure*." In this case *misura* refers to the combinations of meter and speed of the music, and its use means that the *moresca*, like the *balli* contained in the treatises, was made up of sections that changed tempo and meter.

The mixture of pantomimic and social dancing continued. In the midst of allegorical processions from the Jewish community at Pesaro, the bride and groom danced together. A second group of twelve young men emerged from the Mountain of the Jews and performed "a joyful dance in the form of a *moresca*" (*uno alegro ballo in forma di moresca*).[106] This dance was a pantomime of agricultural pursuits: digging the ground, sowing seeds (scattering flowers throughout the hall), all with implements of silver and gold. All of the mimed agricultural tasks were once again danced "*a tempo et ad mesura*," in time with the music and the *misura* of the dance, with all the twelve young men dancing continuously with "the most beautiful order" (*sempre ballando cum bellissimo ordine*).

Often the performers or the servers who carried in the food for the banquet entered the hall dancing. In the latter case the banquet itself was heralded by the shawms playing a *piva*, to the sound of which 120 young men entered the hall in a line, one behind the other, all dancing a *piva* and carrying various castles of sugar and chests of confectionary and spices. A *piva* was a very fast dance in which only *doppi* were performed. Because of the speed of the music the *doppi* were performed without any of the extra bodily movements, such as raising or lowering the body or shading the shoulders, that were normally part of the *doppi* in other dance genres, such as *bassadanza* and *saltarello*. Keeping their bodies relatively motionless would certainly make it easier for the dancers to safely carry the sugar castles and chests of confectionary. Because there was not enough room in the hall for all of the 120 young men to enter in a straight line, they danced "like a snake" (*quasi come uno bissone*), or like the shape of the letter S (*o in forma de questa littera S*).[107] When all were in the hall, still dancing the *piva*, they all made a *riverenza* together, then rose, all at the same time, which presented the "most splendid and most magnificent spectacle that had ever been seen."[108]

Once the confectionary had been distributed to all the noble guests and to everyone in the hall according to their rank, the young men started to dance among themselves, "jumping with the greatest grace and pleasure" (*saltando cum grandissima gratia et piacere*).[109] The food having been consumed, Costanzo led Camilla onto the floor to dance, and then they were followed by all "the noble lords, gentlemen, knights, and learned men, who each took a lady to dance, making a long and grand ball."[110]

The wedding festivities of Costanzo and Camilla give us a very clear picture of the amount of dancing that occurred during these theatrical spectacles. It was not confined to just one short period, before or after eating, for example; rather, it occurred continuously throughout the day's entertainments. The *moresche* and other types of dancing were part of the overall scheme of the spectacle, along with music, the recitation of verses, and the entrances of allegorical carts and figures. Their wedding also illustrates the number of different types of dancing that often occurred during these large celebratory festivities. There was social, couple dancing, led by the bride and groom, and in which the leading members of the court participated. Dancing occurred as part of the processions into and around the hall, and there was also single-sex dancing and the theatrical *moresche*.

As the fifteenth century drew to a close, the choreographic elements of these wedding spectacles became increasingly integrated into the total dramatic spectacle. The beginning of 1487 in Bologna saw the celebration of the wedding of Annibale Bentivoglio (heir to Bologna) and Lucrezia d'Este, the illegitimate daughter of Ercole d'Este.[111] The balls, dancing, and banquets lasted for five days, but the most important event in choreographic terms was the banquet on 29 January, which included an allegorical performance with ten different sections, seven of which were all danced. The representation opened with a dance by a six-year-old Florentine girl and a man, who performed with such virtuosity, lightness, and dexterity that everyone was amazed. Having focused the audience's attention on the performance space, this dance was then followed by another dance "procession," in which all the scenic effects and scenery, and all the allegorical and mythological figures who were to feature in the remainder of the drama, entered the hall. The point I wish to emphasize is that all the scenic effects and figures entered the hall *dancing*.

> When this young girl had finished dancing, suddenly, to the sound of the trumpets, a hairy man appeared in the hall, dressed as a sylvan with a hairy long beard, and horrible hair, with a truncheon in his hand, with which he created space among the people for a tower of wood, that was craftily brought in and placed at the foot of the room opposite the rich dresser, and in which tower was the goddess Juno with two charming young men, one of whom represented the person of the most noble husband. When the tower was set down [on the floor], without delay a palace came dancing [into the hall] that truly looked as if it were moving itself, as it was not possible to see who carried it. In this palace was Venus with a quivered Cupid and two ladies: one was large and had an ugly face, and this one was Infamy, the other was of a distempered aspect and was dressed in garments full of countless eyes, and this one was Jealousy. And there were [also] four emperors accompanied by a most beautiful lady. And thus the said palace was set down near to the tower. And then likewise there came a mountain surrounded by a wood, in whose interior was a type of cavern, where Diana with eight nymphs was dwelling, and then the whole mountain went dancing and was set down close to the tower on its other side. And then came a crag, also dancing. In it was a beautiful girl with eight [companions] dressed in the Moorish style.[112]

The drama continued, with the action being sustained mainly by choreographed dances. In its fourth and fifth sections, Diana and her nymphs danced to the music of a hunting song, and then, to instrumental accompaniment, they all danced a *bassadanza*. Later on Juno and the two young men performed a dance called *Vivo lieta*, while a *moresca* formed the centerpiece of the concluding section.[113] The dance *Vivo lieta* could well have been similar to the choreographies recorded in the dance treatises, in that it has a specific name and it involved one woman and two men, a common format for the *balli* and the *bassadanze*.

Not only was dancing an integral part of the festivities associated with an actual wedding ceremony, but balls and more theatrical dance performances were also part of the spectacles offered by various cities at which a betrothed noblewoman halted on her journey to meet her affianced husband. These events included grand balls—social dancing for dozens of a city's young gentlewomen and gentlemen—as well as *moresche*. When Ippolita Sforza stopped at Siena in 1465 on her way to Naples, the Sienese organized a dance and a banquet in her honor. While most of the dancing was performed by the flower of Sienese youth (of both sexes), it did include a *moresca* of twelve dancers.[114] Siena repeated its efforts eight years later when Eleonora d'Aragona stayed in the city for four days on her way to Ferrara. At the ball held in her honor, the dancing opened with a procession of ninety-eight of the most beautiful women in Siena, accompanied by as many young men.[115] When Eleonora stopped in Rome, Cardinal Pietro Riario organized a stupendous banquet in her honor. The banquet itself lasted seven hours, from dawn to midday, and concluded with a dance performed by eight couples dressed as mythological characters, including Jason and Medea. These couples danced together until they were interrupted by the arrival of dancing centaurs. The mythological figures, led by Hercules, then fought a "beautiful battle" with the centaurs, defeating them. But the centaurs returned after their loss, to perform another dance for Eleonora and the guests.[116]

Important state visits by a neighboring ruler or his ambassadors were constantly celebrated with dance in fifteenth-century Italy. In 1433 Florence welcomed the ambassadors of the Holy Roman Emperor Sigismund to the city. In order to honor them, and to provide entertainment, a ball was organized in the Piazza della Signoria. Two young women from leading Florentine families, Alessandra Bardi and Francesca Serristori, were chosen to dance in public with the leading ambassador, in a choreography for the familiar grouping of three performers.[117] In 1452 and 1469 the Holy Roman Emperor Frederick III visited Ferrara, and on both occasions he was entertained with a ball attended by all the noble ladies of Ferrara, the leading *signori*, and ambassadors from the other Italian states.[118]

One of the most famous state visits of *quattrocento* Italy was that made to Florence in 1459 by the heir to the duchy of Milan, Galeazzo Maria Sforza. On this occasion the dancing occurred on Monday 30 April, the day after the jousting, and was held outdoors in the Mercato Nuovo. All the participants, both men and women, were sumptuously dressed, covered with jewels and pearls from their tunics down to their hose, which was also covered with silver embroidery. Many of the women had sleeves of gold brocade or other beautiful and precious fabrics.[119] After the arrival of Galeazzo and his entourage, when all were seated, the musicians began to play a *saltarello*, with noble squires taking a married lady or young girl to dance. The description of the dancing is worth quoting at some length.

> That was the time when the shawms and the trombone began to play a *saltarello* artistically designed in all its proportions. Then each noble and nimble squire took a married lady or a young girl and began to dance, first one, then the other. Some promenade around, hop, or exchange hands, some take leave from a lady while others invite one, some make up a beautiful dance in two or three parts. Two young girls, united in their courteous purpose, and with a smiling mien, and with their radiant polished face went to invite the noble count, showing how ready they were to pay formal homage to him by making a bow down to the ground. The warlike leader stood up straight, bowing back to them in his turn, then made his way on to the middle of the floor, danced, and in dancing did not make a mistake. While the count was dancing with these ladies, every time he passed before any man or woman each one of them would get up and bow. Having danced that characteristic dance, the ladies escorted him back to his seat using every means they knew to do him honor. After that the count did not wait much before he got up and invited two ladies [to dance] whose cheeks at once turned to fire. Yet each one worthily honored him, placing him in between them and dancing with him; and as they passed everyone would get up. Subsequently Messer Tiberto and the other great lords also danced in this manner, each one placed between two ladies.[120]

The dancing began with couples performing a *saltarello*, a dance type not described in the treatises but which is assumed to be much freer in its choreography than the *ballo* or *bassadanza* genres. Yet at this extremely important public event, the dancers performing the *saltarello* were choreographed, as the anonymous chronicler describes the dance as being carefully planned.[121] Presumably the extra preparation was thought necessary to avoid any mistakes or mishaps during such a significant event.

The description given of the dance by the young squires and the Florentine ladies is especially interesting, as it strongly resembles a general description of the common floor patterns and interactions between partners as found in the notated *balli*. Once again the courtiers are dancing in groups of two or three for the *saltarello*, and then in groups of three, that is, two ladies with a gentleman in the middle, as Galeazzo did with the two Florentine ladies. The next phrase used to describe dancing courtiers is *"passeggia d'intorno"* (promenade around). This phrase could imply that the dancers were walking in circles, one around the other, or that both were describing a circle together. Certainly, partners circling around each other is a common floor pattern in the *balli*. The *ballo Pizochara* (see appendix 3) is for four couples, one behind the other, and the first two-thirds of the dance is taken up with circling maneuvers. After the opening sequence of twelve *piva doppi*, each man circles around his partner, a pattern that is immediately repeated by the women. The men then all make a *riverenza* to the women before starting a long section in the slow *bassadanza misura*, in which the men circle around the line of women in a file, passing in front of and then behind each lady in a continuous S shape, ending up on the opposite side of their partners. The women then repeat the spiraling pattern around the men in the faster *saltarello misura*, by which time two-thirds of the dance has been completed.

Often the middle dancer in a choreography for three takes the hand of the person on his or her left while they circle around each other to return to their place, and then repeats the circling maneuver with the dancer on the right. This pattern is often found in dances for three when the three dancers are standing next to each other, as in the *ballo Ingrata* (appendix 3), and in dances for two, like *Marchesana*, in which the couple take right or left hands and *"andagando d'intorno,"* circle each other to return to their place. A very common variation on this pattern is for the dancer in the middle to circle the one to the left and then the one to the right, while those being circled stand still, as for example at the end of the first section of the *ballo Leonçello novo*, a dance for two men and one woman.

The dancing in the Mercato Nuovo continued for an hour (*"un ora era durato gia il danzare"*),[122] until the sound of trumpets announced the beginning of the processional entry of the wine and confectionary. After all these ceremonies were completed, and the young men had returned wearing new and luxurious outfits, the dancing resumed for a further hour. The anonymous chronicler of this *festa* records that another *saltarello* was danced, and then "a variety of dances as one or the other desired."[123] He then lists some of the dances that were performed: *La chirintana*, very decorated, *Rostiboli, Laura, Mummia, Carbonata, Lioncielo, Belriguardo, La speranza, L'angiola bella*, and *La danza del re*,[124] the majority of which are found in the dance treatises. Here we have unequivocal proof that the dances composed by Domenico and Guglielmo, and recorded in all dance treatises, were actually performed on public, state occasions. It is also interesting to note that although there are no records of Domenico or Guglielmo working in Florence, it was still their choreographies that were being performed in the Mercato Nuovo. It seems certain, therefore, that the popularity and reach of their choreographies was much more widespread geographically than the area of their known professional activities. Furthermore, these dances must have been very well known for the author to remember and name them in his description of the event. A sonnet on the *feste* for the patron saint of the town of Pergola, five years earlier, gives a similar list of dances performed: a *bassadanza*, a *piva*, and a *saltarello*, as well as the *balli Lioncello*, *Rostiboli*, and *Gioioso*, and a new version of *Gelosia*.[125] This sonnet supports the conclusion that Domenico's dance tradition had a wide currency by the middle of the fifteenth century, as the dances are those found in his treatise.

Dancing was part of carnival festivities, when masked balls were held at the houses of the leading members of the elite.[126] There are also records of public dancing competitions held during the carnival season in Florence in the Mercato Nuovo or the Piazza del Signori for young men and young women. Participants were specifically invited, and prizes were awarded to the best male and female dancers. For the competition held in 1419 there were four female judges for the women's competition, but men acted as judges for the brigade's male competitors. All the judges sat on a tall bench, high above the area especially fenced off for the dancing competition.[127] The brigades that organized these events themselves numbered only twelve members, so invitations were issued to numbers of young ladies and men. On one occasion in 1415 around six hundred ladies and a great many men were invited to participate in the *festa di danzare*.[128]

In fifteenth-century Italy dancing was often associated with martial activities—dances were often held either before or after jousts—and combat appeared as subject matter for individual choreographies. Practical considerations, such as both events using the same area, was probably one of the reasons for the close temporal association of the dances and the jousts. For example, in Florence in 1419 and 1421 the dancing immediately preceded the displays of combat and knightly prowess.[129] However, the two events were not always held on the same day, especially if each event by itself took up most of the daylight hours. During the celebrations for Galeazzo Sforza's visit to Florence in 1459 the joust was held on Sunday 29 April and the public dance spectacle on the day after. Both forms of entertainment had a competitive aspect, and the judges for the jousts and the dancing competitions of the brigades were seated on a platform above the fenced-off area for the participants.[130] Both events were also held in an enclosed space, with a physical barrier between the spectators and the participants.

The dance masters often used battle as a theme for their choreographies. Cornazano says that *Verçeppe* is "like a skirmish," in this case a skirmish between the two sexes: many of the floor patterns of this dance constitute a choreographed engagement between the two opposing camps. *Verçeppe* is danced in a file, with three men and two women alternating one behind the other. Often two men circle around the two women in front of them (an exercise in harrying the enemy troops), with the women repeating the exercise. The idea of danced combat was even more popular in sixteenth-century Italy, with half a dozen or so dances bearing titles such as *Barriera* or *La battaglia*.[131] Their music was often full of battle calls and their choreography full of martial patterns: advances and retreats, dancers moving past each other like two knights in a joust, and confrontations with symbolic hand-slapping in place of swords or lances striking shields.

All the occasions for dance performances discussed above are large-scale public events. But dancing was also a part of smaller, more intimate gatherings held among a few members of the court. In his later years, Alfonso of Aragon spent many of his afternoons relaxing in the palace gardens with his mistress. Impatient ambassadors would report home that "He now spends much of the day at archery and in the garden; afterwards there is dancing . . . and so time passes."[132] Dancing was also a common part of after-dinner entertainment at country residences, as in the case of Galeazzo's stay at the Medici villa at Careggi, where he was entertained by watching dancing by some of the women from the Medici family and a few country women.[133]

The Significance of Dance in Society

Dance was ever-present in the lives of the elite in fifteenth-century Italy: it was a means of entertainment and enjoyment, and a pleasant diversion from official duties. But dancing was also a part of official duties for many of the patriciate. Dance was an important element of large state spectacles, and through it the rulers and their courts, and those who governed the republican city-states, presented an image of themselves and sent coded messages to society at large. First and foremost, dance was a symbol of civilized, educated behavior. In a fourteenth-century Sienese fresco by Ambrogio Lorenzetti, the nine dancing figures[134] have been seen as representing the harmony and stability that good government can achieve in a well-ordered state. The dancers are seen as an allegory of concord, emphasizing that the inhabitants are content with their place in society.[135] Certainly there are no scenes of dancing in the opposing fresco that depicts the effects of bad government on the city. In the centuries before Domenico, dance had always been regarded as a normal aristocratic pastime, but in the fifteenth century the art of dance became associated with the civilizing educational program of the humanists. Therefore, knowledge of and skill in dance became a sign of education and intellectual ability. Dancers were increasingly seen as participating in one of the liberal arts. Second, the art of dance as advocated by the *maestri di ballo* became a sign of membership in the upper levels of society. The rules and postural codes of courtly dance were part of the mechanisms by which the court made itself appear superior and inaccessible to the rest of society. The courtiers believed that their superiority should be demonstrated to the rest of society by the different way in which they moved, walked, danced, and even stood in repose. Their carriage and demeanor when on the dance floor did not change once they finished dancing: it remained with them, as it was their normal posture. Dancing taught people control over their bodies and over all their actions, both when dancing and in day-to-day interactions with their colleagues and superiors. Dancing was visible evidence that the dancers were capable of appearing in public without making an exhibition of themselves. Those who could control their outward bodily movements were capable of controlling their inner emotions as well. Dancing, therefore, functioned as a social marker, as one of the ways a certain group in society defined itself and excluded others. A stark example of how dance was used to define the elite in society comes from Nuremberg in 1521. In this year those who held political power wished to further limit the numbers of citizens entitled to vote. Therefore they defined the voting elite as "those families who used to dance in the *Rathaus* in the olden days, and who still dance there."[136] In Nuremberg it was the ability to dance that was used to exclude people from the group who exercised political power.

In fifteenth-century Italy the power of the ruler and his court was publicly expressed through ritual. Dance was part of such ritual, and so it was one of the ways a ruler consolidated and magnified his self-image as a powerful, princely figure. When a duke and leading members of his court danced in public before thousands of his subjects in the main piazza he was displaying his magnificence, and in doing so he was displaying his power. The Italians were obsessed with protocol and ceremony—with "order"[137]—and one of the chief means of indicating rank was by the spatial relationships among people. Thus dance, an art form with spatial relationships as its basis, was a significant tool in this presentation of power and rank through rituals and ceremonies.

The dancing of the elite also represented the relationships between men and women. The vast majority of the dances were devised for both men and women,[138] and the dances themselves chronicle the interaction between the male and female participants. As we have seen, single-sex dances did occur in fifteenth-century Italy, but none of the dance masters chose to record them in their treatises. It seems logical to assume that if the dance masters had not been concerned with portraying the interaction between men and women, then choreographies would have been written specifically for one sex only, or at least a larger number of choreographies would have remained *ad libitum* in this respect, as happens in the late-fifteenth-century English dances found in the Derbyshire Record Office.[139] Furthermore, all the *balli* and the *bassadanze* which are recorded in the treatises are for small numbers of performers, between one and six couples, with over three-quarters of them having only two, three, or four performers.[140] In other words, the dance masters were interested in choreographing the relationships between small groups of men and women.

Dance as a Sign of Communal Identity

Dance functioned as a sign of communal identity, since part of the purpose of these spectacles, of which the *moresche* were a part, was the impact they made on foreign visitors. As Trexler has argued, the public nature of these rituals was intended to consolidate and enhance the "image" or "honor" of the state. One way of defining who one is, is to state what one is not. Thus the *feste*, and the *moresche* in particular, were "danced dramas" in the sense that in them the elite members of society dramatically defined before the eyes of foreigners who they were: their civilized identity was demonstrated by showing scenes of both civilization and barbarism. The scenes of the wild men, savages, or barbarians in the *moresche* were one way of declaring, "This is what we are not."[141] This type of statement was not new, as it was part of the tradition inherited from the ancient Greeks.[142] For the spectators and participants at the festivals the wild men (the other) would be "exotic," that is, outlandish, barbarous, strange, and uncouth.[143] Blackness contributed to the Renaissance sense of the "exotic."[144] Thus the blackened faces and hands of the *moresca* dancers could be seen as representing the barbarian, the person who exists outside the limits of society.

A pantomime of agricultural society was also a way of expressing the civilized identity of the participants. Today we think of urban and rural lifestyles as quite distinct, with the typical image of the city as more sophisticated and therefore more "civilized." But in the Renaissance, agriculture was seen as the "oldest of the civilized arts, and the key to civilization itself."[145] The country was seen as civilized; it was the place where one retired for reflection and philosophic thought, to escape the polluting influences of the city, which was primarily devoted to commerce. The rural world was seen as embodying serenity and order, a place full of "pleasure, wholesomeness, loveliness and grace,"[146] while the urban life was essentially disordered and artificial, a place of confusion, intrigue, and conflict. This attitude was inherited from the ancient Roman tradition. Therefore, when the courtiers mimed the labors of the field in their silken garments and golden mattocks they were creating a scene which implied that even though the center of their political organization was urban, their society was truly civilized because it was based on agriculture. They were identifying not with the reality of the average farm laborer's daily grind of poverty, but with agriculture as civilization.

Dance as Affirming Familial Ties

Just as a specific dance genre, the *moresca*, was an expression of communal identity by its participants and those who watched, so too were specific dances used to affirm family ties and to strengthen

a family's identity. Around 1500 the Roman nobleman Marco Antonio Altieri wrote *Li nuptiali*, a dialogue on the proper conduct
of Roman wedding festivities.[147] In the discussion of the various
rites and ceremonies associated with a wedding is an explanation
of the *giaranzana*, a dance for all the wedding guests that was performed once before and once after the wedding ceremony.[148] The
dance was performed by a long line of couples, who were ordered
by how nearly they were related to the groom and by their rank.[149]
The dance, which could last for over an hour, involved complicated
patterns and turnings, and it required many "modest, gracious, and
honorable gestures" ("*con modesti, gratiosi et honorevil gesti*").[150] Each
couple had to meet and acknowledge every other participant in the
dance by taking their hand as a symbol of happiness at the new
marriage, and as a demonstration of joy for and gratitude toward
all the other members of the family.[151] The dance and what it represented were taken seriously, as Altieri reports that the risk of
incorrectly placing the family members, or of inadvertently insult-
ing a relative by a too hasty acknowledgment or an incorrect movement, caused all who performed it to do so with diffidence and
fear ("*sospecto et timoroso*").[152] No one wanted to be the cause of a
family quarrel over precedence and honor.

The dance was obviously a long-standing tradition, as choreographies with the same name (*Chirintana, Chiaranzana*) are found
in both the fifteenth- and sixteenth-century Italian dance treatises.[153] Both the fifteenth- and sixteenth-century choreographies
bear strong resemblances to Altieri's *giaranzana*. All three are for
a long line of couples, and all three involve the couples, one at a
time, moving between the two lines of the other couples. The
fifteenth-century *Chirintana* is a dance for six couples, and while
the choreographic description is rather brief, the majority of the
dance is a lengthy sequence in which the odd-numbered couples
move down the line between the other couples, while the even-
numbered couples, after they have met the first couple, move up
the line between the couples ahead of them. This sequence is repeated many times until all the couples have returned to their original places, thus ensuring a great number of opportunities for every
couple to meet and acknowledge every other couple. In the
sixteenth-century version of the dance, several of the *mutanze* (variations) involve passing under the raised hands of the other couples
as they move down the line. That this dance could continue for a
long time is emphasized in Caroso's *Chiaranzana*, where, after giv-

ing instructions for three *mutanze*, he says that many other *mutanze* could be danced, but so as not to bore his readers he will not describe them.[154] The fact that Caroso did not feel it was necessary for him to record any more of the many *mutanze* for *Chiaranzana* attests to the widespread knowledge and enduring popularity of this dance.

Dance as an Expression of Power

Fifteenth-century Italy was a society in which rituals and ceremonies mattered. The ordered formal behavior demanded by these rituals was the foundation stone of a state's identity, and the way in which a city or state's relationship with foreigners was constructed and maintained.[155] Thus authors of chronicles and diaries recorded ceremonial events with often astonishing attention to detail, and in 1475 the *Signoria* of Florence instructed Francesco Filarete to record the protocols that had obtained during the visits of foreigners for the last twenty years, and to continue with that record for future visits. Florence's concern with the observation of the correct protocols for ceremonial events did not begin with Filarete's official appointment. Filarete was one in a long line of civic heralds, starting in the second decade of the fourteenth century, whose job included the oversight of all "the practical arrangements necessary to assure the proper decorum at any official ceremony."[156] From the end of the fourteenth century onward, the *Signoria*'s desire for ceremony and ritual increased, and the duties of the herald reflected this change in traditional observances.[157] In contrast to Florentine society in particular and to Italian society in general, the French court at the end of the fifteenth century was much less ceremonial and formal. When the French invaded Italy in 1494 and 1499 the Italians were shocked by the "disorder" in the French court: "Cardinals were not shown all due respect. The king's counselors ate, played cards, or casually sat around in his presence. He was swayed too easily and without ceremony."[158]

Dance was an important constituent of the rituals associated with these state events, and as such described the power relationships between the host government and the visitors. To acknowledge this function of dance is not to deny that other elements of these rituals also functioned in this way: the clothes and the jewels that were worn, the spoken forms of address and gestures associated with meeting others, the gifts that were given to the guests, all functioned as indications of subtle differences in position in the social hierarchy. By the late fifteenth century, for example, Florentine ceremonial recognized twenty-three different forms of address for people of different rank, from a pope to a knight, and seven forms of address for ambassadors.[159] At Costanzo Sforza's wedding the castles and other creations of sugar were presented strictly in order of social precedence, and exactly what gift one received depended upon one's position in the social hierarchy.[160] All these elements helped to project an image of the ruler as a powerful prince among princes, or, in the case of the Florentines, helped to assert the right of the governing body to be included among the nobility. The greater the rituals and ceremonies, the greater the parade of luxurious ostentation, then the greater the power and influence a prince was believed to possess.[161] Filarete himself states this in his *Libro ceremoniale*, where, in his account of Galeazzo Maria Sforza's 1459 visit to Florence, he comments that the quantity of pearls and jewels showed to everyone the gentility of the Florentines, and how the number of noble women, the propriety of the young men, and the mode of dancing and feasting made very plain to the foreign visitors the virtues of the Florentines.[162]

The rituals and official ceremonies for state visits, of which dance was a part, were mostly enacted in the public gaze. The anonymous chronicler of the 1459 *gran ballo* in the Mercato Nuovo was overwhelmingly concerned to describe the presence, behavior, and appearance of the Milanese court and the invited Florentine elite, and the effect they had on those who were watching. When Galeazzo danced with the two Florentine ladies, a very clear signal was being sent about the enormity of the gulf that existed between the dancers and those who watched from afar. Not only were the dancers' clothes and hats groaning with jewels and embroidery, but they were also moving in a manner that was unfamiliar and strange. The dances that were performed were strange to the observers on the periphery, the vast bulk of the city's population. The latter did not know how to perform the dances, nor even how to move in the manner they saw displayed in front of them.

Some of the messages conveyed by these rituals and ceremonial behavior were encoded in spatial relationships—the distances between people. As we have seen, the exact spot at which a foreign visitor would dismount from his horse in relation to the position of the welcoming party of the *Signoria* was crucial. The further the visitor dismounted from the platform on which the *Signoria* sat, the greater the courtesy he was showing them.[163] Similarly, the distance from the city gates at which a visitor would be met by the welcoming party of illustrious Florentine citizens was significant. In 1460 the marquis of Mantua, Luigi Gonzaga, was greeted three miles from the gates of Florence, while Galeazzo Maria Sforza, as the duke of the richer and more powerful duchy of Milan, was met eight miles from the city.[164] Distance mattered in fifteenth-century Italy. Therefore dance, an art form that is bounded by spatial considerations, was an excellent vehicle for the subtle expression of differences in rank and power. Dance also required close physical contact between its participants. Thus when a prince visited a neighboring court that was not as rich or as powerful as his own, and was seen dancing in public with young ladies from his host's family or court, a strong message was conveyed to those watching. The proximity of the honored guest and his dancing partner(s) symbolized a temporary equality of status between the richer and more powerful guest and his hosts. Certainly the Florentine elite recognized this when Galeazzo Sforza invited two Florentine ladies to dance with him. So aware were the women of the honor done to them that they blushed violently: "After that the count did not wait much before he got up and invited two ladies [to dance] whose cheeks at once turned to fire."[165]

Those participating in a ball would be seated according to their rank. This is made very clear in the description of the ball held in the Mercato Nuovo in 1459: "His lords and all his retinue sat down on the dais, each one where his rank allowed."[166] Furthermore, when the ladies, "as beautiful as the sun," entered the space enclosed for the dancing, they also seated themselves in pre-ordained places.[167] As the honored guest and heir to the duchy of Milan, it was Galeazzo who was first invited to dance, by two Florentine ladies. Not until after Galeazzo had finished did the members of his court join the dancing. And then it was not until this group had finished that the ambassadors of the duke of Burgundy were invited to dance.[168] Thus the social order was reflected in the order of those invited to dance by the Florentine young ladies. That it was normal practice for the order of those dancing to reflect the differing social relationships among those present is illustrated by the court of the king of Naples. Toward the end of his life, Alfonso became enamored of Lucrezia d'Alagnos, and made her his mistress. Lucrezia manoeuvred herself to Naples and took up residence at the court. During a visit of the Holy Roman Emperor and his wife her status was publicly affirmed by the fact that "in the dancing she took third place behind the empress and the duchess of Calabria."[169]

Dance as Courtship

The Renaissance has often been portrayed as a period when the individual was paramount. Probably the first, and certainly the most influential, proponent of this view was the nineteenth-century historian Jacob Burckhardt. He saw the Renaissance as a period when people ceased to be tightly bound into allegiances of family, guild, state, and religion, but fought to express their own identity and "to shape themselves into beautiful, powerful, virtuous, and wise individuals."[170] Burckhardt's view of the Renaissance in turn influenced many twentieth-century scholars, including Hans Baron, whose ideas gained public prominence with the 1955 publication of his *Crisis of the Early Italian Renaissance: Civic Humanism and Republican Liberty in an Age of Classicism and Tyranny*, and whose legacy is still being debated by scholars today.[171] This attention to individuals, however, can be overemphasized. While more attention was paid to the individual in the Renaissance than in previous centuries, the primary medium through which the individual interacted with society was still the family. Individuals' positions in society were primarily determined by the standing of their families or the families into which they had married, and an individual's actions, whether honorable or dishonorable, would affect all family members. This view that the position of a family could affect the success of individuals within that family, whatever their personal merit and virtues, was certainly expressed at the time. For example, for most of the first decade of the fifteenth century, the Florentine Giovanni Morelli struggled to improve his position in the competition for political offices in Florence. In 1409 he eventually did achieve a political post, but the reason that the honor was so long in coming to him, according to Morelli, was that he had married into the wrong family. In 1396 he was forced to abandon the hope of marrying the girl with whom he was in love, because of the opposition of her father,[172] and was constrained to marry Caterina Alberti, whose family had fallen out of favor. Families imposed a number of important obligations and duties upon individuals, such as the duty to marry well, since marriage was a means of social advancement for the whole family.[173] Marriage was not a private, personal arrangement between two people, but a legal contract that affected two groups in society. Marriage, and the process leading up to it, was the point at which the dance practice of the upper levels of society intersected with the family.

Balls and informal dances were occasions at which men and women were able to meet and interact with each other. They were a common activity in a society in which men's and women's lives were far more segregated and controlled than is the case today. The opportunities that balls afforded for dalliance with the opposite sex are clearly demonstrated in the anonymous account of Galeazzo's visit to Florence in 1459. In his poem the author describes the women who are participating in the *festa* as "*vezzose*," an adjective that is perhaps best translated as "coquettish." The women present were certainly beautiful, but they were well aware of their beauty and the effect they were having on the male courtiers and *signori* who were watching them:

> That day was when one could satisfy one's hunger for the sight of beautiful women and lovely things, and examine in detail all their guiles. In this form the coquettish ladies were all sitting in the first rank: a lovely mixture of unmarried and married women.[174]

In these lines the author creates a vivid image of the ladies and young girls, all sitting in their allotted seats close to the dance space. Yet all of them, in many subtle ways, by their gestures, facial expressions, and bodily demeanor, showed that they were well aware of the interest of the men and doing their best to draw attention to themselves and their expensive clothes, hairstyles, and jewelry. Later on the author describes how joyful all the participants were, how they were so intoxicated by the dancing that everyone present could not help but fall in love:

> That joyful dance seemed like a paradise of dancing angelic hierarchies, and everyone was full of joy and laughter. . . . I believe that the great and worthy ladies made a thousand fires burn on that day without tinder-box, flint, sulphur, or wood.[175]

The whole occasion was one for "making love with one's eyes," for sending and receiving desiring glances, for inciting passion in the courtiers so that there was "no breast in which the heart did not burn with a fierce flame."[176] There is nothing ambiguous here about the actions of the dancers and their response to each other. The ball was an opportunity for flirtation and coquetry, for inciting desire, and for pursuing the object of one's own desires.

Thus if a ball itself provided the opportunity for each sex to pursue the other, the actual choreographies, the step sequences and floor patterns as created by the dance masters, also aided in the ritual of courtship.[177] When viewed in these terms the dances are revealed as a series of social events, most of which provide opportunities for interaction with one's partner, or with all the members of the opposite sex in the dance.[178] A detailed study of the *balli* reveals seven major categories of social events: "opening sequence," "formal greeting," "inspection," "social progress," "confrontation," "chase," and "imitation." The category "opening sequence" is so called because it often occurs at the beginning of the *balli*. It is a sequence of movements in which all the dancers perform the same steps. There is no definite path stated in the choreography for this category.

The acknowledgment of one's partner (or of those watching the dancing), when a couple meet each other and leave again, forms the category I have called "formal greeting." This category includes the *riverenza* and *continenza* steps, and sometimes the *ripresa* step.[179] While the pattern is often found at the beginning of dances, it is also interspersed throughout the choreography. One example of this latter use is in the *ballo Prexonera*, which alternates formal greetings with another social event. *Prexonera* begins with the couple standing side by side and holding hands. Unusually for a *ballo*, the dance begins with two *continenze* to the side, and then a forward sequence of three *sempi* and one *doppio*, rather than the usual series of *saltarello doppi*. Another "formal greeting" pattern then occurs, as both dancers perform a *riverenza* to each other, and another two *continenze*. The forward-moving sequence of three *sempi* and one *doppio* is repeated, followed by the third "formal greeting," that is, another *riverenza*.

The inspection or perusal of one sex by the other was an important part of court life. The inspection in a dance often occurs when the lady or gentleman (or one half of a line of couples) circles around the partner(s). The *ballo Anello* is a good example of this category, as after the opening sequence the rest of the dance all falls into the inspection category. *Anello* is choreographed for two couples who stand behind one another. (The floor track of *Anello* is given in appendix 3.) At the end of the opening section the four dancers move away from each other to form a square, all looking inward. The dance continues with a repeated sequence of two *movimenti*—performed first by one sex and then by the other—then two *saltarello doppi* in which first the men, then the women, parade in front of their partners while changing places. This "inspection" continues with more exchanges of signals between the men and the women—the *movimenti*[180]—and further circling around each other—the *volta tonda*—and then around the opposite sex—the four *piva doppi*—until everyone returns to their original partners.

The movement pattern associated with the category of "social progress" is a long spiral path among and around lines of dancers that allows each dancer to meet others, acknowledge their presence, and pass on to the next. One example of a dance which is constructed around a sequence of patterns like this is the *ballo Jupiter*, in which the first four social events are "opening sequence," "social progress," "opening sequence," and "social progress." The opposite of "social progress" is "confrontation." This category represents the battle between the sexes, with advances and retreats by both sides. The common movement pattern associated with this category normally starts with a woman facing two men. The three dancers first move forward to meet one another, then cross over and move away from one another. At the end of this forward path all three turn 180 degrees to face one another. The movement pattern is concluded as they move toward each other to meet for a second time. Much of the choreography of the *ballo Ingrata* portrays "confrontation." The confrontation occurs in the middle of the dance, after the opening sequence and the chase section. (See appendix 3 for the floor track of *Ingrata*. The confrontation occurs in musical sections 3, 4, and 5.)

The category of "chase" occurs when one sex chases the other: for example, when the man goes forward, and then stands still while the woman follows him, or vice versa. In the "imitation" category, each couple (or each dancer) simply repeats the actions of those in front of them.

These seven social events represent common movement patterns found in almost every *ballo*. Not all the steps in each dance are involved in the portrayal of social events, as dancing was a multi-faceted art. Thus a choreography can be seen as a sequence of movement patterns linked together to form a complete work. Since a choreography was more than just a mirror of the upper level of society, there are some parts of each dance which do not fall into any of these seven categories, and which were not part of the dance masters' portrayal of the social interaction between women and men, but were included for other reasons. The sequence of steps with which Guglielmo liked to conclude his *balli*, that is, one *doppio* behind, then a *volta tonda*, is one example of this.

When the *balli* are analyzed in terms of the social events that they portray in the choreographies, it is clear that the dance masters had definite rules and procedures which they followed when constructing these dances: they did not haphazardly place movements one after the other with no regard to the path traced out on the floor, or to the interaction of the performers. For example, not all the different social events were used in every dance. Generally each dance consists of three or four different events.[181] The largest number in any one dance is six, and only nine dances have this many.[182] The dance masters, however, did not limit themselves to using a social event only once in a dance, as the same one can occur several times in one dance. Many of the *balli* alternate two social events. A good example of this is the *ballo Jupiter*, which involves three pairs of "opening sequence" and "social progress," followed by two pairs of "opening sequence" and "inspection," and finishes with a "formal greeting." Thus, while there are eleven social events in this *ballo*, only four different ones are used.[183]

The dance masters had definite preferences among the social events categorized in the *balli*. Some rarely occur (constituting about one percent of the total number), while others are used frequently. The three most commonly used social events are "opening sequence," "inspection," and "formal greeting."[184] The dance masters built their choreographies around these three social events, which occur in most *balli* not once, but several times.

The dance masters also had clear preferences for the way in which their dances began, as more than three-quarters begin with an "opening sequence" and all but one of the rest with a "formal greeting." Similarly, most of the second social events are either "chase" or "inspection."[185] However, unlike those at the start, the step sequences at the end of the *balli* do not (with two exceptions) fall into any consistent patterns.[186]

When the *balli* are analyzed in this way, another preference of the dance masters in composing them is revealed: they preferred to have all the performers participate in one event at the same time. One can only speculate as to the reason for this preference. It may be that their sense of order was offended by several events taking place at once: that such a situation was not *varietà*, but merely *copia*. They may not have considered it aesthetically pleasing, for example, to have one couple involved in "chasing" one another, while at the same time a second couple were involved in a "confrontation" and a third couple were in the middle of an "inspection" sequence.[187] The dance masters' preference for all the performers to be involved in the same social event is also more realistic, as in real life people in small groups are usually all involved in the same type of interaction at the same time: for example, all greeting each other.

At court a person's success depended upon his or her ability to create an attractive image which could smooth the paths of social interaction. A courtier's appearance had to inspire trust and convince others that it did indeed reflect the true nature within: no disjunction was permitted between surface appearance and the reality beneath. Dealing with a constant parade of people, and avoiding the dangerous undercurrents created by clashes of precedence and family rivalries, required a supreme mastery of the intricacies of the social conventions, especially in the meeting and recognition of all the other members of the court with whom courtiers came into contact on a daily basis. The members of a court were on display at all times, not just when dancing, and the "usual courtesies" applied off as well as on the dance floor. The realities of life at court were portrayed by the dance masters in their choreographies. The frequent use of the "formal greeting" in the dances reflected the importance of successfully negotiating the hazards of interacting with everyone one met at court. Their preference for the social event of "inspection" reflected the importance of the dance as an occasion where men and women could mix together, and where political intrigues could defer to the amorous nature of court life. Court dance mirrored the life of the court, but it was also a part of that life. Art and daily reality were one, with no distance between them.

2

The Dance Treatises and Humanist Ideals

The fact that Domenico, and later on Guglielmo and Cornazano, wrote dance treatises at all, let alone treatises that included substantial material on the philosophical basis of the dance practice, is a strong argument for the view that humanist thought influenced the art of dance in fifteenth-century Italy, that the dance masters were aware of the current ideas and attitudes of the humanists, and that their work was a response to those concerns. The fact that the dance masters chose to write treatises, a literary preoccupation in itself, in order to advance their dance practice to the status of a liberal art indicates a strong familiarity with, and acceptance of, the norms and values of the Italian humanists. Up until this time dance instruction had presumably been an oral practice, with courtiers learning new dances directly from those most skilled. Teachers of dance seem to have been uninterested in committing their choreographies to paper, whether to produce instruction manuals outlining the basic steps and principles of the dance style or to produce treatises on dance as gifts to their patrons. The *maestri di ballo* do not appear to have had literary mindsets; dance was a physical skill, not a written one, and it was not considered necessary to be able to write about dance and describe it in anything other than general, descriptive terms. In literary works the words used to describe scenes of people dancing were those words in common usage, rather than any specialized vocabulary. In *The Divine Comedy* Dante mainly used the words *danza, danzando, ballo,* and *tripudio,* generic terms for dances and dancing. He did not employ any more specialized adjectives in an effort to describe the type of dancing, or the quality of the dancers' movements.

A similar situation with regard to dance terminology is found in Middle High German literature and thirteenth- and fourteenth-century French and English literature. Before the mid-fifteenth century the vocabulary used to describe dancing in German texts was limited to a few common terms, and no detailed descriptions were ever given.[1] From her analysis of dance terminology in Middle High German texts from 1150 to 1450, Ann Harding has concluded that "there is no technical dancing vocabulary in MHG, but only a number of descriptive verbs and nouns,"[2] and that the terms which were used before 1400 all refer to general actions of processing, leaping, or turning. In thirteenth-century English literature several verbs are used to signify dancing—including "sailen" and "hoppen"—while "trippen" and "skippen" appear in the fourteenth century, along with the names of dance genres such as carole and houe dance.[3] The verb "to dance" only appears in English texts in the late fourteenth century.[4] It is not until the fifteenth century that specific step names, like "trace," "trett" and "retrett," "hornpepy," "hertt," "flowrdelice," and "rak," appear.[5] In France the dance terminology found in the works of literary figures, including Adam de la Halle, Guillaume Machaut, Jean Froissart, and Eustache Deschamps, concentrates on a small number of words that refer to specific genres of dance: *bal, carole, tresche,* and *danse.*[6] Ecclesiastical texts similarly use general terminology (*saltatio, tripudium,* and *choreas*) to refer to dancing.[7]

It was not until the 1440s that this oral or non-literary mindset was challenged by the writing of Domenico's treatise, with the next two decades seeing the appearance of Cornazano's and Guglielmo's treatises. All three treatises are written in the vernacular rather than Latin, which at first glance might seem to distance the dance masters from the circle of the Latin-orientated humanists. But in spite of their championing of the revival of classical Latin, humanists were also deeply concerned with the promotion of the vernacular as a language worthy of literary merit and production, and men such as Bruni, Palmieri, Cornazano, and Alberti exemplified this attitude in their own literary output.[8]

Florentine humanists such as Colucio Salutati and Bruni were consistent in their praise for Dante's vernacular poetry. His rhymed verses were of an exceptional standard that elevated the vernacular to a "language of art," and Salutati considered him equal with the great writers of antiquity as an ideal model for contemporary humanists.[9] Salutati's letter of 1399 is typical of his praise for Dante's *Commedia*:

> Distinguished man, excellent brother, dear friend, I am anxious to have a correct copy of our Dante's divine work. Believe me, no poem so far is loftier in style or more elegant in invention or of greater weight, when you consider the subject, the diction or the treatment. . . . Where could you find more important matters set forth in more fitting words? In short, dear Niccolò, we can point out nothing loftier, nothing more embellished, nothing more polished and nothing more profound in knowledge than those three cantiche. . . . [T]here rhetorical figures of thought and language are evident in such splendor that you would be hard put to find such great embellishment elsewhere, even in the greatest authors.[10]

Bruni thought that Dante would never be surpassed in rhymed poetry because the "greatness and sweetness of his poetry is truly marvelous; it is prudent, meaningful and serious."[11] Matteo Palmieri shared Salutati and Bruni's opinion of Dante's poetry:

> Others have written works in the vulgar tongue, [but] few are of such skill. The first, and most worthy above all others, is our poet Dante. He in every way so much exceeds the other vernacular writers, that it is not worthy to compare him to them, because apart from the language he is found only a little behind the greatest Latin poets.[12]

The stature of Dante did not diminish among humanists as the century progressed, with later scholars continuing to praise him:

> All men agree that Dante first brought back to the light the ornaments of poetry and rhetoric; and the elegance, temperance and dignity of the ancients, which had been extinguished for many years. . . . [H]e was the first who ennobled with fullness and

elegance, with erudition and ornament our own native tongue, which until his times was coarse and unused. . . . He first showed how suitable was the Florentine tongue not only to express but also to fill out and decorate all that which falls into discussion.[13]

These learned men, who were dedicated to the revitalization of classical Latin, did not scorn literary production in their own native tongue. Cristoforo Landino, for example, praised Alberti as he did Dante:

> [Leon] Baptista Alberti has expanded our language very much, and in loose oration and prose has surpassed and defeated all his superiors; and his eclogues written in Tuscan verses show how learned he is in poetics and with how much judgment he abounds.[14]

Alberti was considered a model in this regard, as he encouraged the development of the vernacular not only by his own literary compositions but also by writing the first book of Tuscan grammar and organizing a public poetry competition for poems in that language.[15] In his *Della famiglia* Alberti explains his reason for championing the vernacular:

> I fully admit that the ancient Latin language was rich and beautiful, but I see no reason why our present-day Tuscan is so contemptible that anything written in it, however excellent, should fail to satisfy us. I think it will do for me if I can say approximately what I want to say and speak in a manner that may be understood. . . . As to the great authority among all nations which my critics attribute to the ancient language, this authority exists simply because many learned men have written in it. Our own tongue will have no less power as soon as learned men decide to refine and polish it by zealous and arduous labors.[16]

Like Alberti, humanists often made a deliberate choice to produce a work in Italian. For example, in the late 1430s Palmieri chose to write his substantial treatise *Vita civile* in Italian so that his fellow citizens who "desired to live well and virtuously," but who did not know Latin, would have a model they were able to follow.[17] At other times the choice of Italian was due to a desire to extend the vernacular literary forms. This desire is exemplified in Cornazano's literary output, which was in both Italian and Latin. Apart from his dance treatise, his major literary works in the vernacular included the *Vita della Vergine Maria*, a life of the Virgin Mary in terza rima, and the twelve books of the *Sforzeide*, which were modeled on Vergil's *Aeneid*, and which celebrated the great achievements of the dukes of Milan. With this work Cornazano was attempting to start a tradition of the epic in the vernacular, while still using the classical model.[18] Other works were written in two versions, Latin and Italian,[19] while other poems included both Italian and Latin text in the same work.[20] Cornazano also produced works solely in Latin, such as his treatise in prose on the art of war. Thus Guglielmo's choice to use both Italian and Latin in his treatise was not uncommon; many other classically literate scholars did the same. Guglielmo used Latin for the treatise's title and some of the chapter headings, as well as including a second dedicatory poem to Galeazzo Maria Sforza in Latin after the first poem in Italian.

The Structure and Content of the Dance Treatises

The response of the dance masters to humanist concerns went further than just writing treatises. The structure and content of their treatises also show an awareness of, and affinity with, humanist writings. In the second half of the theoretical part of his treatise Guglielmo presents his arguments as a dialogue between a censorious, doubting pupil and Guglielmo himself. The pupil contests every point that Guglielmo makes, allowing the latter a second opportunity to reiterate his arguments and thus convert the pupil to his point of view. Guglielmo was not alone in his adoption of the humanist practice of structuring his treatise as a dialogue. Antonio Averlino, or, as he was more commonly known, Filarete, wrote his treatise on architecture in the early 1460s. It too was written in the vernacular (Tuscan), not Latin, and took the form of a dialogue.[21] The dialogue form was a common one among humanist texts as the authors sought to imitate the ancient, classical texts that favored this form. One has only to think of the dialogues that Poggio Bracciolini wrote throughout his life, from his early work, *On Avarice* (composed 1428–29), to the later works written in the 1440s and 1450s.[22] Guglielmo was starting his career, establishing himself at the various courts and choreographing dances for important festivities and celebrations, in the same period that Poggio and other humanists were producing works in the dialogue form. Poggio's dialogues are obviously more sophisticated than that of Guglielmo. For example, *On Nobility* opens with a gracious description of the setting for the debate, Poggio's country villa, and the participants—Lorenzo de' Medici and the Florentine humanist Niccolo Niccoli. But in spite of this difference in tone and writing style, there still remains the fact that Guglielmo did choose to use the form of a dialogue to structure this part of his treatise. He could have chosen another form, such as the straightforward explanatory approach he adopted in book 1, which was indeed used by Domenico and Cornazano in their dance treatises. The fact that he did not do so indicates that he was aware of the general structure of treatises written by his humanist contemporaries.

Like most humanist writing, the dance treatises contain appeals to ancient authorities. The preface to Guglielmo's treatise begins by citing ancient authorities to support the author's positive view of the power and virtue of dance, its good effect on human beings, and its status as a liberal art through its close association with music. Guglielmo begins by canvassing figures from the world of antiquity who were believed to have been responsible for the invention of music: Apollo, Syrinx, Pan, and many others. Whoever was responsible for the beginning of this science deserves praise, according to Guglielmo, because music is one of the seven liberal arts, and as such is one of the paths to true knowledge just as much as any of the other liberal arts:

> But whichever of these, or whoever was the originator or founder of this science, he is worthy of excellent praise and remembrance. This art is not the least among the seven, rather as a liberal science it shows itself to be sublime and profound, and as worthy to be followed as the others.[23]

Guglielmo argues that, of all the liberal arts, music is most suitable to human nature, because it offers solace to all its hearers' senses, just as if it was the ideal food for their souls:

> [A]nd it is the most apt, and conforms itself to human nature almost more than do the other [arts]. Because, being formed by and composed of four main concordant voices corresponding to our four main elements, it offers through listening to it great comfort to all our senses, almost as if it were the most natural food of our souls.[24]

In this passage Guglielmo is referring to the Pythagorean tetrad of elements: earth, air, fire, and water.[25] It was with these four elements that God created the universe, and they were believed to be the basis of every part of nature: the building blocks of every animate and inanimate object on the earth.[26] The four elements were determined by the four basic qualities of hot, cold, moist, and dry; that is, air was produced by the interaction of the hot and moist qualities, water by the interaction of moist and cold, earth by the interaction of cold and dry, and fire by the interaction of dry and hot. It was through the pattern of the tetrad (one manifestation of which was these four elements) that nature—the human world—was bound together with the heavenly world, and, as a consequence of this shared pattern, divine nature resonated through every level of God's entire creation. This concept of the cosmos was endorsed by every major medieval scholar from Macrobius onward, and it continued to be accepted by the majority of Renaissance scientists. In fact, it became one of the most frequent scientific commonplaces during the Renaissance, as the belief continued to be expressed in popular treatises until well into the seventeenth century. Therefore, Guglielmo's reference to this cosmological picture was standard for his day, as it was part of the intellectual heritage of his society. Later on in his treatise Guglielmo elaborates on this same point:

> Now in order to have a full appreciation and understanding of these things mentioned above, we must note, as has been mentioned before in the preface, that instrumental music or song is mainly founded and based on four principal voices. These [voices] are concordant with, and conform to, our four elements. Through this concordance we have the being and the sustenance of our life, in such a way and in such a measure that when, by an accident, one of these four principal substances (called elements), of which we are composed and formed, is missing in us immediately our life will cease.[27]

By referring to the four elements in these two passages, Guglielmo is positioning music, and therefore dance (since dance is a natural consequence of music), right in the center of the Pythagorean view of the nature of the cosmos. Thus Guglielmo is using the authority of classical learning in two ways here: by referring to individual figures and their associations, and by linking music and dance with the relationship between God and his creation.

Guglielmo continues to use references to ancient mythological and Biblical figures to argue that music has a powerful effect on human beings, wild beasts, gods of the underworld, and inanimate objects. Dance is specifically introduced in the example of King David and the Israelites, who by their dignified dancing moved their angry and powerful god to a mood of mercy and peace:

> And also like the glorious King David, who many times with his loving and holy psaltery gathered together [his] troubled people with festive and virtuous dancing, and with the harmony of [his] sweet song he moved an irate and powerful God to a compassionate and most pleasant peace.[28]

In concluding, he states that dance proceeds naturally from music, and explains how this procession takes place:

> These things show us the great excellence and supreme dignity of the science [that is, music] from which the joyful art, and the sweet effect of dancing, naturally follow. This virtue of the dance is none other than an external action reflecting interior spiritual movements [or "movements of the soul"]. These movements must agree with the measured and perfect consonances of a harmony that descends with delight through our hearing to our intellect and to our welcoming senses, where it then generates certain sweet emotions. These sweet emotions, just as if they are constrained against their nature, try as much as possible to escape and make themselves visible in active movement. This active movement, drawn out by its own sweetness and melody to the exterior parts of the dancer's body, manifests itself almost as if it were joined and combined with the voice and harmony that emerges from the concordant and sweet song or from the heard and measured sound.[29]

Throughout the prologue Guglielmo presents the central thesis of his treatise: that dance is an art which is the outward, physical realization of the harmony of music. Since dance proceeds from music, it also shares the characteristics of music; that is, it too is a realization of the proportions that govern all the cosmos, and which tie human beings into the harmony of the universe. Guglielmo presents his arguments in a humanistic framework by supporting them with appeals to ancient authorities and mythological figures.

Italian humanists of the early to mid-fifteenth century were also quite happy to use carefully selected portions of classical texts to bolster their own intellectual agendas. They defended their arguments more often by appeals to ancient, classical authorities than by logical arguments or empirical evidence.[30] Whatever type of work was produced by the humanists, the text was peppered with references to classical heroes and mythological figures. Mario Filelfo's poem in praise of Guglielmo is an extreme example of this tendency. In almost every line Filelfo refers to a figure from the ancient world: to Socrates, Plato, and Aristotle; to Scipio and Cato; to the Biblical figures Solomon, Judith, and David; and to mythological personages, both well known (Apollo, Mars, and Diana) and very obscure.

Yet while Filelfo's poem may seem to us today to be an empty catalogue of names, the humanists' appeal to ancient authority was serious. The treatise on education by Aeneas Silvius Piccolomini, later Pope Pius II, is another example of a work that uses this technique. Throughout *De liberorum educatione* Piccolomini uses the ancient figures and stories from history as exemplars from which his reader will learn the necessary lessons. To give just one example, at the beginning of his treatise Piccolomini argues that "[n]o one needs wisdom more than a sovereign,"[31] and this is why the prince to whom the treatise is addressed, Ladislaus, should during his younger years be constantly imbued with the highest ideals of virtue. Piccolomini strengthens his point by referring to the Roman emperors of the period when "learning prevailed."[32] He then quotes Socrates' advice that "commonwealths were happy if their rulers were lovers of wisdom."[33] Princes must fulfill their public duties but also act according to the wisdom (or philosophy) that they have learnt. Piccolomini then marshals Pericles, Architas of Tarentum, Dion of Syracuse, and Epaminondas, as well as the "Scipios, Fabii, Catos, Marcelli and Caesars, all of whom had the greatest glory and learning," as exemplars for Ladislaus, so that when he becomes king he will be able to "rule after their fashion, so that Hungary, wearied by great disasters . . . under [his] . . . leadership may breathe once more and be restored to [its] . . . ancient splendor."[34]

Between 1422 and 1429 Bruni wrote a treatise on education dedicated to Battista Malatesta. In this work he defended the study of the *studia humanitatis*, and part of this defense was the appeal to ancient authorities. In the section where he argues for the value of studying poetry, for example, his first argument is that Aristotle frequently cited the verses of poets such as Homer, Pindarus, and Euripides in his writings.[35] Alberti is another humanist who used the authority of the Latin authors to support his arguments. When explaining why painting is worthy of study he points out that painting possesses a "divine power," illustrating his argument with a story from Plutarch concerning one of Alexander the Great's generals.[36]

Dance and the Humanist Dialogue on Art: Informed versus Uninformed Viewers

References to ancient authorities are not the only evidence of humanist influence on the content of the dance treatises. In their discussion of dance Domenico and his two pupils also promoted the concepts used by the humanists in the latter's writings on painting and sculpture. These concepts were first established by Petrarch in the mid-fourteenth century, who arranged them in contrasting pairs: oppositions between classical antiquity and the present, between the informed and the uninformed viewer, between sensuous delight in art and a more useful pleasure that results from a knowledge of the art, between matter and form and between matter and skill, and finally the contrast between art and nature.[37] The majority of these contrasting pairs of concepts also appear throughout the dance treatises.

The opposition between a group of informed viewers and an uninformed group was central to both the dance masters and the humanists. The latter were committed to the idea of a literary elite who had knowledge of and mastery over literary activities, as well as an understanding of artistic pursuits such as painting. The humanists' literary work, just like the work of painters and sculptors, was for the "informed" section of society, those who had the intellectual capacity to appreciate it. The same attitude pervaded the dance treatises. The dances the *maestri di ballo* created, and the practice they taught and advocated, were only for the "informed" group in society, that is, the noble elite, rather than the uninformed populace:

> We come to these *balli* and *bassadanze* which are removed from the populace, and are composed for the noble halls, and are to be danced only by the most worthy ladies, and not by the common multitude of people.[38]

The distinction between an uninformed group of people and an informed elite who have the advantage of an intellectual appreciation of their dance practice occurs again in Cornazano's treatise when he is discussing the *piva*. In the past the *piva* was commonly performed by the elite in society, but no longer, says Cornazano, because of the greater education and intellectual understanding of the nobility in his day than in previous times:

> Although this [*piva*] was the main music to which our ancestors danced, today, because our intellects have flourished in many things, [the *piva*] is [seen as] contemptible and is despised by good dancers and noble persons.[39]

Guglielmo expresses sentiments similar to Cornazano's at the end of the theoretical section of his treatise. He closes by reiterating that his dance style is only for those who can appreciate it, who fully understand and have mastered all the exercises and skills he has discussed in the treatise;[40] that is, his dance practice is only for the informed section of society, not the uninformed. Guglielmo even cautions against the harm that can arise if those uninformed, ignorant persons attempt to participate in the dance properly belonging to the elite:

> For it happens [that] many times some men, seeing themselves [as] a little knowledgeable in the dance, presume, in a shameful, dissolute, and corrupt spirit, to be presumptuous and foolhardy beyond measure. And these people are the ones who turn this most worthy art into something contemptible and dishonest.[41]

Indeed the possibility of abuse by the ignorant was a common reason why clerics and other moralists argued against dance.[42] Their argument is put forward by Guglielmo's pupil very clearly, in order that Guglielmo can refute the calumny that dance gives rise to every imaginable evil, especially lust and murder. It is only when dance is practiced by "dissolute, evil, base, and lecherous men" that evil consequences will occur, argues Guglielmo: in other words, when the dance is abused by the uninformed sections of society. When practiced by virtuous and noble men, who are informed about its style, structure, and philosophical framework, it will have only positive and beneficial consequences:

> You should think how wicked and culpable it is, because infinite evils and vexation descend from the dance, of which we clearly see examples every day. And you cannot still deny that it is a seducer and a stimulus to lust. Through it the most terrible mur-

ders, quarrels, and hatreds come about, which are most displeas-
ing not only to God, but also to mankind. . . . [Guglielmo then
responds to his pupil:] As regards the second point, I do not deny
that many murders, sins, and other evils have descended from the
dance, [but] this is when the art is performed and practiced by
dissolute, vile, lustful and common, plebeian men, to whom (if
you have well understood and carefully read [what I have written]
previously) I prohibit and deny it. But when it is practiced by
noble, virtuous, and honest men, I say that this science and art
is good, virtuous, and worthy of commendation and praise.[43]

The possibility that the ignorant might abuse artistic works or
objects was also discussed by the humanists. One example is Salutati's *De fato et fortuna*, in which he admits that religious images
can be misunderstood by the uninformed, vulgar multitude, and
therefore the images may be abused or give rise to undesirable
consequences.[44]

Dance and the Humanist Dialogue on Art: Matter and Form

The opposition between informed and uninformed is crucial
to two of the other contrasting pairs: matter and form, and sensuous pleasure and useful pleasure. According to the humanist dialogue on the visual arts, when looking at a painting a viewer was
supposed to resist the "charms of matter" and appreciate the "sub-
tlety of form" and the skill of the artist.[45] But of course this appreciation of, and reaction to, a painting or sculpture was only
possible for an informed viewer, a point made by Giovanni da Ra-
venna:

When a painting is exhibited, the knowledgeable beholder expresses approval not so much of the purity and exquisite quality
of the colours as about the arrangement and the proportion of
its parts, and it is the ignorant man who is attracted simply by
the colour.[46]

Guglielmo makes a similar point in his treatise when he argues
against his pupil's negative and simplistic view of the art of dance.
The pupil is ignorant, and therefore is incapable of appreciating
the subtleties of the art. He can see only the surface requirements,

like dancing in time and remembering the correct step sequence, not the far more complex principles such as *misura*:

> You do not have [any] true knowledge and understanding of the particularities and subtleties of the aforesaid art, and [because] these are lacking it is not possible for you to fully understand the perfection that it requires. Therefore, nothing of your arguments surprises me, to which I will briefly respond. For [the dance] to become a perfect art it is necessary that it should contain the six previously mentioned things, for without them the science will be worthless. And the greatest [of these things] are *memoria* and *misura*, since they are used not only in this art, but in all the liberal arts.[47]

The subtleties of form, as opposed to the more obvious technical elements, also feature in Cornazano's discussion of *bassadanza misura*:

> In the *bassadanza* . . . sometimes it is not ugly to rest for a *tempo* and to be as if dead, and then to enter into the following [*tempo*] in any airy fashion, almost like a person who has risen from the dead. In this Misser Domenichino, your good servant and my master, has the most considerate judgment [when] he says that to dance specially in the slow *misura* is to be like a dream-like shadow. In this comparison one intends so many things to be explained that one cannot say them all. The masters of juggling tricks and the foot-heavy tappers should hold their tongue, because only this manner is refined, and once the *bassadanza* is removed from it, it changes into vulgar movements, and loses its natural propriety.[48]

The movement called a *fantasmata*—an infinitesimal pause at the end of a step, and then a resumption of movement in an incredibly light and airy manner—cannot be understood by the ignorant and superficially minded, the "masters of juggling tricks and the foot-heavy tappers." Even though the execution of *fantasmata* is subtle, it is also so essential to any noble and graceful performance of a *bassadanza* that its absence will destroy the character of the dance, just as an artist's inappropriate arrangement of figures in a painting, or the absence of the correct proportions, would destroy the work of art and ruin the moral effect it had on its viewers.

Dance and the Humanist Dialogue on Art:
Sensuous Pleasure and Useful Pleasure

The contrast between sensuous pleasure and useful pleasure also rested upon the division between the informed and uninformed viewer. To the humanists it was only "the informed beholder who was in a position to distinguish between crude sensuous pleasure and some more complex and intellectual enjoyment offered by a painting or statue."[49] Part of the intellectual pleasure offered by a painting was the moral pleasure which could be gained from viewing and meditating upon religious and virtuous scenes. Guglielmo repeats the same sentiment when he explains how dance, when properly performed, is capable of enriching and delighting the souls of all those who have a true appreciation of it:

> Also you who intend to perform it must strive to give pleasure to the spirits of those people who take delight in it, and deny it to those who, by their incapacity and ineptitude, disapprove and condemn the dance.[50]

Guglielmo acknowledges that dance can provide ample opportunities for sensual pleasure, but once again only to those who are uneducated and ignorant of its true qualities:

> But it is totally alien, and a deadly enemy, to the vicious and base common people, who mostly with corrupt souls and ungodly and lewd minds make this liberal art and virtuous science [into] an adulterous and servile [affair]. And many times, under the semblance of honesty, they make the dance a pimp for their shameful lust in order that they can bastardize it, so that they can cautiously enjoy each voluptuous effect that comes from the dance.[51]

On those who have the knowledge to appreciate and understand it, dance has a virtuous effect:

> But when it is practiced by noble, virtuous, and honest men, I say that this science and art is good, virtuous, and worthy of commendation and praise. And moreover not only does it turn virtuous and upright men into noble and refined persons, but it also makes those who are ill-mannered and boorish and born into a low station into sufficiently noble people.[52]

Dance and the Humanist Dialogue on Art: Nature and Art

The last contrasting pair of concepts which underlie Petrarch's discussion of painting and sculpture are nature and art. According to Petrarch, painting is to be esteemed above other crafts (or the other artificial pursuits of mankind) because it is closer to nature, while sculpture is even closer to nature than painting, as it has a three-dimensional solidity to it not found in painting.[53] Petrarch acknowledges the human ingenuity and skill—the art—which contributes to the close depiction of nature, whether in portraits of men's faces or figures or the more substantial representations of human figures by sculptors. Painting and sculpture depend upon both "art" and "nature," the true representation of which is the goal of the artist.

The contrast between "nature" and "art" also lay at the center of the debate on the nature of rhetoric. In the second book of *Institutio oratoria*, Quintilian examines the question of whether or not rhetoric is an art, concluding in the affirmative: "[t]hat rhetoric is an art may, however, be proved in a very few words."[54] He then continues, "I quite realise that there is a further question as to whether eloquence derives most from nature or from education."[55] According to Quintilian, both an innate ability and a rigorous training are necessary for the successful orator. A certain amount of eloquence in speaking is innate in some practitioners, but the perfect orator owes more to art—to training and education—for while "material without art does possess a certain value, . . . the perfection of art is better than the best material."[56]

The dichotomy between nature and art pervades the different parts of rhetoric, as well as rhetoric as a whole. To take just one example, memory,[57] one of the five parts of rhetoric, is seen both as natural (an innate ability) and as an art (the product of training and disciplined practice).

> There are, then, two kinds of memory: one natural, and the other the product of art. The natural memory is that memory which is embedded in our minds, born simultaneously with thought. The artificial memory is that memory which is strengthened by a kind of training and system of discipline. But just as in everything else the merit of natural excellence often rivals acquired learning, and art, in its turn, reinforces and develops the natural advantages, so does it happen in this instance.[58]

Furthermore, the whole structure of the grammar school curriculum was underpinned by the contrast between a natural activity altered by human skill and the simple, unadorned activity itself. Grammar school students began their study of Latin by learning the rules for word order and syntax of what we now call medieval Latin. This language, called *ordo naturalis*, was considered appropriate for children, but not for older, more advanced students. These students were expected to artfully and skillfully vary their written expression, to ornament it, so that an elegant discourse, or *ordo artificialis*, was produced. There were many ways in which this could be achieved, such as by altering the natural word order, or by extending or abbreviating it, or by the use of rhetorical figures.[59] It is this type of prose composition that was considered an "art": a natural activity that was transformed by human ingenuity and skill.

The dance masters adopt the same distinction between "art" and "nature" in their discussion of the dance practice. From the title of his treatise onward, Guglielmo asserts that what he is discussing is an art, as throughout his treatise he continually refers to the dance practice about which he is writing as "the science and art of dance." Guglielmo specifically elaborates on the opposition between art and nature in book 2 of his treatise. Here he explains how dance is both natural and also an art, a product of human ingenuity and skill:

> I will respond to that which you have said against the practice and art of dance as briefly as it will be possible with my small intellect. And first I say and confirm that this science is serious and virtuous, as you have more fully seen above, proving to you by true reasoning that it is both innate and learnt (as you will understand below). And as regards your first point about dancing without music, I answer that if eight or ten people are dancing without music, [but] with steps that are harmonized and measured together, then it is a natural thing. And when a musician plays and those dancing harmonize and measure their steps to the music, then it is an acquired skill. Since this science of dance is both innate and learnt, it is also perfect and worthy of praise.[60]

Dance is a part of the natural world, as it is a natural activity which happens when people move together with measured steps that are in harmony with one another. Dance moves into the realm of an art when music is played and the dancers adjust their steps to fit the music. It is through this act that human skill enters the equation, and natural dancing becomes part of the art of dance. In the latter scenario the dancers are imitating a natural activity, but human skill and knowledge transform this natural activity, or order, into a man-made order. For Guglielmo dance is a natural practice, and innate ability to dance is found in people in varying degrees. But for this natural practice to be truly perfect it needs the refining layer of human application and skill, of training and education. In adopting this attitude Guglielmo was following the standpoint found in the classical rhetorical treatises:

> [T]he natural memory must be strengthened by discipline so as to become exceptional, and, on the other hand, this memory provided by discipline requires natural ability. It is neither more nor less true in this instance than in the other arts that science thrives by the aid of innate ability, and nature by the aid of the rules of art.[61]

The opposition between art and nature, so fundamental to the theoretical discussion of dance, also permeates the choreographies themselves. For example, the steps are divided into two groups: "natural" or "innate" steps, and the "man-made" or "learnt" steps. Domenico lists nine natural steps: the *sempio, doppio, ripresa, continentia, riverenza, meza volta, volta tonda, movimento,* and *salto,* and three man-made steps: the *frappamento, scorsa,* and *escambiamente.*[62] Cornazano's division of the step vocabulary is almost identical to Domenico's. He classifies the *sempio, doppio, continentia, contrapassi, movemento, volta tonda, meza volta,* and *scambi* as natural steps and the *trascorsa, frappamento,* and *piçigamenti* as man-made steps.[63] The natural steps are the basic, simple, unadorned steps that when performed in their own order form the backbone of the choreographic step sequences. An example of a natural step performed in its own order is a *bassadanza doppio* performed in *bassadanza misura.* The man-made steps are the quick, ornamental movements that add grace and decorate the basic step sequences. Performers were usually free to choose which and how many of these man-made steps they would perform, and where they would perform them. Thus these man-made steps can be seen to represent the extra layer that human skill and inventiveness brings to the dance, that is, the "art" side of the art/nature divide.[64]

3

Eloquent Movement—
Eloquent Prose

An important part of humanist culture's effect on the dance practice of fifteenth-century Italy was the dance masters' realization that language was absolutely necessary to the status of dance as an art. They were acutely aware that for dance to be included as a liberal art, with a claim to true knowledge and wisdom, then it had to be more than just a body of physical skills; it was now essential to be able to talk about dance in addition to being a good practitioner. In realizing this, the dance masters were responding to one of the central concerns of the humanists. Ever since the late fourteenth century the Italian humanists had been passionately concerned with words, with eloquence in the spoken and written text, and with rhetoric, the art of effective and persuasive public speaking and writing. The humanists' interest in language, and their belief that it was the most powerful tool to move the passions of mankind, resonated throughout the educated elite, influencing not only dance but also other artistic practices, such as architecture and painting. One example of the strength of the humanists' feeling about the position of language can be seen in Lorenzo Valla's treatise, *Elegantiae linguae latinae*, in which he describes classical Latin as

> the noblest and the truly divine fruit, food not of the body but of the soul. . . . For this language introduced those nations and all peoples to all the arts which are called liberal; it taught the best laws, prepared the way for all wisdom; and finally, made it possible for them no longer to be called barbarians. . . . The Roman dominion, the peoples and nations long ago threw off as an unwelcome burden; the language of Rome they have thought sweeter than any nectar, more splendid than any silk, more precious than any gold or gems, and they have embraced it as if it were a god sent from Paradise.[1]

For Valla, and the humanists in general, the importance of Latin as a language went far beyond its literary style. Latin was seen as the cornerstone of civilization, the basis of a civil society regulated by laws and based on wisdom—a knowledge of the divine. Their appreciation was not merely aesthetic, but had very practical, day-to-day consequences for the society in which they lived. Thus to the humanists proficiency, if not excellence, in the use of language was essential for the good running of the state. The comments of Francesco Patrizi of Siena (1413–94) are typical in this regard:

> No quality is of more vital concern to the state than public speaking, especially that aspect which relates to civil discussion. For the ends of the state depend upon the ability of men of affairs to persuade others into or out of a proposed course of action.[2]

The ability to understand and to manipulate language was considered to be of such importance that the major part of the humanists' system of education was directed toward this end. Guarino Guarini (1374–1460) taught in Florence, Venice, and Verona before establishing a school at Ferrara on the invitation of the d'Este family. Guarino intended his pupils to be able to use Latin competently, securely, and, more importantly, discerningly, with a mastery of the elegant nuances of the language so beloved of the classical Latin authors.[3] To achieve this aim he oriented his educational program toward mastery of the Latin language, and in order that his pupils gain this fluency Guarino "amassed an elaborate corpus of linguistic information essential for an elegant Latin style,"[4] so that his pupils graduated with the "ability to speak *extempore* on any subject in classical Latin, [and] the ability to compose formal letters to order in the classical idiom."[5]

Guarino's concern with eloquence in the spoken and written language is echoed in the humanist educational treatises. In *De liberorum educatione*, for example, Aeneas Silvius Piccolomini wrote of the importance of fluent speech to members of the governing elite:

> Now since speech comes from practice, we think that something must be said about the manner in which the faculty of speech ought to be formed in a boy, that when he has assumed a man's estate he can not only speak *but speak elegantly and well*, which accomplishment no one thinks a king should neglect. They who excel others in the art of speaking procure the greatest praise for themselves.[6]

It was within the milieu that placed such an emphasis on language skills, both spoken and written, that the dance masters began to compose their own treatises.

The Development of a Technical Vocabulary

In order to produce a dance treatise that was more than just a compilation of choreographies, the dance masters needed to develop a technical vocabulary in which to discuss their subject. When I use the term "technical vocabulary" here I am referring to the language used to describe the quality of the dance movements in the theoretical sections of the treatises, rather than the vocabulary used in the choreographic descriptions to refer to the actual steps. In their development of such a vocabulary they used everyday terms, but in new and specialized ways, and they also borrowed and adapted terms from other arts, such as painting and rhetoric. Words such as *misura*, *maniera*, and *aiere* had common meanings in the fifteenth century, but the dance masters greatly extended and developed their significance. For example, *misura*, according to the earliest Italian-English dictionary (by John Florio), meant "a measure, a rule, a direction, a method, a proportion," while *maniera* was a "manner, fashion, use, custome, or woont," and *aiere* meant a "countenance, a looke, a cheere, an aspect, a presence or appearance of a man or woman" as well as having a musical meaning and referring to the air one breathes.[7] The best example of the dance masters' taking a term already in use and extending its meaning is found in the word *misura*. As it is explained in the dance treatises, *misura* was fundamental to the art espoused by Domenico, Cornazano, and Guglielmo, and it was also the link that bound dance to the cultural and intellectual framework of fifteenth-century Italy. *Misura* embodied the idea of proportion: a proportioning of the space around a dancer's body through the movements of the body, a proportioning of the ground on which the floor patterns were traced out, and a proportioning of the music. It is this concept of proportion that linked the art of dance (and the other arts) to the Pythagorean and Platonic idea of the nature of the cosmos.

One meaning of *misura* referred to the proportioning of the movements of the dancer's body. In this context the dance masters used a wide vocabulary of terms in their treatises to describe particular movements of the dancer's body. The terms included *maniera, aiere, ondeggiare, campeggiare*, and *gratia*. The meaning of *misura*, when applied to movements of the body, is made clear by Cornazano:

> Also in the dance one does not only observe the *misura* of the sounds, but also a *misura* which is not musical, but is different from the others. It is a measure of space in the elevation of the rise and fall; that is, one must always rise in such a way as not to break the *misura*. *Ondeggiare* is nothing other than a slow rising of the whole person and a quick descent.[8]

Cornazano is saying that proportioning of the body comes about through the whole body's rising slowly and descending quickly.

Domenico also uses the word *misura* in relation to the apportioning of the movements of the body, but in his treatise he introduces another element to the concept of *misura*, that is, measure in the Aristotelian sense of always keeping to the mean and avoiding extremes:

> There is another *misura*, that which is composed (all with the grace of *maniera*) by the carriage of the whole person. It is different from the musical *misura* mentioned above. This *misura el tereno* is a light *misura*, and this is the one that keeps the whole of your body within the mean of the movement. And this movement is neither too much nor too little. And you must avoid the extremes of movement according to what has been said here above.[9]

This is a very important principle of Domenico's art of dancing (and one that he often returns to in his treatise): the movements the dancers make should be measured, moderated, always avoiding the extremes of excessive movement or too little movement.

So far we have seen that the word *misura*, as used in the dance treatises, refers to a concept of proportion which applied to the space (both aerial and terrestrial) in which the dancers found themselves, and to the movements of their bodies within that space. But for the dance masters, *misura* had yet another level of meaning, found in the proportioning of the music. For Domenico, the foundation of the art of dancing is *misura*, that is, quickness and slowness according to the music.[10] Guglielmo, in his treatise, repeats this claim:

> And note that all these experiments or practices exist in order to understand perfectly the *misura* upon which is founded all the aforesaid art of dance.[11]

Domenico and his pupils regard the science of musical proportioning as the foundation of dance because they believe that dance itself came from music. Guglielmo explicitly states this in the prologue to his treatise, when, after a long discourse on the origins of music and the effects of music on the human spirit, he affirms,

> These things show us the great excellence and supreme dignity of the science [that is, music] from which the joyful art, and the sweet effect of dancing, naturally follow.[12]

In linking the proportions of music with the movements of the dance, Guglielmo and his colleagues were not presenting any radical new ideas. They were merely expressing in their own words the traditional music theory and moral philosophy of the Middle Ages; that is, the essential nature of music theory was the study of proportion and relation, and for them, the perfect practical art was one in which this proportion was expressed simultaneously in sound and movement: in poetry which was sung and danced. All the manifestations of *misura* were ways of expressing in both sound and movement the fundamental truth and beauty of the cosmos— its numerical essence. Dance was an ordering of movements of the human body that was concordant with the proportioning of the music which accompanied it.[13]

Thus the musical *misura* referred to by Domenico, Guglielmo, and Cornazano is a rhythmic proportioning of the music in the same ratios that the medieval and Renaissance West believed represented virtue, the noble ideal of temperance and moderation. In keeping with the accepted beliefs of their day, the dance masters describe four *misure*, related to each other in the ratios of 1:2, 2:3, and 3:4.[14] Domenico called the *misura* from which all the others were derived *bassadanza misura*, while the three ratios based on *bassadanza misura* were called *piva misura, saltarello misura,* and *quaternaria misura* respectively. The dance masters explained, in both words and diagrams, the relationships between the speeds of these four *misure*. As mentioned above, the *misure* were not regarded as purely technical categories. The fifteenth-century dancing masters were concerned to present dance as both an art and a science, and as an honorable and virtuous discipline. Consequently, the four *misure* also embodied aesthetic qualities: the *piva misura*, for example, which was seen as having peasant origins, was regarded as the least graceful of the four *misure*,[15] while *bassadanza misura* was seen as the queen of all the *misure* and the most difficult of all to perform, for that reason requiring the greatest *virtù* in execution.[16]

The dance masters were not the only ones to appropriate and extend everyday terms in order to develop a technical vocabulary for their own art. Alberti took standard terms from the arts of the trivium and used them in new ways in his treatise on the art of painting.[17] Book 2 of Alberti's *De pictura* discusses pictorial composition (*compositio*), that is, how a painting can be organized from its individual parts to produce an effective whole. Alberti's account of composition was a reworking of the theory of composition that was part of both grammar and rhetoric.[18] *Compositio* in grammar was the method every schoolboy was taught to produce a complicated sentence: words were combined into phrases, which were in turn combined to produce clauses, and clauses were combined to produce the finished sentence. For Alberti *compositio* in painting was

> the procedure in painting whereby the parts are composed together in the picture. . . . The principal parts of the work are the surfaces, because from these come the members, from the members the bodies, from the bodies the 'historia', and finally the finished work of the painter.[19]

Thus the grammatical hierarchy of words-phrases-clauses-sentence was replaced in painting by the hierarchy of surfaces-members-bodies-*historia*-finished painting.

Even if the dance masters did not adopt the theory of composition,[20] they did take over terms from rhetoric in their effort to build a specialized vocabulary in which to describe the art of dance. One such term was *varietà* (variety), which was discussed by Cornazano (but not by Domenico or Guglielmo) under the name *diversità di cose* (a diversity of things):

> *Diversità di cose* is to know how to dance the dances with variations, and not always to perform them the one way; and thus to have the steps . . . [performed] in diverse ways: and that which is done once must not be done immediately a second time.[21]

Diversità de cose is another overarching principle which must be applied in every dance and to all steps. According to Cornazano, subtle variations among performances of sequences of the same dance steps were essential if a dancer wished to achieve recognition for the skill of his or her performance.

The concept of *varietà* came from rhetoric. Quintilian considered it one of the essential characteristics of a good delivery:

> For the first essential of a good delivery is evenness. . . . The second essential is variety of tone, and it is in this alone that delivery really consists.[22]

When Cicero describes the style of delivery of Marcus Antonius (143–87 B.C.), who was considered one of the greatest orators of his day, variety of expression forms part of his excellence.

> You know what Antonius' type of oratory is like. It is vigorous, vehement, excited in delivery, fortified and protected on every side of the case, intense, precise, to the point, lingering on each and every aspect, giving ground without dishonor, pursuing vigorously, intimidating, begging, *displaying the greatest possible variety of expression, without ever satiating our ears.*[23]

Quintilian also believed that variety was essential in an orator's carriage, as well as in his expression, the movements of his hands, and the language he used:

> But it is often expedient and occasionally becoming to make some modification in the time-honoured order. We see the same thing in pictures and statues. Dress, expression and attitude are frequently varied. . . . [T]he hands will not always be represented in the same position, and the variety given to the expression will be infinite. . . . A similar impression of grace and charm is produced

by rhetorical figures . . . [f]or they involve a certain departure
from the straight line and have the merit of variation from the
ordinary usage.[24]

All these areas needed variety in order for the orator to increase
his grace and effectiveness. Just as the dance masters advocated
varietà for added grace in a performance, so Quintilian argued for
variety in the bodily movements of the orator for him to be truly
effective.

Variety was also considered important in the theory of painting
in fifteenth-century Italy, where it had the same meaning as in the
dance treatises. From Alberti's *De pictura* it is clear that *varietà*
meant a diversity of matter, especially in the hues chosen by the
artist and in the number and contrasting arrangement of figures in
a painting. It was never merely a large number of objects or figures
in a picture, as this was just *copia*, a profusion of matter:[25]

> The first thing that gives pleasure in a 'historia' is a plentiful
> variety. . . . So, in painting, variety of bodies and colours is pleas-
> ing. . . . But I would have this abundance not only furnished with
> variety, but restrained and full of dignity and modesty. I disap-
> prove of those painters who, in their desire to appear rich or to
> leave no space empty, follow no system of composition, but scat-
> ter everything about in random confusion with the result that
> their 'historia' does not appear to be doing anything but merely
> to be in a turmoil.[26]

Alberti's discussion of *varietà* in painting fleshes out for us the practical implications of Cornazano's use of this rhetorical concept.
Cornazano is saying that the interest in a dance performance and
the skill of the dancers lie in the *diversità di cose*, and that this variety
is more than just a large number of different steps strung together.
It is a more subtle quality of individual variation of each step, so
that repeated steps all appear to be slightly different, with each
step providing a contrast with that which went before it.

Elegance in Word and Body

In all their literary activities the humanists were concerned to
imitate the classical literary styles, especially the elegance they believed was a characteristic of classical texts. Part of their enthusiasm
for the writings of Plato, for example, derived from their percep-

tion of him as one of the "most elegant writers of antiquity."[27] The opinion of Lorenzo Valla, one of the humanists whose writings had an enormous impact on the development of the neo-classical Latin literary style, is typical in this respect: he comments on "the elegance of the Latin language, from which there is nevertheless just a short step to eloquence itself."[28] The humanists' passion for the eloquence of classical texts was echoed by the passion of the dance masters for eloquent movements. The humanists' professional activity was the use of words, and so the production of elegant prose or poetry was one of their chief aims. The professional métier of the dance masters was movement of the human body; this was their poetry and prose, and this was where they strove to inculcate elegance.

The gulf between the bodily movement of the dance masters and the literary activities of the humanists was not as great in fifteenth-century Italy as one might imagine, since there were classical precedents for a connection between these two activities. The connection came from the rhetorical writings of Cicero and Quintilian, works which were part of the canon treasured by humanists in the first half of the fifteenth century.[29] Both authors argued in their writings on rhetoric that gesture, voice, and pronunciation were, in effect, corporeal eloquence.[30] In the third chapter of the eleventh book of *Institutio oratoria* Quintilian states,

> *Delivery* is often styled *action*. But the first name is derived from the voice, the second from the gesture. For Cicero in one passage speaks of *action* as being a *form of speech*, and in another as being a *kind of physical eloquence*,[31]

while in *De oratore* Cicero defines delivery as "the language of the body."[32]

For Quintilian, bodily movement, the manner in which a person walks, and his or her facial expressions convey meaning, just as if words had been spoken:

> [T]here are many things which [gesture] can express without the assistance of words. For we can indicate our will not merely by a gesture of the hands, but also with a nod from the head: signs take the place of language in the dumb, and the movements of the dance are frequently full of meaning, and appeal to the emotions without any aid from words. The temper of the mind can be inferred from the glance and the gait.[33]

Thus the fifteenth-century humanists, as well as the dance masters, believed that a person's gestures, deportment, facial expressions, and manner of walking, that is, a person's bodily movements, were a silent language that carried a rich treasury of meaning, just as did the spoken and written word. Given the concern of the dance masters with the imitation of elegant and virtuous patterns of movement, it is not surprising that a large part of the specialized technical vocabulary developed in their treatises dealt with the nuances of these eloquent movements.

Maniera and *aiere* were two of the terms the dance masters used to describe these movements.[34] Domenico's description of *maniera* is given to the reader in the form of a picture of the movement of a gondola which, pushed by two oars over the little waves of a quiet sea, rises slowly and falls quickly. This *maniera*, says Domenico, must never be adopted in the extreme: dancers must always practice moderation in their movements, neither moving so little as to appear wooden, nor too much.[35]

Cornazano defines *maniera* as a rising and falling movement of the body, *ondeggiare*,[36] and also as another movement of the body which he calls *campeggiare*.[37] The meaning of *campeggiare* is not entirely clear, although the word seems to refer to a horizontal shading movement of the body above the foot which makes the step.[38]

Guglielmo suggests that this lateral movement is what is meant by *maniera*,[39] while *aiere* refers to the rising and falling movement of the body:

> [*Aiere*] is an act of airy presence and elevated movement, with one's own person showing with agility a sweet and gentle rising movement in the dance. . . . Because keeping [the steps] low to the ground, without rising and without *aiere*, the dance will be shown to be imperfect and outside of its nature. Nor will it appear to the bystanders as worthy of grace and of true praise.[40]

For Cornazano *aiere* is another grace of movement which will render the dancer pleasing in the eyes of the onlookers.[41] Unfortunately Cornazano does not state what sort of movement will produce the grace he calls *aiere*.

With Cornazano's description of *aiere* we come to another of the basic but extremely important principles of court dance: *gratia* (grace). In the fifteenth-century Italian dance treatises the word *gratia* is associated with the bodily movements necessary to perform the dances properly.[42] Judging from Domenico's discussion of *maniera* and Cornazano's and Guglielmo's statements on *aiere*, *gratia* is most commonly used with reference to bodily movements, which should not be performed in an extreme manner: neither so large and expansive that the dancer appears ungainly, nor so small that the performance is judged to be wooden and lifeless. From Guglielmo we learn that these bodily movements involved rising movements during the steps, and from Domenico's description of *maniera* that they involved a slow rise with a quicker descent.

Not all the steps, however, were performed with this slow rise and quick descent. As mentioned above, *bassadanza misura* was regarded as the most graceful of the four *misure*, and so these rising and falling movements were an essential part of the *doppio* step when performed in *bassadanza misura*. Since this was the slowest *misura*, dancers had time to raise and lower their whole body during the step, without making jerky, staccato movements that would be contrary to Domenico's idea of keeping to the mean (or measure) of the movement. *Piva doppi*, on the other hand, did not have these rising and falling movements. *Piva doppi* were performed so quickly that there was no time to add any additional movements to the three small, quick steps on the ball of the foot which made up the step. *Quaternaria doppi* also did not have the rising and falling movements of the body,[43] which perhaps explains why this step was not much liked by the Italians.[44] The performance of *saltarello doppi*, however, followed that of *bassadanza doppi* in that it included these rising and falling movements.

Elegant movements, according to the dance masters, involved a fluidity and flexibility in the dancer's body so that her or his rising and falling throughout the length of a step was always controlled. Dancers had to be able to control their body so that their elevation at the beginning of a step was slow and gradual, while the descent at the end of a step was quicker. Keeping the body rigid and stiff would hinder a dancer's *maniera*, and usually any such performance would be viewed as totally lacking in grace. The dance masters' insistence on flexibility in the dancer's body is similar to Quintilian's judgment on the graceful and inelegant postures of statues and figures in painting:

> The body when held bolt upright has but little grace, for the face looks straight forward, the arms hang by the side, the feet are joined and the whole figure is stiff from top to toe. But that curve,

I might almost call it motion, with which we are so familiar, gives
an impression of action and animation.[45]

Part of the grace of elegant movement was also to be achieved
through the use of *fantasmata*. Both Domenico and Cornazano
mention the principle of *fantasmata*,[46] or *ombra phantasmatica*,[47] in
their discussions of the essential qualities of the dance style. *Fantasmata* is an elusive, subtle quality, which even Cornazano says is
difficult to put into words.[48] *Fantasmata* is concerned with the way
in which each step is phrased, especially when these steps are
danced in *bassadanza misura*. At the end of every step the dancer
must freeze briefly for a fraction of a second, just as if he or she
had seen the head of the Medusa, before moving on to the next
step with so little effort it is like a falcon taking wing.[49] The quality
of movement that Domenico and Cornazano were describing by
this term was a very important part of the eloquent movement they
advocated. It is paradoxical in that it is a characteristic of a dancer's
movement, yet it involved a momentary cessation of all movement.[50] The word itself is similar to the Renaissance Italian *fan-
tasma*, which referred to a ghost, hag, hobgoblin, or sprite,[51] and
it may well be the elusive, transient, and ethereal nature of these
spirits that Domenico was seeking to evoke by his use of this word
in his dance treatise. The medieval Latin word *phantasma* refers to
one of the five kinds of dreams:

> A *phantasma* is when a person who is just beginning to sleep, and
> up to this time thinks he is still awake, seems to see things rush-
> ing at him or diverse and changing shapes wandering hither and
> thither, either joyful or disturbed. Amongst this kind of dream
> are nightmares.[52]

While it is not possible to state with any certainty why Domenico
chose this term for this grace of movement, perhaps he did know
of the medieval Latin meaning of *phantasma* and wanted to capture
some of the sudden, quickly changing motions of the shapes of the
dream state in his dancers' performance. The fifteenth-century
dancer's application of this grace had to be so subtle, so light, the
moment of repose so quick as to seem almost insubstantial, almost
as if it were just a dream.

Humanist authors also discussed movement: not movement
while dancing, but people's carriage, their gestures, and their general demeanor while attending to their everyday activities.[53] The

sentiments expressed in these works are very similar to those expressed by Domenico and his two students in their more specialized discourse on movement. A good illustration of the sentiments shared by the dance masters and the humanists is found in Palmieri's 1439 treatise, *Vita civile*. In the second book of this work, as part of a discussion of justice, prudence, fortitude, and temperance (or keeping to the mean), Palmieri discusses the appropriate movements and gestures of the body, in a passage which echoes Quintilian's thoughts on gesture:

> Now I will discuss that which is appropriate to the body, both in its movements and when it is at rest. . . . One must flee from every movement and whatever condition of the body which deforms it from its natural use and makes it appear ugly. . . . Often it happens that by small signs one recognizes great vices, and these signs give to us a true indication of the state of our soul, as for example, a haughty glance signifies arrogance, a lowered mien signifies humility, while to lean to one side indicates sorrow. . . . In walking one must consider one's age and rank. One must not walk too upright, nor make one's steps slow, hesitant, and of such gravity that one appears pompous, like those in a procession of ecclesiastical dignitaries. Neither should one spread one's clothes or walk so swollen and rounded that the street appears not capable of holding one. . . . Neither does one wish to walk too quickly, as this signifies fickleness, and demonstrates that one is lacking in constancy, but rather every movement should express an ordered modesty, in which is observed one's proper dignity, having nature always as our teacher and guide.[54]

Moderation in movement was seen by Palmieri as natural, while excessive movement or lack of movement was regarded as unnatural, ugly, and a sign of the vices or defects in a person's character. Palmieri, like the dance masters, believed that the nature of a person's soul was revealed by movements and facial expressions. Thus the body should be neither rigid nor excessively floppy, but well controlled. The gaze should be level, the head neither hanging low on the chest nor constantly looking up, as an elevated glance signifies arrogance. One should walk neither too slowly nor so fast that one appears always to be in danger of tripping and, even worse, of indicating to others one's lack of constancy.

The belief that a person's character was revealed by deportment and gestures was widespread among the humanists. Piccolomini, in his treatise on the education and studies suitable for a prince, expresses similar sentiments and agrees that control over one's bodily movements is necessary. Piccolomini urges Ladislaus

> that your countenance be not thrown backward, that your eyes be not cast down upon the ground, that your neck be not inclined to either side, that your hands may not seem awkward, your stature unbecoming, and that your sitting posture be not ridiculous. The motions of the eyelids must be suitably restrained; the arms must be straight; let there be no awkwardness in walking.[55]

The belief was so common that it pervaded all areas of humanist writing, not just educational treatises. In Carlo Marsuppini's poem on the nature of nobility, for example, the people who are "false nobles" reveal their hollow character by the manner in which they walk:

> If a person has more wealth than Croesus
> fills his many pastures with sheep and cattle,
>
> dwells in palaces with Priam's gilded beams or Menelaus's golden tapestries,
> and while fancying himself noble, scorning the less fortunate,
> aroused by anger, *he struts pompously with affected gait*,
>
> then let him be as greedy as he likes
> while anxiously striving to accumulate more treasure.[56]

The sentiments expressed by Palmieri and Piccolomini are very similar to those of the dance masters. Throughout their treatises the latter constantly insist on the importance of moderation in the movements of the dance, of always keeping to the mean and avoiding both too little movement and excessive movement. Following Cicero and Quintilian, and then the humanists, the dance masters also paid particular attention to the carriage of the head. It was important that those in the social elite carry themselves so that their head neither hung low on their chest, nor tilted up, with the chin in the air. It should be held level at all times, with young ladies especially remembering to keep their eyes, but not their heads, modestly lowered.[57]

The concerns over control of one's body, over moderation in movement, over the importance of the carriage of one's head and the significance of this for one's character, all of which are present in the writings of the dance masters and the humanists, have their source in classical authors like Quintilian, who discusses how an orator's bodily movements and gestures contribute to the meaning and effectiveness of his speech:

> The head, being the chief member of the body, has a correspond-ing importance in delivery, serving not merely to produce grace-ful effect, but to illustrate our meaning as well. To secure grace it is essential that the head should be carried naturally and erect. For a droop suggests humility, while if it be thrown back it seems to express arrogance, if inclined to one side it gives an impression of languor, while if it is held too stiffly and rigidly it appears to indicate a rude and savage temper.[58]

Moderation was a central component in the dance masters' un-derstanding of what constituted eloquent movement. The concept of moderation adopted by the dance masters and the humanists came from the teachings of Aristotle (384–23 B.C.), as well as from rhetorical texts. Domenico acknowledges this in his treatise when he refers specifically to Aristotle's *Ethics:*[59]

> In the second book of the *Ethics* he argues against it, saying that all things corrupt themselves and spoil themselves if they are led and brought in a different manner; that is, by the operation of the extremes. And the mean conserves them.[60]

> This virtue consists in avoiding the extremes and the bad things, remembering that Aristotle in the second book [of the *Ethics*] praises *eutrapelia*, which holds the virtue of the middle while flee-ing the extremes of the rural peasant and of the person who is a juggler and minstrel.[61]

Aristotle's doctrine of the mean was expounded in the second book of the *Nicomachean Ethics*, where he discusses the nature of virtue, part of which is found in the doctrine of the mean:

> In this way, then, every knowledgeable person avoids excess and deficiency, but looks for the mean and chooses it. . . . If, then, every science performs its function well only when it observes the mean and refers its products to it (which is why it is custom-ary to say of well-executed works that nothing can be added to them or taken away, the implication being that excess and defi-ciency alike destroy perfection, while the mean preserves it)—if good craftsmen . . . work with the mean in view; and if virtue, like nature, is more exact and more efficient than any art, it fol-lows that virtue aims to hit the mean.[62]

Aristotle then gives concrete examples of the doctrine of the mean as it applies to human actions or feelings. For example, the mean of "conversation" is "wittiness," or *eutrapelia*, the same Greek term used by Domenico in his treatise, while the two extremes of this action are "buffoonery" and "boorishness." The mean of the human emotion of "anger" is "patience," while an excess of "anger" is "irascibility" and a deficiency of it is "lack of spirit."[63] Aristotle's doctrine of the mean was adopted by the Latin writers on rhetoric. Quintilian says that the speech of an orator should be neither too fast and hurried, nor too slow.[64] Similarly, his gestures should also be moderate, avoiding all the extremes of movement:

> Nor yet again must we adopt all the gestures and movements of the actor. Within certain limits the orator must be a master of both, but he must rigorously avoid staginess and all extravagance of facial expression, gesture and gait. For if an orator does command a certain art in such matters, its highest expression will be in the concealment of its existence.[65]

Domenico's references to Aristotle are further evidence of contact between humanists and the dance masters. Domenico's use of the actual Greek term and his adaptation of Aristotle's teaching to the art of dance imply that he had some sort of contact with university teaching and the humanist studia. Certainly the court at Ferrara, where Domenico worked for so many years, was the home of Guarino's studium. Furthermore, Leonello d'Este was one of the members of the learned circle at Ferrara.

The similarity in opinion between the dance masters and the humanists on this point indicates a widespread concern with control over one's body that went beyond the specialized field of dance teaching. Within humanist circles generally in the fifteenth century, and therefore among the elite with whom they lived, worked, and taught, there was an emphasis on measured movement and control over one's body, since these were outward signs of a person's moral nature. Moderation in movement signified a virtuous soul, a person who was neither dominated by an excess of vice nor skewed by an excessive amount of one particular virtue. Thus a person's gestures and bodily movements, both when dancing and when engaged in day-to-day activities, had to be controlled and had to conform to a certain set of rules or standards. Just as the most eloquent written or spoken language had to conform to a certain set of rules (the grammatical structure and style of classical

Latin), so too did the language of gesture and movement for those of the elite in society. Just as eloquence in prose or poetry was necessary in order to persuade readers of the moral lesson behind what they were reading, so too was elegant movement necessary to convince one's associates of the moral nature of one's character. Just as the readers of history (that is, history as the retelling of the lives of past heroes and virtuous men) should benefit from the moral instruction contained in these works, so too could virtue be acquired by watching and imitating the elegant gestures and movements of those skilled in this art.

Movements of the Soul—Movements of the Body

Part of the reason for the cultivation of, and insistence on, elegant movements was the belief, common to both the humanists and the dance masters, that movements of the body were an outward manifestation of the movements of a person's soul.[66] Those who moved in an ungraceful and inelegant manner in public exposed their inner nature for all to see. There was more at stake than momentary ridicule for one's clumsiness. Vulgar movements that were not eloquent would be a clear sign to those watching that a person's soul was not virtuous and was out of harmony with the world soul. Just as an ungraceful dancer could often be out of step with the music, so too would her or his soul be out of step with the movement of the cosmos that bound heaven and earth together. The fact that movements of the soul are reflected in movements of the body is stated explicitly by Guglielmo in the preface to his treatise:

> This virtue of the dance is none other than an external action reflecting interior spiritual movements [or "movements of the soul"]. These movements must agree with the measured and perfect consonances of a harmony that descends with delight through our hearing to our intellect and to our welcoming senses, where it then generates certain sweet emotions. These sweet emotions, just as if they are constrained against their nature, try as much as possible to escape and make themselves visible in active movement.[67]

In other words, for Guglielmo, movements of the body were reflections of movements of the soul; and, therefore, those movements had a double reason to appear graceful. The same belief that

movements of the body were an exterior manifestation of movements of the soul is found in a letter written by Manuel Chrysoloras between 1411 and 1413, in which he discusses how a person
can obtain rational pleasure from painting and sculpture by recognizing the human emotional and moral conditions portrayed by
the artist:[68]

> [A]nd just as the soul of each man disposes his body . . . so that
> its own disposition—distress or joy or anger—is seen in the body,
> so too the artist disposes the outward form of the stone . . . or of
> the bronze or pigments . . . so that through portrayal and skill the
> passions of the soul can be seen in them.[69]

For Chrysoloras it is part of the virtuosity and skill of artists that
they can render into stone or paint a commonplace human ability,
that is, the way human beings externalize movements of the soul
in movements of their own body. Just as a painter could "move the
soul of the beholder when each man painted there clearly shows
the movements of his own soul . . . [that] are made known by
movements of the body,"[70] so too could dancers move those who
saw their performance to sorrow, anger, happiness, or laughter.
The emotions of the dancers were made visible through the movements of their body, thus giving them both a tremendous power
and a responsibility: a power to affect the emotions of those who
watched, and the responsibility to represent only morally edifying
emotions.

Dance, Nobility, and Ethical Behavior

To the *quattrocento* mind, dance had the ability to teach ethical
behavior. A person watching a dance performance could learn to
recognize virtues by observing their physical representations. Since
a virtuous person when dancing would be imitating in his or her
movements various positive ethical states, these would then be recognized by the spectators, who could then learn to imitate these
virtues in their own lives. Naturally the reverse was also true; that
is, a dancer's movements could represent negative emotional states.
Guglielmo did not seek to deny that the art of dance could be
abused and used for immoral or improper purposes. But he also
argued that when used by virtuous, noble, and moral men, it could

have a positive ethical effect on its practitioners and on those who observed it.[71] Therefore, the dance masters had an interest in promoting the moral virtues of the art of dance and in emphasizing its benefits for society as a whole, as is illustrated by the following passage from Guglielmo's treatise:

> But when it is practiced by noble, virtuous, and honest men, I say that this science and art is good, virtuous, and worthy of commendation and praise. And moreover not only does it turn virtuous and upright men into noble and refined persons, but it also makes those who are ill-mannered and boorish and born into a low station into sufficiently noble people. The character of everyone is made known by the dance.[72]

In the passage quoted above, Guglielmo is advancing a serious claim for his art of dance: that it makes men noble (*gentile*). The definition of exactly what constituted "nobility" in fifteenth-century Italy varied, ranging from the possession of great wealth, to membership in an ancient lineage, to holding a public office or being trained to bear arms.[73] The definition of nobility was also a subject for debate in humanist circles, with several of the leading humanists writing on the subject, including Poggio Bracciolini, Carlo Marsuppini, Bartolomeo Sacchi (Il Platina), and Cristoforo Landino. Although their emphases varied slightly, all these four men agreed that for a person to be truly noble she or he had to be virtuous:

> For virtue and goodness alone
> are the marks of true nobility.[74]

Nobility was not created by great wealth or an old family name, they argued, but issued "from virtue alone,"[75] a virtue that was due to the efforts of each individual, not external causes, or the actions of others in the past.[76] Platina described nobility as

> a certain distinction that comes from nothing other than virtue itself, by which we separate good from evil, worthiness from unworthiness. If it is noble to be steeped in the liberal arts, to have learned to observe justice, duty, and wisdom, and to persevere in all things, how is it at all possible to consider anyone noble who has allied himself, without learning or erudition, to intemperance, injustice, disregard for obligation, and prodigality?[77]

Both Platina and Landino include in their dialogues a discussion of what virtues lead to true nobility, that is, wisdom or prudence, courage or fortitude, moderation and temperance, and justice.[78]

Thus when Guglielmo says that dance makes men noble, he is claiming, I argue, that dance helps those who practice it to cultivate all the virtues that bestow true nobility. In his treatise Guglielmo is adopting the humanist ideal of nobility, and all that this ideal entailed, rather than merely claiming that dance makes men noble by teaching them to walk and move in a manner suitable for a member of an old or wealthy family. I base this argument on three grounds: other statements in the dance treatises that ally dance with the virtues that bestow nobility, particularly prudence and moderation; on the attention Poggio's ideas about nobility received when they were published; and on the unanimity with which the humanists who wrote after Poggio continued (and enlarged upon) his central theme of how the practice of virtue leads to nobility.

I will address these grounds in reverse order, beginning with the popularity of Poggio's ideas. Poggio's and Marsuppini's texts were written close together, that is, before September 1440. Platina's and Landino's works were not written until the 1470s, after Guglielmo had completed the 1463 presentation version of his treatise. Yet, while both Platina and Landino expanded on Poggio's arguments, their central thesis was still the same. Furthermore, Marsuppini was appointed professor of poetry, rhetoric, philosophy, Greek, and ethics in the Florentine studium in 1431, a post he held for many years, and through which he taught many of the next generation of scholars, including Landino. Thus Landino had strong links with the earlier generation of humanist scholars whose work appeared in the 1440s and 1450s, that is, in the two decades that the dance treatises were also being written.[79]

While Poggio (unlike Platina and Landino, later on) does not discuss in great detail the virtues that lead to nobility, these virtues do form part of many other humanist writings of the 1430s, 1440s, and 1450s. For example, Palmieri, in his treatise *Vita civile* of 1439, devotes many pages to a thorough discussion and analysis of the four cardinal virtues of prudence and wisdom (*prudentia*), fortitude (*forteza*), justice (*giustitia*), and temperance or moderation (*temperantia*). Palmieri divides each of the four principal virtues into further subsections: prudence, for example, is composed of memory (*memoria*), intelligence or knowledge (*intelligentia*), and foresight (*providentia*).[80] Thus a person who is truly noble will excel in prudence, the exercise of reason that facilitates a person's choices between good and evil in thought and action. Memory is a necessary component of prudence, because it is through memory that a person learns lessons from past events, and through these lessons present and future actions are judged.[81] As Platina says, "[P]rudence . . . is in these respects the mistress of the other virtues."[82]

Therefore, the first part of Guglielmo's claim that dance makes men noble is that dance helps them to choose prudently between good and evil. Certainly *memoria* occupies a central part in the theoretical foundation of the art of dance, just as it does in the art of rhetoric.[83] It is one of the essential characteristics or qualities of the art of dance, without which the dance would be imperfect:

> [W]e have understood that wishing to have this [art] perfect, six principal things are required, that is, *misura*, memory, the proportioning of the ground,[84] *aiere*, *maniera*, and bodily movement,[85] and especially memory and *misura*.[86]

Memory is essential for the art of dance, as it is for the other liberal arts,[87] as one needs to be able to remember all the elements that combine to produce an elegant and graceful performance, while at the same time concentrating on the music and adjusting one's steps, gestures, and movements to it as it changes:

> And in the second place one needs to have a perfect memory; that is, a constant diligence in assembling into one's mind the parts necessary to the said memory, paying close attention with great concentration to the rhythmical sound corresponding to the steps. Because if the music changes in some way, becoming either slower or faster, then he who has begun to dance may be despised for his lapse in concentration or lack of memory.[88]

Thus those trained in dance would have learnt to perfect their memory, a training that could then be utilized in other aspects of their lives. Domenico also insists that a "large and profound memory" (*una grande e perfonda memoria*) is essential, and he describes it as a "treasury of all the bodily movements, natural and learnt" (*texorera de tutti Li motti corporali Naturali e Acidentali*),[89] a phrase strongly reminiscent of the description of memory in the Roman rhetorical treatises:

> Now let me turn to the treasure-house of the ideas supplied by
> Invention, to the guardian of all the parts of rhetoric, the Mem-
> ory.[90]

> What shall I say about that universal treasure-house, the mem-
> ory?[91]

But Domenico also explicitly links memory and prudence in his
discussion of Aristotle's virtue of the mean, where he says that
"memory is the mother of prudence":

> But do we not know that *misura* is part of prudence and it is in
> the liberal arts? We know that memory is the mother of pru-
> dence, which is itself acquired by long experience.[92]

In this passage Domenico brings together the virtues of moderation, prudence, and memory in a way that is echoed by Platina in
his work on nobility a generation later: "Moderation is not without
reason joined to prudence."[93] Thus the second virtue that conferred
true nobility on a person, and which is discussed in the dance treatises, was that of temperance or moderation. In saying that the art
of dance makes a person noble, Guglielmo is claiming that dance
encourages its practitioners to cultivate moderation and temperance. The importance of moderation to the dance masters' philosophical justification of their dance practice has been discussed
above, and, as we have seen, it was a recurring theme in all the
dance treatises.[94] Moderation in movement was one way dancers
could avoid the evils of sexual license and depravity.[95] Once again
this is very close to the humanists' understanding of the virtue of
temperance,

> which we are accustomed to call sometimes restraint, sometimes
> even moderation. This virtue calms and guides the desires of our
> minds and *moderates against lust.* . . . One whom we designate as
> noble ought to be self-controlled and temperate.[96]

Half a century after the death of Guglielmo, the ability of
dance to teach moral truths was carried even further by the northern European humanists. The status of dance as a medium of moral
instruction was elevated by the publication of such works as Thomas Elyot's *The Boke Named the Governour.*[97] Elyot's book was a
treatise on the education of young boys for careers in the country's
administration. Elyot was strongly influenced by the educational

writings of the fifteenth-century Italian humanists, and he too firmly believed that virtue was to be developed through a program of education and training. According to Elyot, dance was a noble and virtuous pastime, as it provided both recreation and a means to learn and comprehend the virtues and noble qualities necessary for adult life, especially the fundamental virtue of prudence, "the porch of the noble palace of man's reason whereby all other virtues shall enter."[98] Through the study and practice of the *basse danse* children could learn the important moral truths that were essential for those engaged in public affairs and in the government of the country. The *basse danse*, according to Elyot, was an exercise in virtue, with each step of the dance signifying a different aspect of prudence.[99] For example, the reverence which begins every *basse danse* signifies the honor due to God, which is the basis of prudence and should be the starting point for all of mankind's actions.[100] The branle step signifies "maturity," by which Elyot means "moderation," that is, the mean between two extremes.[101] The two single steps signify providence and industry. By "industry" Elyot means the combination of intelligence and experience, while "providence" refers to the ability to foresee what is necessary for a good outcome for the public one is governing and then to act to ensure that this outcome is achieved.[102] The reprise step signifies "circumspection," that is, knowledge of the causes of past disasters and the outcome of present actions. "Circumspection" means being able to evaluate events and their consequences, so that one can decide whether a course of behavior should be continued or abandoned.[103] Because the double step of the *basse danse* was made up of three forward movements (or steps), it signified the three branches of prudence: natural authority, experience, and modesty.[104]

The Physical Expression of Virtuous Movements

Elyot clearly specified which step of the *basse danse* was associated with each virtue. The fifteenth-century Italian dance treatises were not so specific, but it is clear what sort of movements Domenico and his colleagues considered virtuous. Central to Domenico's ideal of morally correct movement was, of course, keeping to the mean. For Domenico excessive movement was a sign of moral weakness as well as low social standing. It is the peasant from the country and the professional entertainer, the minstrel, and the juggler who exhibit extremes of movement.[105] Thus large leaps from the ground, extravagant gestures with the arms, bending the body at a wide angle from the vertical axis, taking large strides so that the body becomes unbalanced, or lifting the legs high in the air would indicate a morally corrupt state. This idea of what constituted virtuous movements was shared by Alberti, as can be seen in his discussion of how painters should portray movement in the figures they draw:

> But because they hear that those figures are most alive that throw their limbs about a great deal, they cast aside all dignity in painting and copy the movement of actors. In consequence their works are not only devoid of beauty and grace, but are expressions of an extravagant artistic temperament.[106]

Alberti is agreeing with Domenico that excessive movements indicate low social standing. If a painter filled his painting with figures contorted by violent actions, then the work of art as a whole would not be capable of expressing virtuous emotions, as only base ones would have been represented. The fact that larger, wider, more spacious movements were commonly associated with persons of low social status is seen in the portrayal of servants, especially young female servants, in fifteenth-century paintings. These women are often depicted taking large steps, with their long, flowing clothes moving and shifting as a result of their rapid movement. By comparison, women of high social status are depicted with very little movement, and their clothes hang simply around them.[107]

While violent contortions of the body were considered the outward expression of an ugly soul, absolute rigidity was just as bad. Dancers who remained immobile were equally at fault; one only has to remember Castiglione's courtiers at Urbino ridiculing Pierpalo's wooden and lifeless dancing.[108] The time Domenico, Guglielmo, and Cornazano devote to explaining the movements of the body which were essential to a graceful performance is testimony to the abhorrence they felt of a dancer who remained totally rigid and immobile.

A person could imitate virtue in her or his movements by keeping them in between these two extremes. The picture Domenico gives of a gondola moving gently up and down on the swell indicates the moderate movements that he considered ideal. The dancer's movements should always be smooth, never jerky, and always smaller rather than larger, so that the dancer does not overbalance and have to lean one way or another to compensate. The dancer's body should always maintain a controlled fluidity, so that its necessary horizontal movements seem natural and unforced, with one gliding smoothly into the next, just as the gondola effortlessly rises and falls with the waves and rocks slightly from side to side, but never too violently, as this could lead to capsizing.

Alberti reiterates Domenico's ideal of the scale of acceptable movement in his treatise on painting. He emphasizes that while people can move and turn their limbs far more than their torso or head, they do not do so. The movements of the arms and legs, while potentially large, are usually on a much smaller scale:

> I have observed from Nature that the hands are very rarely raised above the head, or the elbow above the shoulders, or the foot lifted higher than the knee, and that one foot is usually no further from the other than the length of a foot.[109]

The movements which Alberti regards as natural are small, and do not cause the body to be pushed far from its vertical or horizontal axis.

Eloquent movements, however, were not produced just by following a set of rules. For movements to be eloquent they also had to be suitable to the occasion and to the music that accompanied them. Guglielmo makes this point very clearly when he discusses the movements that are suitable for men dancing in long tunics, as opposed to those dancing in short tunics.

> Note that the person who dances in a long garment should dance with gravity, and in a different manner than one does if dancing in a short garment. Because dancing as if he were going about in a short garment would not be acceptable. And it is necessary that all his gestures and movements be grave and as refined as is in keeping with what he is wearing, so that the *turcha* or long gown he is wearing does not move around too much, here and there. And be aware that greater posture control, slower rhythm, and more time are necessary when dancing in a long garment, since a short garment requires a little more vigorous dancing. And be aware that whoever dances in a short garment must dance in a different manner than if he dances in a long one. It is required that he perform jumps, full turns, and flourishes with *misura* and in time [with the music]. And this attire of a short robe is very well suited to these [movements and gestures]. . . . And also note that other considerations are necessary when dancing in a short cape. . . . And the reason is that the short cape catches the wind

so that when you make a jump or a turn the cape moves about. It is necessary that for certain gestures and for certain movements and at certain tempi you seize hold of the cape on one side, and at other tempi you must hold both its sides.[110]

From this passage it is clear that part of the skill of a good dancer is the ability to harmonize his movements and steps with the clothes he is wearing as befits the occasion. Movements that would look dignified and seemly when dancing in a long garment appear slightly ridiculous when dancing in a short tunic. Similarly, the jumps, turns, and flourishes that appear elegant when wearing a short garment would have the opposite effect if observed on a dancer in a long tunic. Elegant movement, therefore, as outlined by the dance masters, was not always slow or stately. The most important criterion was that a dancer's movements had to be in harmony with the music, and suitable to each occasion and to the garments worn. From the passage quoted above, it is clear that the elegant, noble dancer had to be able to dance in a vigorous and lively manner when it was appropriate, since jumps and three-hundred-and-sixty-degree turns were an expected part of a performance.

Furthermore, the steps and gestures of the dancers had to be suitable to the music which accompanied them. Certain steps were more fitting to be performed to certain *misure*. When dancing to *piva misura* only the *doppio* step should be performed, because of the fast speed of this *misura*, but when the *bassadanza misura* is heard the dancers could perform all the nine natural steps (except for the *movimento*).[111] A constant refrain in Guglielmo's treatise is that the gestures of the dancers should be in harmony with the music:

> Carrying himself freely [that is, easily, in a natural, unforced manner] with his gestures moving in harmony with the *misura*, according to the accompanying music.[112]

Humanists, also, often considered concordance between a person's movements and the external circumstances necessary. Quintilian has a long passage on how the orator's gestures should conform to his voice, that is, how his movements should be in harmony with the content of his speech:

> [I] will proceed first to the discussion of gesture, which conforms to the voice and, like it, obeys the impulse of the mind. . . .[113]

Further, it should derive appropriate motion from the subject of our pleading, maintaining harmony with the gesture and following the movement of the hands and side.[114]

Alberti expressed a similar view of the depiction of figures in a painting, saying, "I believe that all the bodies should move in relation to one another with a certain harmony in accordance with the action."[115]

It is appropriate for a running man to throw his hands about as well as his feet. But I prefer a philosopher, when speaking, to show a modesty in every limb rather than the attitudes of a wrestler. . . .[116] A painting should have pleasing and graceful movements that are suited to the subject of the action. . . . each person's bodily movements, in keeping with dignity, should be related to the emotions you wish to express. And the greatest emotions must be expressed by the most powerful physical indications.[117]

Thus the dance masters were refashioning common humanist ideals to fit them to the art which they taught. Just as painters would be considered unskilled or deficient if the movements of the figures they depicted were not in sympathy with the subject of the painting, so too did the dancers have to ensure that their movements were in harmony with the music and appropriate to the circumstances of the performance.

Both the dance masters and the humanists believed in the existence and efficacy of a corporeal eloquence, a silent language of the body that had the power to move one's emotions just as did the spoken word. They also agreed that mastery of this eloquence in corporeal and verbal language was achieved through the teaching of a master. Thus both nature and art were necessary for eloquent movements. Guglielmo admits that those who are born with an ability to move gracefully have an advantage over those not similarly gifted, but maintains that it is essential for anyone who wishes to perfect the art of dance to learn all the required skills and practice them:

These things are very much easier and more pleasant to those who have their noble nature and constitution disposed to it by a divine gift, and [who have] a well-proportioned body [that is] healthy, light, and full of agility, without any defect in their limbs, but young, beautiful, agile, nimble, and well studied in grace. In

these people all the aforesaid parts can, with study, be freely demonstrated [to cause] more lasting pleasure. . . . Having seen the
above and fully understood how much the fundamental principle
and the elements are necessary and pertain to the aforesaid art
of dance, without which, as has been said, no one can have perfect
knowledge, nor will he have a praiseworthy reputation among
people of intellect, now it is necessary to note some other most
essential points helpful to turn that knowledge into practice. . . .
Because observing well the said *misure*, and knowing how to divide them up and how to put them into action, is a sign of a
good intelligence and the beginning of true practice, for which
it is necessary to measure oneself with these tests and exercises,
which, if they are well performed, as described below, will lead
to perfection in performance.[118]

For Domenico, Guglielmo, and Cornazano, the dances they describe in their treatises require far more than just the knowledge
of how to do each step. In order to present an elegant, noble, and
assured performance, fifteenth-century dancers had to possess a
thorough understanding of the interaction between the music and
the dance, the ability to adapt the patterns of each dance to the
space available, the wit and invention to subtly vary each step so
that it was not performed the same way several times in a row, a
knowledge of movements of the body which accompanied many of
the steps, an awareness of the phrasing of each step, and the agility
and "bodily quickness" to carry them out. Without any of these
principles the art of dance would not be perfect, and all of them
had to be learnt and practiced in order to be understood and per-
fected.

Good teaching was also crucial for the mastery of rhetorical
eloquence. Quintilian knew this, and book 2 of *Institutio oratoria* is
centered on the teaching of rhetoric, with chapters on the choice
of a teacher (ii), the importance of avoiding inferior teachers (iii),
and arguments against the view that instruction and good teaching
are not a necessity (xi). For Quintilian the art of speaking could
only be mastered by "hard work and assiduity of study," and by "a
variety of exercises and repeated trials,"[119] all under the guidance
of an eloquent teacher.[120]

But as regards the practice of rhetoric, it is not merely the case
that the trained speaker will get the better of the untrained. For
even the trained man will prove inferior to one who has received

a better training. If this were not so, there would not be so many rhetorical rules, nor would so many great men have come forward to teach them.[121]

The fifteenth-century humanists also understood the importance of good teaching, as illustrated by the time devoted to the teaching of rhetorical skills in their schools, as well as by their statements. For instance, Antonio da Rho, a Milanese humanist, declared,

> Neither by nature nor through art will we at once attain what we are seeking. Without some brilliant and excellent man whose footsteps we may follow in our diction, we shall not be able to be impressive in the thoughts we state or elegant in the refinement and brilliance of our language.[122]

Alberti also emphasized the importance of teaching and study in the pursuit of the art of painting:

> [T]he means of perfecting our art will be found in diligence, study and application. . . . [123] Nature gave to each mind its own gifts; but we should not be so content with these that we leave unattempted whatever we can do beyond them. The gifts of Nature should be cultivated and increased by industry, study and practice.[124]

By stressing the necessity for teaching and practice, as well as ability, the dance masters were once again placing themselves within the humanist dialogue on the arts, whether this dialogue was the art of rhetoric or the art of painting.

4

Dance and the Intellect

In this matter [the education of the mind] we desire you to be convinced that there is nothing that men possess on earth more precious than intellect, and that other goods of human life which we pursue are truly insignificant and unworthy. Nobility is beautiful but it is a good not one's own; riches are precious but they are the possession of fortune; glory is pleasant but it is inconstant; beauty is becoming but it is fleeting and ephemeral; health is desirable but indeed subject to change; you desire strength but it easily declines in sickness or old age. Nothing is more excellent than intellect and reason. These no attack of fortune may take away, no calumny may tear asunder. And although all the others are lessened by time, yet age increases knowledge and reason.[1]

These words were written by Piccolomini in his educational treatise, *De liberorum educatione*, but the sentiments expressed by him were widely shared by the fifteenth-century Italian humanists. These sentiments were also one of the main preoccupations of the dance masters, and the importance of intellectually understanding the dance practice is brought out very clearly in their treatises. Unless one engaged one's intellect and reason, the art of dance would never be perfect. For these men dance was far more than physical movement. It was one way in which the truth of the cosmos and therefore the nature of God, the creator of the cosmos, was revealed to human beings and could be understood by them. As we have seen, in their treatises the dance masters argued strongly that dance was an art, an art which was closely linked to music, one of the seven liberal arts. The dance masters were so concerned to establish this link because those who understood and participated in the four mathematical arts of the quadrivium—music, arithmetic, geometry, and astronomy—were engaged in the pursuit of wisdom. Practitioners of these four arts were considered to exercise true knowledge, rather than just a particular skill or ability that could be taught, as, for example, could be the skills of a stonemason or carpenter.

Dance (through music) was one of the liberal arts, and therefore Domenico devotes a substantial part of the theoretical section of his treatise to explaining how dance shared the numerical basis of music and the other mathematical arts of the quadrivium. This chapter is a detailed analysis of Domenico's argument as it is found in his treatise, as well as Cornazano's and Guglielmo's treatments of the subject. The argument rests heavily on fifteenth-century Italian mensural theory, and although this material may not be familiar to every reader, its inclusion here is unavoidable, as this is the way the subject is presented in the dance treatises. The dance masters stated that dance was linked to the liberal arts through music in general, and in particular through the proportions (or ratios) that formed the basis of music at this time, and which were believed also to order the cosmos. In order to understand the importance of the theoretical basis of the dance treatises, and the reason the dance masters argued so vehemently that dance was an art, it is necessary to understand the origin and principles of these beliefs, the Pythagorean and Platonic ideas of the nature of the cosmos. The dance masters were not philosophic thinkers or innovators. Their worldview was that of the Pythagorean and Platonic tradition, which had been transmitted to the medieval West through the writings of St. Ambrose, St. Augustine, and Boethius, and through the commentary and partial translation of Plato's *Timeaus* by Chalcidius.[2] From this tradition the dance masters inherited their belief that dance revealed the ultimate truth of the cosmos. Therefore, before beginning the detailed examination of the proportions found in the art of dance, and how they were expressed in this art, I will provide a short summary of the Pythagorean tradition inherited by the dance masters for those readers unfamiliar with these concepts, in order that they may better appreciate the importance that these proportions held for Domenico and his two pupils.

The Philosophical Basis of Fifteenth-Century Italian Dance: Pythagoras and Plato

Pythagoras, a Greek philosopher and mystic who was born c. 570 B.C., taught that the basis of reality was number, and that every part of nature, both in the earthly world and in the wider cosmos, was organized according to numerical proportions.[3] Numbers themselves, and by extension the mathematical proportions or ratios they formed, were held to represent ethical and aesthetic values; that is, they were true, beautiful, and good. The study and contemplation of numbers was a means for human beings to move beyond the earthly world to knowledge of, and participation in, the divine world.[4] Through this belief that numbers were the "principles and elements" of all things,[5] Pythagoras and his followers were able to form a united system in which all parts of nature, including mankind, were connected through number and proportion. Music was one way these numbers or ratios were expressed in the cosmos.

The numbers which the Pythagoreans believed constituted reality were one, two, three, and four. The number one represented a point, the number two a line, the number three a surface (or area), and the number four represented volume, that is, a three-dimensional figure. No other numbers were necessary, as in the physical world there is nothing greater than a three-dimensional figure. Therefore, perfection was equated to ten—the sum of the numbers which constituted reality.[6] For the Pythagoreans the numerical reality of the universe was expressed in music through the ratios or proportions that produced the notes of the scale. Since they believed that the number ten defined the limit of the physical world, the only proportions that could form the concordant intervals of the musical scale were the proportions between one, two, three, and four: 1:2, 1:3, 1:4, 2:3, 2:4, and 3:4.[7] Some of these are redundant: 2:4 is the same as 1:2, 1:3 is a combination of 1:2 and 2:3, and 1:4 is a combination of 1:2 and 1:2. Thus the concordant intervals of the musical scale for the ancient Greeks (and the medieval West) were those formed by those that remain: the octave (2:1), the fifth (3:2), and the fourth (4:3).

The teachings of Pythagoras were extended by the philosopher Plato, who was born into an aristocratic Athenian family in 427 B.C. Plato accepted the Pythagorean belief in the numerical basis of the universe, and his concept of the cosmos was very close to that of the Pythagoreans. In the *Timaeus*, the only Platonic work known to the pre-fifteenth-century West, Plato describes the creation of the world soul, which was based on a division of the whole into parts. These parts were related by the series of 1:2:4:8 and 1:3:9:27, and the ratios obtainable from these two series, that is, 3:4, 4:3, 9:8, etc.[8] Furthermore, in *Timaeus* Plato presented the view that the human soul is ordered in the same proportions as the world soul.[9] These same ratios are heard in music and are those which sound pleasing to the human ear, since they are those that order the human soul and body.

> Moreover, so much of music as is adapted to the sound of the voice and to the sense of hearing is granted to us for the sake of harmony. And harmony, which has motions akin to the revolutions of our souls, is not regarded by the intelligent votary of the Muses as given by them with a view to irrational pleasure, which is deemed to be the purpose of it in our day, but as meant to correct any discord which may have arisen in the courses of the soul, and to be our ally in bringing her into harmony and agreement with herself, and rhythm too was given by them for the same reason, on account of the irregular and graceless ways which prevail among mankind generally, and to help us against them.[10]

According to Plato the musical intervals and rhythms that were based on these ratios had specific ethical effects; they could "correct" defects in the movement of the soul, and bring it back into concord with the movements of the world soul.

Boethius, born c. 480 A.D. into one of the leading Roman families, was the major conduit through which the teachings of Pythagoras and Plato were transmitted to the medieval West. In his works *De institutione musica* and *De institutione arithmetica* Boethius both codified and summarized Pythagorean and Platonic thought, as well as integrating those beliefs with Christian teachings. These two works of Boethius influenced the teaching of both music and arithmetic as arts of the quadrivium throughout the Middle Ages, because they were used as standard texts until the fifteenth century. Boethius's work remained influential because it discussed music as an example of Pythagorean proportions rather than simply describing performance practice of the fifth century A.D., a subject which would have fast lost its relevance for musicians of later centuries. Thus as long as the Pythagorean ratios remained vital, Boethius's work could be used by both musicians and philosophers.[11]

For Boethius, music, along with the other three arts of the quadrivium, was concerned with the search for truth:

> From this it follows that, since there happen to be four mathematical disciplines, the other three share with music the task of searching for truth; but music is associated not only with speculation but with morality as well.[12]

Music was associated with morality because it had the power to move men's and women's minds and actions toward virtuous or evil deeds: "Plato holds music of the highest moral character."[13] Boethius then gives examples of music's power over mankind: "It is common knowledge that song has many times calmed rages, and that it has often worked great wonders on the affections of bodies or minds."[14] He continues to repeat the Pythagorean and Platonic beliefs that humans are numerically united with the cosmos, and that each person's physical body is connected to his or her spiritual soul by the reality of mathematical relationships:

> [F]or they [the Pythagoreans] knew that the whole structure of our soul and body has been joined by means of musical coalescence. . . . [T]here can be no doubt that the order of our soul and body seems to be related somehow through those same ratios by which . . . sets of pitches, suitable for melody, are joined together and united.[15]

For Boethius the numerical truth of the cosmos was expressed in three different kinds of music, all of which were bound together by the same numerical proportions. *Musica mundana* was the music of the cosmos, inaudible to human ears. *Musica humana* was the musical proportions found in the human body, which united the human soul with the cosmos. *Musica instrumentalis* was the audible pitches (that is, music) produced by human instruments and voices.[16] Boethius's argument that the human soul was bound to the world soul—the *musica mundana*—was very attractive to the philosophers, scholars, and artists of the fifteenth century, as it provided the basis for the widespread analogy that human beings were a microcosm of the broader relationships found in the cosmos.

It was this intellectual heritage that was inherited by the dance masters, and which they used in the theoretical sections of the dance treatises to present dance as an art like music, as a pathway to knowledge of the divine, and as an ethical activity that needed to be understood by the intellect.

The Pythagorean and Platonic Tradition in the Dance Treatises

As previously discussed, Guglielmo's treatise begins with praise of the art of music, and with examples of music's power to move mankind's emotions and to produce the most marvelous effects in the world.[17] He then repeats the traditional belief that through music the human soul is linked to the underlying reality of the cosmos, both earthly and celestial.[18] Guglielmo argues that dance is also an art, one which is no less than the outward, physical realization of the harmony of music.[19] Thus, since dance proceeds from music, dance must also share the characteristics of music; that is, it too is a realization of the proportions which govern all the cosmos, and which tie human beings into the harmony of the universe. In expounding these arguments, Guglielmo is repeating the traditional viewpoint that dance is a human manifestation of the divine nature. It is a path to understanding the nature of God, and to contemplating divine things, because both dance and the cosmos are based on number and proportion. Domenico, on the other hand, adopts a more practical approach in his treatise. His concern when discussing the relationship between dance and music is to explain how the two are related in the actual performance of the dances. Domenico recognizes that the two arts are linked through proportion (*misura*) and thereby bound to the proportions which order the cosmos, but in his treatise he focuses on how these proportions are manifested in the dances themselves. But no matter in what terms Guglielmo and Domenico address the subject, their insistence on the intellectual understanding of dance is essential to their claim that dance is one of the liberal arts. It is this claim that echoes Boethius's stance on music in *De institutione musica*:

> From all these accounts it appears beyond doubt that music is so naturally united with us that we cannot be free from it even if we so desired. For this reason the power of the intellect ought to be summoned, so that this art, innate through nature, *may also be mastered, comprehended through knowledge.* For just as in seeing it does not suffice for the learned to perceive colors and forms without also searching out their properties, so it does not suffice

for musicians to find pleasure in melodies without also coming
to know how they are structured internally by means of ratio of
pitches.[20]

The Four Misure: *Domenico da Piacenza*

Domenico, Guglielmo, and Cornazano all recorded two genres
of dance in their treatises, the *ballo* and the *bassadanza*, and it is in
the former that the Pythagorean ratios or proportions are most
evident. The *balli* were dances composed of short sections of contrasting speed and meter, called *misure*. There were four *misure*:[21]
bassadanza misura, the slowest in speed; *quaternaria misura*, the next
fastest; *saltarello misura*; and finally *piva misura*, the fastest. Domenico goes to great lengths to describe the relative speeds of the
four *misure*, as it is the ratios between these relative speeds that
duplicate the Pythagorean ratios. This subject is so important for
Domenico that he describes the relationship between the four *misure* in two ways: in words, and through the use of symbols.[22]

Domenico's first explanation of the four *misure* is given in
words as follows:

> Note well (and I beseech you to open the virtue of your intellect
> in order to understand) what the *misura* of motion is, and also
> how movements are composed upon the *misure*. . . . And above
> all, under the general heading of *misura* there are four particular
> kinds. The first, which is slower than the others, is called by the
> name *bassadanza*. . . . The second *misura* is called *quaternaria* . . .
> and its speed is one-sixth faster than *bassadanza*. The third *misura*
> is called *saltarello* . . . and this *misura* is one-sixth faster than *qua-
> ternaria* and one-third faster than *bassadanza misura*. The fourth
> *misura* is called *piva* . . . which is one-sixth faster than *saltarello*
> and three-sixths faster than *bassadanza misura*. . . . In these four
> *misure* consist the movement of the dancer and of the musician,
> from the slowest to the fastest.[23]

In this passage Domenico gives the relative speeds of the four *misure*. The *bassadanza misura*, the slowest of the four *misure*, is the
one against which all the others are measured. *Piva misura* is the
fastest *misura*, and it is three-sixths faster, or twice the speed of
bassadanza misura. Thus every three breves (or bars) of *bassadanza
misura* take the same time to play or dance as six breves of *piva
misura*. Thus the ratio of the speed of *bassadanza misura* to that of

piva misura is 1:2. *Saltarello misura* is the second-fastest *misura*. It is two-sixths faster than *bassadanza misura*. Therefore, for every four breves of *bassadanza misura* one can perform six breves of *saltarello misura*, creating the ratio 4:6 or 2:3. *Quaternaria misura* is one-sixth faster than *bassadanza misura*. This means that for every five breves of *bassadanza misura* one can perform six breves of *quaternaria misura*, creating the ratio 5:6. Thus the three ratios or proportions of the different speeds are 1:2 (*bassadanza* to *piva*), 2:3 (*bassadanza* to *saltarello*), and 5:6 (*bassadanza* to *quaternaria*).

In the same passage Domenico also describes the relationship between the four *misure* by using the symbols (or mensuration signs) of fifteenth-century music theory for the division of the breve and the semibreve. This information is embedded in Domenico's description of the ratios between the four *misure*. Here he describes *bassadanza misura* as major imperfect, *quaternaria misura* as minor imperfect, *saltarello misura* as major perfect, and *piva misura* as minor perfect. In fifteenth-century music theory the terms "perfect" and "imperfect" referred to the division of the breve into either three or two semibreves respectively, and the terms "major" and "minor" to the division of the semibreve into three or two minima respectively. This division of the breve and semibreve was called the mensuration and was represented by the four symbols ⊙, ○, ₵, ℂ (see figure 2).

At first glance it seems that by using the terms "major"/"mi-

perfect major ⊙	breve = 3 semibreves
	semibreve = 3 minima
perfect minor ○	breve = 3 semibreves
	semibreve = 2 minima
imperfect major ₵	breve = 2 semibreves
	semibreve = 3 minima
imperfect minor ℂ	breve = 2 semibreves
	semibreve = 2 minima

Figure 2. Division of the breve and semibreve

nor" and "perfect"/"imperfect" Domenico was giving the mensuration of the four *misure*. But this interpretation conflicts with the
mensuration signs found in the notated music. Given the context
of these phrases in the text, one should consider the possibility that
Domenico is still referring to the relative speeds of the *misure*, and
that these terms (or symbols) are another way of describing the
ratios or proportions between the four *misure*. When these terms
are interpreted in this way, most conflict with the signs in the music
disappears.

When he uses the terms "major imperfect" and the others in
the same passage that discusses the relative speeds of the four *misure*, Domenico is still talking about the ratios between the *misure*.
These terms do not describe the time signature of each *misura*,
that is, the division of the breve and the semibreve, but still refer
to the proportions between the four *misure*. In other words, Domenico is using these symbols not as mensuration signs (as one
would commonly expect), but as proportion signs.[24] (A detailed
examination of how Domenico has used these symbols as proportion signs is given in appendix 2 for those who wish to follow the
musicological arguments.)

The Four Misure: *Antonio Cornazano*

The establishment of dance as a liberal art was also important
to Cornazano. Even though, at the insistence of his father, his education at the University of Siena was in law (c. 1445–47), Cornazano himself preferred literary studies.[25] While the University of
Siena did not concentrate on humanistic studies during the fifteenth century, Francesco Filelfo taught in Siena for a few years
in the mid-1430s, during which time he "immediately animated
Sienese humanistic studies both in and outside the university."[26]
Cornazano arrived in Siena less than a decade later, and the interest
in Greek and Latin literature generated by Filelfo's residency could
well have continued, and have been the source of Cornazano's interest in humanistic studies, the fruit of which was seen in his later
life. But while the exact details of his time in Siena are not known,
it is clear that Cornazano would have been well aware of the Pythagorean and Platonic belief in the numerical basis of the cosmos,
and how these proportions were expressed in the quadrivial arts.
For dance to be included in this group it too would have to be
based on the same proportions that ordered the cosmos. In the art

of dance the numerical structure of the cosmos was represented by the ratios between the four *misure*, a topic that Cornazano discusses quite explicitly in his treatise, in two forms—in words, and with the aid of a diagram. On f. 10r of his treatise Cornazano has drawn a diagram in the shape of a ladder. Each rung of the ladder represents one of the four *misure*. If one measures the rungs of the ladder in this illustration one finds that the ratio of their lengths is the same as the ratios of the relative speeds of the four *misure* as expressed by Domenico in his written description of the relationship: "one-sixth faster, two-sixths faster, three-sixths faster." The ratio of the length of the *piva* rung to that of the *bassadanza* rung is 1:2, of the *saltarello* to the *bassadanza* is 2:3, and of the *quaternaria* to the *bassadanza* is 5:6. This exactitude cannot be coincidence.

At the end of his treatise Cornazano lists the *misure* again (f. 34r–34v). Here he states that in *bassadanza misura* each note is doubled, so that three notes are worth six, and six notes are worth twelve (f. 34v). Since he has already said (on f. 10v) that *piva misura* is the first rung of the ladder, and therefore is the *misura* from which the others are measured, his ratios are consistent with Domenico's. Thus, all Cornazano is saying on f. 34v is that what were three notes in *piva misura*, when played in *bassadanza misura* take the same time as six notes played in *piva misura*.

Cornazano's ladder diagram also has text attached to it. In this text Cornazano is following Domenico's "symbolic" usage; that is, he is employing mensural terminology (the terms "major imperfect" and the rest) to refer to the proportions between the four *misure*, not to their mensuration. For example, on his ladder diagram Cornazano (f. 10r) says that *piva misura* is "perfect minor" and that *saltarello misura* is "perfect major," thus agreeing with Domenico's symbolic description of the relationship between the four *misure*. Cornazano describes *quaternaria misura* as "*quattro per tre di perfecto magiore*" [four for three of perfect major]. Perfect major is represented by the sign ⊙, which means that the breve is divided into three semibreves. Following Cornazano's instructions, if four semibreves are played in the time of three, the ratio 3:4 is produced, the same ratio as Domenico gives. (See figure 10 in appendix 2.) The meaning of Cornazano's description of *bassadanza misura* as "*perfecto magiore in ragione di canto*" is unclear, but the size of the rungs in the ladder diagram are in the ratios given by Domenico.

The Four Misure: *Guglielmo Ebreo*

Guglielmo introduces the four *misure* in book 1 of the theoretical section of his treatise, in the chapter entitled *Aliud experimentum [V]*. After stating that *misura* is the foundation of the art of dance, Guglielmo says that there are four "rules" or types of *misura: perfetto magiore, perfetto minore, imperfetto minore*, and *quaternario*.[27] Later on, in the other versions of his treatise, the four *misure* are described as "*si balla*."[28] In these manuscripts *bassadanza misura* is described as perfect major, *quaternaria* and *piva* as imperfect minor, and *saltarello* as perfect minor. I have taken the phrase "*si balla*" to mean that the *misure* are being described as they occur in the music. This is indeed the case for *quaternaria, saltarello*, and *piva misure*, as *quaternaria* and *piva* do commonly appear in the music in the mensuration of imperfect minor (C), and *saltarello* in the mensuration of perfect minor (O). As with Cornazano, the problem occurs with *bassadanza misura*, which is described as perfect major (☉), while in the music its mensuration is imperfect major (₵). On the basis of the Siena and Modena versions of Guglielmo's treatise, we can reasonably assume that in the 1463 presentation version he is referring to *bassadanza misura* as "*perfetto magiore*," *saltarello misura* as "*perfetto minore*," and *piva misura* as "*imperfetto minore*"; that is, he is giving the mensuration of the four *misure* as they appear in the music, not the ratios of their speeds.

In the version of his treatise held in the dance collection of the New York Public Library, the passage referring to the four *misure* near the end of the manuscript is as follows:

> *Bassadanza* when one dances it is perfect major, or as others say, imperfect major, while *saltarello* is perfect major and *piva* and *quaternaria* are imperfect major.[29]

This is the only occasion in which *bassadanza misura* is given two appellations: it is called both "perfect major," as in all the other versions of Guglielmo's treatise, and "imperfect major," the mensuration given by Domenico in his treatise. Thus in this manuscript, information from Domenico's description of the *bassadanza misura* is conflated with Guglielmo's description. Whether the remainder of this passage further mixes Domenico's usage of mensuration signs to indicate the proportions between the *misure* (that is, "*saltarello* is perfect major") with an inaccurate rendering of

Guglielmo's description of the mensuration of *piva* and *quaternaria*, or whether all three *misure* (*saltarello, piva*, and *quaternaria*) have been inaccurately named, is unclear.

The Four Misure: *A Summary*

In summary, the three treatises do not contradict or disagree with one another about the relative speeds of the *bassadanza* and *saltarello misura*, or of the *bassadanza* and *piva misura*. Both Domenico and Cornazano are quite explicit that the ratio of *saltarello* to *bassadanza* is 3:2, and that of *piva* to *bassadanza* is 2:1. Guglielmo cannot be said to contradict this position, as he does not discuss the relative speeds of the four *misure*. He only gives their mensuration.

The ratio of *bassadanza misura* to *quaternaria misura* is given by Domenico and Cornazano as both 5:6 and 3:4. The first ratio is derived from the written description of "one-sixth, two-sixths, three-sixths faster," while the second is derived from the "symbolic" description, that is, the use of mensural terminology to indicate proportions. Half a millennium after the flowering of this dance practice, it is unclear which ratio was meant by the dance masters, or indeed what the exact relationship was between the speeds of *bassadanza* and *quaternaria misure* when they were performed for a *ballo* in the ducal palace. Certainly Domenico's scheme of "one-sixth, two-sixths, three-sixths faster" is simple and elegant, and could be easily remembered by practical dancers. On the other hand, the concept of proportion was vitally important to the dance masters. It may well have been the case that in the time needed for five breves' worth of *bassadanza* steps a dancer did perform six breves' worth of *quaternaria* steps. But in mensural notation the ratio 3:4 is as close as one can come to 5:6, since mensuration signs can represent only ratios of numbers divisible by two or three.[30]

Both Cornazano and Guglielmo use the words "perfecto magiore" to refer to *bassadanza misura*. In his discussion of the four *misure* Guglielmo is giving the mensuration of each *misura*, that is, the division of the breve and semibreve when each *misura* occurs in the music. This is indeed the case for *quaternaria, saltarello*, and *piva misura. Bassadanza misura*, however, does not usually appear in the surviving music as "perfecto magiore" (◉). Why one of the four *misure* is not described by, or given, its mensuration as it appears in the music is not clear. John Caldwell has suggested that on this occasion Guglielmo may well be using "perfecto magiore" to mean only the slowest of the four *misure*.[31] This explanation may well be correct. But whatever the case may be, one thing is clear: the dance masters were skilful enough to adapt existing musical conventions and value systems in order to achieve the practical result that they wanted. In their treatises they have constructed a genre of dance based on a system of proportions that ties their dance practice back to the Platonic reality. This connection with the Platonic conception of the cosmos was essential for their dance practice to qualify as an art, and for it to be superior to the other current dance practices.

The Practical Implications

Domenico was concerned to place dance within the medieval system of the seven liberal arts, in order to lay claim to the inherent truths of these arts for the dance practice he taught and participated in. Thus the numerical ratios which were found in all three levels of music (*musica mundana*, *musica humana*, and *musica instrumentalis*) found expression in the *balli* in the ratios of the speeds between the four *misure*. But Domenico was a practicing choreographer and dancer as well as a theorist, and therefore had a pragmatic purpose in writing his dance treatise, namely to specify the ratios which were actually used in dancing. The ratios between the four *misure*, 2:1, 3:2, and 4:3, were part of the standard conventions of *musica mundana*, the music of the heavenly spheres. It is these ratios which Domenico describes by his use of the standard mensuration signs as proportion signs. It is the connection with *musica mundana*, and all that that entailed, which was important to Domenico. If the consequences of this particular use of mensural terminology, when worked out in actual dance practice, did not fit exactly and precisely into the theory of practical, contemporary music-making in Italy c. 1400–50, this was of secondary importance.

When Domenico explains the ratios between the four *misure*, he is talking about the ratios at the minima level, not at the semibreve level. This concentration on the minima level is deliberate because it is this level that is of most concern to the dancer. Dancers must be aware of the speed of individual minima, as it is on the minima beats that the movements of the different dance steps occur. For example, the three forward-moving steps which form a *doppio* occur on the first, third, and fourth minima of every breve. Thus, in his explanation of the four *misure*, Domenico has married the practical concerns of the dancer to the intellectual ideas about the nature of the cosmos. He has achieved this by applying fifteenth-century Italian music theory to the needs of the dance practice.

Thus John Caldwell is quite correct when he points out that Domenico's explanation of the four *misure* "amounts to an idiosyncratic use of mensural terminology," because it "implies that the minims of 'major perfect' can then be taken out of their mensural context and performed that much faster in a different mensural context."[32] This does not mean that Domenico was confused about the standard use of mensural terminology, or ignorant of fifteenth-century music theory. It only means that he was using the "rules" and "conventions" developed over several centuries for one art—music—to explain the procedures of another art—dance. Domenico used the conventions of music theory to indicate how much faster the minima of one *misura* should be played and danced than the minima of *bassadanza misura*. In his treatise Domenico does not discuss the mensuration of the four *misure* as they appear in the music for the *balli*.

In actual performance of the *balli* the minima of the four *misure* are all at different speeds. Every *doppio* step takes six or eight minima to perform, whether one is dancing a series of *doppi* in *bassadanza, saltarello, piva,* or *quaternaria misura*. The mensuration of each *misura* as found in the music of the *balli* is given in figure 3. Thus a *doppio* in *bassadanza misura* would take one breve of ₵, or six minima, to perform. A *doppio* in *saltarello misura* would also take one breve of ○ or ₵ to perform, but in this case the six minima

Misura	Mensuration Sign	Semibreve Division	Minima Division
Bassadanza	₵	◊·◊·	♪ ♪ ♪ ♪ ♪ ♪
Quaternaria	₵	◊ ◊ ◊ ◊	♪ ♪ ♪ ♪ ♪ ♪ ♪ ♪
Saltarello	○ or ₵	◊ ◊ ◊ or ◊·◊·	♪ ♪ ♪ ♪ ♪ ♪
Piva	₵ or C	◊·◊· or ◊ ◊	♪ ♪ ♪ ♪ ♪ ♪ or ♪ ♪ ♪ ♪

Figure 3. The mensuration of the four *misure*

Bassadanza		$\dot{\quad}\!\cdot = 56\text{mm}$	$\frac{6}{8}$	$\flat = 168\text{mm}$
Quaternaria	(6:8)	$\dot{\quad} = 56\text{mm}$	$2 \times \frac{2}{4}$	$\flat = 224\text{mm}$
	(5:6)	$\dot{\quad} = 50\text{mm}$	$2 \times \frac{2}{4}$	$\flat = 201\text{mm}$
Saltarello	(6:9)	$\dot{\quad}\!\cdot = 84\text{mm}$	$\frac{6}{8}$	$\flat = 252\text{mm}$
		$\dot{\quad} = 126\text{mm}$	$\frac{3}{4}$	$\flat = 252\text{mm}$
Piva	(6:12)	$\dot{\quad}\!\cdot = 112\text{mm}$	$\frac{6}{8}$	$\flat = 336\text{mm}$
		$\dot{\quad} = 168\text{mm}$	$\frac{2}{4}$	$\flat = 336\text{mm}$

Figure 4. Metronome markings for the four *misure*

would all be moving one-third faster than the minima of the *bas-sadanza doppio*. Figure 4 shows how the speed of the minima of each of the four *misure*, assuming one starts with a value of one semibreve in *bassadanza misura*, equals 56mm. One must always remember that there is a distinction between the mensuration of the *misure* (how many minima are needed to complete one breve of that *misura*, or one *doppio* step) and Domenico's use of mensuration signs to signify the proportions, or different speeds, between the four *misure*. The breves of *saltarello misura*, for example, always have six minima, not nine, as the "major perfect" is used only to symbolize the increase in speed between *bassadanza* and *saltarello*, not to show the mensuration of *saltarello misura*.

5

Order and Virtue

The old notion of synonymity between geometric and
moral rectitude was so ingrained in the Western mind
that people took it for granted that anyone fortunate
enough to be raised in a geometrically ordered environment would be morally superior to anyone who lived
amid the twisting cowpaths of an amorphous village.[1]

Geometric order equals moral virtue. This idea, encapsulated in
one sentence from a footnote in Samuel Y. Edgerton Jr.'s discussion
of the relationship between art and science in Western Europe,
forms the framework of this chapter. The idea is expressed by the
humanist Leonardo Bruni early in the fifteenth century in his panegyric on the city of Florence. It is found even more clearly
throughout the architectural treatises of Alberti and Filarete. The
idea was also adopted by the dance masters in their treatises, both
in their theoretical foundation for the art of dance and in the practical end-product of their work, the choreographic patterns of their
dances.

In *Laudatio florentinae urbis* Bruni presents a picture of Florence
as a round shield, whose center is the Palazzo Vecchio, and which
in turn is surrounded by a number of concentric circles consisting
of the inner city, the city's walls, the houses outside the walls, the
country villas, and the smaller country towns that lie in the out-
ermost circle, along with the castles between them:

> The city itself stands in the center, like a guardian and lord, while the towns surround Florence on the periphery, each in its own place. A poet might well compare it to the moon surrounded by the stars. . . . Just as on a round buckler . . . here we see the regions lying like rings surrounding and enclosing one another. Within them Florence is first . . . the center of the whole orbit. The city itself is ringed by walls and suburbs. Around the suburbs, in turn, lies a ring of country houses, and around them the circle of towns. The whole outermost region is enclosed in a still larger orbit and circle. Between the towns there are castles.[2]

While Bruni's picture of Florence does indeed follow the topography of the city and its surrounds,[3] it is also idealized in that it is presented in the geometrically ordered plan of concentric circles.[4] Just as the cosmos was seen as a series of concentric circles radiating outward from the fixed, immobile Earth, through the spheres of the planets and fixed stars, to the crystalline sphere, then the sphere of the *primum mobile* that formed the boundary of the finite universe, to the empyrean, the realm of God and the angels and archangels, so too is Florence viewed according to this divine geometry. Bruni alludes to this picture of the cosmos in his image of Florence as "the moon surrounded by the stars." Florence is a city built on "great moderation" and "solid proportion"[5] and is unsurpassed in its "splendor and architecture," in the "nobility of its citizens," and in all the "virtues and accomplishments."[6] Florence is constructed according to divine geometry—the rings of concentric circles and the well-proportioned buildings—and this geometric order and proportion is emulated throughout the city: each part is in harmony with every other part. "[T]his very prudent city is harmonized in all its parts, so there results a single great, harmonious constitution whose harmony pleases both the eyes and minds of men."[7] The order and harmony of its setting, architectural design, and construction make its citizens virtuous: "[h]ere are outstanding officials, outstanding magistrates, an outstanding judiciary, and outstanding social classes."[8]

Geometric Order in Architecture

Nearly half a century later, Alberti was to expand on the idea that geometric order resulted in moral virtue in his treatise *De re aedificatoria*. In this work Alberti argued that it was the responsibility of the architect to design and construct an ordered environment for his fellow citizens, since "without order there can be nothing commodious, graceful, or noble."⁹ For Alberti an ordered environment was one in which the buildings, the squares, indeed the whole city was designed and laid out according to the geometric figures that are found in nature, and which underlie the whole cosmos. And it was in the judicious selection and management of these geometric shapes, as well as their numerical expressions in the proportions of a building, room, or column, that the beauty of a building resided:

> Beauty is a form of sympathy and consonance of the parts within a body, according to definite number, outline, and position, as dictated by *concinnitas*, the absolute and fundamental rule in Nature. This is the main object of the art of building, and the source of her dignity, charm, authority, and worth.¹⁰

The beauty produced by the proportional forms found in nature was conveyed to human beings through their senses. Whether through sight or hearing, the same ideal of beauty was recognized. Therefore it was clear to Alberti that the "very same numbers that cause sounds to have that *concinnitas*, pleasing to the ears, can also fill the eyes and mind with wondrous delight."¹¹ If the architect wished to produce a built environment that conveyed the ideal of beauty to the "eyes and mind" of its inhabitants, then he had to use the same numerical proportions in his buildings that produced the musical consonances. In chapters 5 and 6 of book 9 Alberti explains what these ratios are, and how they can be measured in terms of the varying lengths of strings. Thus the ratios of the lengths of strings that produce an audible harmony can, when transposed to ratios of the length, width, and height of a building and all its parts, produce a visual harmony:

> [T]he musical numbers are one, two, three, and four. . . . Architects employ all these numbers in the most convenient manner possible: they use them in pairs, as in laying out a forum, place, or open space, where only two dimensions are considered, width and length; and they use them also in threes, such as in a public sitting room, senate house, hall, and so on, when width relates to length and they want the height to relate harmoniously to both.¹²

Thus Alberti recommends that in designing a piazza or open area, such as a garden, the ratio of width to length that the architect should use is the 1:1 ratio of the square, or the musical consonances of the fifth (2:3), or the fourth (3:4).[13] Furthermore, flat surfaces like the paving in a church should be decorated with the same musical proportions and geometric shapes: "I strongly approve of patterning the pavement with musical and geometric lines and shapes, so that the mind may receive stimuli from every side."[14] The ideal shape of a church building as a whole should imitate basic geometric shapes: circles, squares, rectangles, or polygonal figures like the hexagon that can be circumscribed by a circle and which are also found in nature.[15]

For Alberti the "natural excellence and perfection" of a building, which "excit[ed] the mind" of its viewers and caused immediate sympathy with it,[16] was the fact that the building was a representation of the cosmos. The architect, through the use of the Pythagorean proportions and geometric figures such as the circle and the square, could create buildings, and indeed whole cities, that were three-dimensional representations of the divine world. The city's inhabitants would naturally respond to this visual representation of divine beauty, desiring virtue and imitating the divine order that they saw before them in their city buildings. Alberti knew that people's "eyes are by their nature greedy for beauty and *concinnitas*."[17] Without the geometric order present in the buildings and in the design of a city, its citizens could not be noble, and, as argued in chapter 3, one of the chief components of nobility was moral virtue. Thus, just as viewers of a painting were moved to experience virtuous emotions and actions, so too were the inhabitants of a geometrically ordered city inspired to virtuous activities.[18]

Geometric Order in Dance and Garden Design

In the medieval and Renaissance West geometric order was one representation of the cosmos. One of the functions of human representations of the cosmos was to further individuals' knowledge of the nature of God. The closer people came to understanding the divine presence, the more they wished to imitate the nature of God, that is, to act in a virtuous manner, in both their private lives and their civic duties and responsibilities. The cosmos could be represented by "many different models based upon the several disciplines of the quadrivium."[19] As we have seen, one of these models was geometric figures, either planes or solids, while another was the "visual depiction of ratios between numbers"[20] that was found in architecture. That the art of dance was an aural as well as visual representation of the ratios between numbers is made clear by Domenico in the theoretical section of his treatise. As has been shown in the previous chapter, one way in which Domenico represented the cosmos in his choreographies was by using the Pythagorean ratios to describe the temporal relationship between the four *misure*. But this was not the only representation of the cosmos found in the art of dance. It was also represented in the choreographic patterns of Domenico and Guglielmo, through which they constructed a visual representation of the macrocosm. The patterns formed by the dancers were predominantly the simple geometric figures that were also found in architecture and in the design of grand gardens: squares, rectangles, circles, and triangles.

Both garden design and choreography are concerned with manipulating, controlling, and ordering space. Dance can be seen as the creation of patterns in space: patterns which form and reform, and trace out shapes in the air and on the ground. Formal gardens can also be viewed as the creation of patterns on the ground: their shapes are static, but they still present changing images as viewers stroll from section to section, and new shapes open up before them. The fundamental principles of order and measure, geometric forms, and the construction of the whole out of small compartments are clearly seen in the Italian gardens and in the contemporary collections of choreographies. The earliest extant garden design of the sixteenth century is a sketch for a small garden by Baldessare Peruzzi from the 1520s.[21] The designs in the compartments are geometric, segments of squares and circles. The now famous Italian gardens of the Medici family and other nobility of sixteenth-century Italy were built from the 1530s onward.[22] Information on the princely gardens of the fifteenth century is less abundant. But from the work of scholars such as David Coffin on the gardens in Rome,[23] and from the architectural treatises of the fifteenth century, such as that of Leon Battista Alberti, it seems clear that the essential characteristics of strongly geometric shapes, compartments enclosed within a finite space and arranged in four quarters, were present. Alberti's treatise on architecture included comments on gardens, since the author believed that the garden was just as much the concern of the architect as the house was, since the same geometric figures should be employed in gardens as in buildings.[24] Lorenzo de' Medici, two of whose choreographies have survived, was very fond of his copy of Alberti's treatise on architecture, and was not eager to lend it to Borso d'Este when the latter requested it in 1484. When the book was printed two years later, sheets of the printed edition were delivered to Lorenzo as soon as they came off the press. The same terms were used in gardening and architecture, and it was not an accident that the great garden designers of the fifteenth and sixteenth centuries were also the famous architects of the day: for example, Francesco di Giorgio Martini, Giuliano da Sangallo, and Bramante. In di Giorgio's designs, for example, the compartments of the gardens are very similar to the rooms of the houses.[25]

Above all, the Renaissance garden was ordered and measured. Through it was expressed the interaction of the artificial culture created by human beings with the natural "culture" created by God. As a reflection of the cosmic order, nature was inherently ordered, and so in the garden the art of mankind had to "imitate not only nature's outward appearance, but also its underlying order."[26] This underlying order was understood to be rendered more perfect by the cultivation of the trees and plants in the garden, and by the addition of sculpture, ornaments, water features, mounds, and grottoes. In topiary work, labyrinths, and trellis constructions, plants—shrubs, vines, and trees—were cultivated into geometric figures like spheres or pyramids; or into shapes reminiscent of sculpture, like ships or human figures; or into natural shapes, like animals. The overwhelming importance of order in fifteenth- and sixteenth-century gardens was the characteristic which distinguished them from the gardens of earlier centuries. It is also the characteristic which they shared with dance.

The order in gardens was expressed not only in the geometric forms of the ornaments, but also through the use of bilateral symmetry: the central paths which bisected each other at right angles, the trees planted in straight lines, and the geometry of the compartments all created a strong rectilinear character. Utens's view of the Medici villa L'Ambrogiana (begun after 1587) clearly illustrates the wide central avenue with symmetrical units on either side of it. Not only does each compartment have its own geometrical space, but each section is divided into four quarters. Even the large trees in the beds at the back of the garden are planted in straight lines. One of the major contributing factors to the ordered, rectilinear nature of the formal gardens was the use of the square. The compartments, while often having circular forms within them, were

invariably square. This shape was further emphasized by the planting of large trees in each corner. Squareness also found expression
in the patterns created by the dancers as they progressed through
the figures of a dance. One example is *Anello* (see appendix 3), in
which the choreography emphasizes the pattern of circles within
squares.[27] This dance begins with the two couples facing one another in a square. The second half of the dance then consists of
the two men, then the two women, tracing out circles as they
exchange places.

Furthermore, in the choreographies the harmony and proportion of the straight walks of espaliered fruit or yew trees were trans-
muted into the long, forward-moving floor tracks of the fifteenth-
century *balli* and *bassadanze*, and the circular figure which was often
interspersed with the rectilinear patterns. (I am referring here to
the figure which is created when a couple take left or right hands
and move around each other, tracing out a circle as they go.) One
example of this type of floor pattern is the *bassadanza Lauro*, which
was choreographed by Lorenzo de' Medici (see figure 1). Many of
the *bassadanze* and *balli* share this type of floor pattern. In *Lauro*
the couple only move forward, with a pause in the middle of the
choreography to describe a circle. The floor track is very similar
to the gardens with their long straight central avenue, often broken
by a circle around which the four compartments are arranged, for
example, at the Medici villas Petraia and Poggio a Caiano. In other
dances the performers move forward *and* backward from the starting position, but usually still in straight lines. As Claudia Lazzaro
remarks, "Throughout the Renaissance, a central avenue traversed
the garden, often covered with a pergola. . . . Movement from one
end of the garden to the other, but not excursions to either side,
was encouraged by such an axis."[28] In the *bassadanza Lauro*, the two
performers move from one end of the dance space to the other,
with only a few small "excursions to either side" with the *riprese*.
One should note that two of the four groups of sideways steps
occur in the central circular space created by the couple's taking
hands and walking around each other. Thus half of the sideways
movements are used to reinforce the circle in the middle of the
long, straight path.[29]

The environment of each dance that was presented to the viewers was certainly ordered, and its order was defined by geometric
shapes. Within the microcosm of their choreographies, the dance
masters were imitating the structure of the macrocosm, so that

through their moving pictures men and women might be led into noble and virtuous behavior. Circles, squares, triangles, and rectangles were present in the choreographic patterns as the result of conscious decisions on the part of the dance masters. These basic geometric shapes were regarded by the dance masters as "thematic figures," that is, as overarching shapes that were formed and maintained through most of the dance, and within which the performers interacted. They were not seen as a sequence of discrete figures out of which the choreography was put together, and between which the dancers moved, forming first one figure, then moving quickly into the next, and the next, until the end of the dance.

This view of the squares and circles as overarching shapes can be seen in the written descriptions of the choreographies, which was the form of dance notation used by the *maestri di ballo* in their treatises. The choreographies were notated in the form of a description of a series of step sequences and direction indicators. The geometric shapes only become apparent when the dance is executed. As the performers progress through a dance they find themselves forming a square, triangle, or circle. The geometric shapes formed by the choreographic instructions are normally not explicitly named, as they are one hundred and fifty years later in the texts of the English Jacobean masques, because in Italy they were not the building blocks of the dance, but the end result of the series of step sequences.

The manner in which these "thematic figures" were worked out in practice can be clearly seen in the dances for three performers.[30] In dances like the *balli Ingrata* and *Spero*, or the *bassadanze Venus*, *Phoebus*, and *Pellegrina*, the three dancers begin the dance in a straight line. Reasonably soon they form a triangle, usually when the middle dancer moves in one direction and the other two outside dancers move in the other (see figure 5). This triangular shape is then maintained for most of the dance as the three move toward each other, pass, move away from each other, and then turn to face each other (see figure 6).

In *Ingrata* [The ungrateful woman] the triangular shape allows the dramatic "plot" of the dance to unfold, that is, the continuing advances of the two men toward the woman, and her constant playing with these advances, first rejecting them, then encouraging them, then deserting the men for a second time, before the final slow advance together that culminates in her circling each man in turn (perhaps to symbolize the final harmony) to finish in a straight

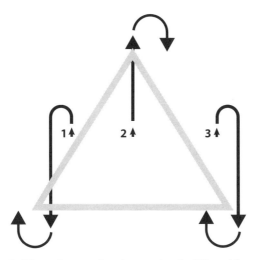

Figure 5. Three dancers forming a triangle. The odd numbers represent the two men and the even number the woman. The small arrow by each number indicates the direction the dancer is facing. The larger arrows indicate the dancers' paths. The gray lines are used to indicate the triangle formed by the dancers' paths.

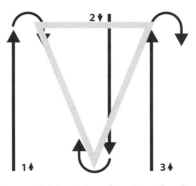

Figure 6. Maintaining the triangular shape

line as they began. The floor track shows (see appendix 3) how the formation of the triangular shape separates the woman from the two men, and the maintenance of the shape throughout most of the dance allows her changing reactions to her partners to be emphasized. Similarly in *Merçantia*, a *ballo* for three men and one woman, the solo woman and the two "spare" men form a triangle after the woman's partner has left her. Although this time the triangular shape does not last as long as it does in *Ingrata*, it is used

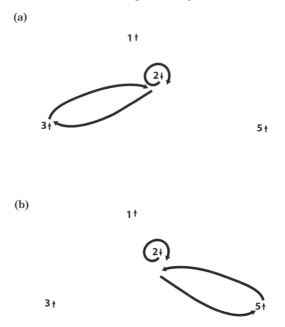

Figure 7. Triangular shape in *Merçantia*

for each of the men's attempts to win the woman, with their advances toward her and subsequent retreat outlining yet again the
geometric figure (see figure 7). Thus, as is illustrated by *Ingrata*
and *Merçantia*, the geometric shapes present in these choreographies are "thematic figures" in that they continue for a reasonable
length of time while the interaction between the performers is
played out.

    One *ballo*, *Santomera*, is built around a single geometric shape
that is specifically mentioned in the dance description. The opening instructions of this dance are for the two women and one man
to arrange themselves into a triangle,[31] which is maintained
throughout most of the dance.[32] Many of the floor patterns involve
the three dancers moving around the perimeter of the triangle,
tracing out this shape as they move. The triangular shape is also
emphasized and maintained by floor patterns in which the three
dancers all move toward each other to meet at the center of the
triangle, then turn 180 degrees to return to their starting positions
at the vertices of the triangle. The floor patterns of this dance do
not cause the dancers to move outside the original formation: there
are no long, rectangular, forward-moving sequences, nor in any of

the step sequences does one of the dancers break away from the triangular formation.

In the fifteenth century the triangle had a number of symbolic meanings. A triangle could be formed by ten points, one at the apex, two in the line below, three in the next, and four forming the base. This arrangement was a diagrammatic way of expressing the reality of the cosmos,[33] and was a sacred symbol for the Pythagoreans. The triangle was later adopted by Christian writers as a symbol of the Trinity. It was also the symbol for the element of fire, while an inverted triangle (with the apex pointing down) represented the element of water. Given the tapering shape of the triangle, this geometric shape was also a symbol of the link, or relationship, between the earthly and divine spheres. It represented movement, or ascent, from the physical, sensual life to an intellectual understanding of the divine realm. While a square figure represented the earth, and a circle the divine world, the perfection of the heavenly realm, the triangle (or pyramid) represented the path from one to the other.[34]

In the *ballo Santomera* it is not possible to state precisely what the choreographer had in mind when devising this dance, but one can assume that those watching would see the triangle and recognize it as a symbol of the Trinity. Furthermore, one can see how this dance, with its overwhelming emphasis on the triangular shape, would illustrate the dance masters' insistence that dance could lead men and women to noble and virtuous behavior. For the educated viewer, the sustained presentation of the geometric figure of the triangle would be a visual reminder of the moral imperative to aspire to a closer knowledge of the divine nature.

Triangles were not the only geometric shape found in the choreographies: squares and circles were also common. Sometimes one figure merged into another, as in the *ballo Anello* (see appendix 3). After the opening sequence of eight *saltarello doppi* in *piva misura*, the two men separate from their partners to form a square.[35] The next few step sequences take place along the perimeter of the square as first the men, then the women, change places. In the second half of the dance a circular shape is emphasized, with the men, and then the women, turning in individual circles. Then the two men change places by moving in a circle behind the women, and once again the women repeat the men's movement. *Colonnese* and *Giloxia* are both dances for three couples, and in them the circular shape predominates, as dancers both circle their own partners (describing small circles) and move around the whole line of couples (describing larger ones). Other dances in which the performers stand in a file one behind the other, like *Verçeppe* and *Jupiter*, combine the two geometric figures of a circle and a long thin rectangle like a column. Rectangular shapes dominate in dances such as *Lauro*, *Leonçello in doi*, and *Rostiboli gioioso*, whose floor tracks show continuous forward movement in a straight line. Many of the *bassadanze*, including *Mignotta nova*, *Mignotta vecchia*, *Corona*, *Reale*, and *Flandresca*, show a variant of this simple rectangular pattern in which the forward movement is interrupted with 180-degree changes of direction.

Dance was a natural activity, but it was also shaped by human intellect and reason in order to produce an end product in which divine order was apparent. Dance, like its sister arts in fifteenth-century Italy, was based on an imitation of nature, and the "laws" that governed the natural world also generated the choreographic compositions of the dance masters. The geometric shapes observed in nature and the numerical ratios that ordered the whole cosmos were present in the art of dance. Men and women, through their participation in the art of dance as either performers or spectators, were able to recognize this order, and by contemplating its beauty were stimulated to imitate that divine order in their own lives. Thus geometric order—a representation of the cosmos—led people toward virtue, and this was true in dance just as it was in music, painting, architecture, and gardening. The dance masters were quite explicit about the fact that dance makes men noble, and that this was one of the characteristics that differentiated their dance practice from the crude caperings of the peasants. In fifteenth-century Italy, nobility had a number of meanings, but chief among them was the possession and practice of virtue, a virtue that was created by the efforts of each individual. To the uninformed or ignorant, dance could be seen as a sequence of steps or movements through space and time: a glorious but ephemeral moving spectacle with no lasting impact, underlying rationality, or consequences for the behavior of women or men. But to the educated, informed viewers, dance was much more than this. They looked for order in its movements, and recognizing such order was both proof of their intellectual activity and standing and a stimulus to a virtuous life.

Conclusion

In their treatises both Cornazano and Guglielmo acknowledged Domenico as their master,[1] but Domenico himself gives no hint as to where, or from whom, he learnt the art of dance. He was certainly not its inventor, since dance had been an aristocratic practice for more than a century before his birth. He was, however, the first person to systematize and to codify the practice, to give it a theoretical and philosophical basis, and to argue for its classification as an art. In this book I have explored some of the reasons why the status of dance and the way dance practice was recorded changed when they did: between the 1430s and the 1450s, the same years in which the humanist Guarino Guarini was working at Ferrara. The dance practice was closely enmeshed with the contemporary intellectual culture and humanistic activity. In their work Domenico and his two colleagues were responding to patterns of thought and intellectual debates that permeated the entire spectrum of society, affecting not only their profession but other artistic practices of the time as well. The court at Ferrara, which during the 1430s "was . . . the most brilliant literary and artistic center in

Italy,"[2] is a useful symbol of these interlocking relationships, for not only was it closely associated with the development of the art of dance, it was also a leading center of humanist activity.

In 1429 Guarino Guarini arrived in Ferrara to be Leonello d'Este's personal tutor. For six years the heir to the marquisate of Ferrara studied under one of the leading humanists of the day, who became a colleague and companion as well as a teacher and mentor. Even when Guarino's official duties as Leonello's tutor were completed in 1435, Guarino continued to live in Ferrara, operating a boarding school and attracting visiting humanists to Ferrara. From 1436 to 1460 he held a chair of rhetoric funded by the communal government,[3] as well as teaching at the University of Ferrara.[4] Leonello himself was a scholar: he knew Greek and Latin and wrote poetry in the latter. His first wife, Margherita Gonzaga, was educated by Vittorino da Feltre at Mantua, and so was able to share his intellectual interests. From the 1430s onward Leonello attracted a circle of learned friends with whom he regularly engaged in philosophical and literary discussions, including the humanist Angelo Decembrio and the artists Pisanello (Antonio Pisano) and Jacopo Bellini. During this decade Leonello also became friends with Alberti, whose treatises on painting and architecture show many parallels with the dance treatises. Indeed, it was at the urging of Leonello d'Este that Alberti began to write his treatise on architecture. Finally, it is at the end of this decade, just before Leonello became the marquis of Ferrara in December 1441, that the dance master Domenico da Piacenza's name first appears in the Ferrarese records. Thus Domenico was associated with a court that was led by a humanist ruler, and which was an active center for scholarly humanist activity, teaching, and debate.

While one cannot point to any direct evidence, such as letters, of contact between Domenico and the humanists at the Ferrarese court, there is a large amount of indirect evidence for contact, the transmission of ideas, and the influence of humanist values on Domenico's work and thought. In his dance treatise Domenico not only referred to Aristotle's *Nicomachean Ethics*, a work that was favored by the humanists and was not regularly taught as part of the university curriculum,[5] but also used Aristotle's term, *eutrapelia*, for the mean of conversation when discussing the concept of keeping to the mean in all one's actions. His use of a precise Greek term is indirect evidence that he was in contact with the humanists at Ferrara. It is extremely unlikely to be a coincidence that Domenico used this term, given that he was working in Ferrara at a court ruled by a man literate in Greek and home to one of the very few humanists who was fluent in Greek, and who was first to learn the language in Byzantium.

Nor is it a coincidence that the dance treatises show such similarities with contemporary treatises on painting and architecture. Domenico shared the preoccupation of other *quattrocento* artists who were trying to consolidate their professions into an art, rather than a physical skill, that is, to make their practice part of the intellectual culture.[6] Once dance, painting, or architecture was an art, it was possible to formulate theories about its nature. One could explain the laws or rules that governed a dance performance, as well as discuss the general principles of the art of dance and its component parts, as Domenico, Guglielmo, and Cornazano did in their treatises. Most importantly, once dance was considered one of the liberal arts it became a method of approaching God, a pathway to understanding the divine as manifested in God's creation on earth, and ultimately the nature of God.

In the treatises of Domenico and his two disciples, dance was provided with a theoretical and philosophical foundation, like all the quadrivial disciplines. Dance was linked to the liberal arts through music, and in particular through the proportions that formed the basis of music at this time. Therefore, through the relationships between the four *misure*, Domenico established that the art of dance was also based on these same numerical proportions, which were found in music and which ordered the cosmos. These proportions were held to be "true, beautiful, and good," since they were the goals in a scholar's pursuit of knowledge, a "spiritual ascent toward experience of essential reality, of absolute truth, of the deity."[7] Dance was not the only profession for which a philosophical framework was being devised. Alberti's aim in writing his treatise on architecture, a version of which was presented to the pope around 1450, was "to confer upon architecture the status of a productive art."[8] As far as Alberti was concerned architecture had the same theoretical principles as did the quadrivial arts. The proportions that were found in beautiful and elegant buildings were the same ratios found in music, dance, arithmetic, geometry, and astronomy:

> The very same numbers that cause sounds to have that *concinnitas*, pleasing to the ears, can also fill the eyes and mind with wondrous

delight. From musicians therefore who have already examined such numbers thoroughly, or from those objects in which Nature has displayed some evident and noble quality, the whole method of outlining is derived.[9]

Filarete endorses Alberti's conception of the discipline of architecture. A good (that is, knowledgeable) architect will "strive to make his building good and beautiful,"[10] and he will achieve this by following the "laws of nature":[11] the proportions which order the cosmos. The proportions that Filarete uses most frequently in designing his ideal city are 1:1, 1:2, and 2:3, followed less frequently by 3:4 and 1:4,[12] all of which fall within the small set of Pythagorean ratios that represent the numerical reality of the cosmos.

If dance was indeed one of the liberal arts, as claimed by the dance masters, then those who practiced it needed to do more than move gracefully and remember the correct step sequences. True *maestri di ballo* needed an intellectual understanding of the dance, as well as physical skills. They needed to understand proportion—*misura*—in all its manifestations, the division of space, all the rules and principles laid down in the dance treatises. This stratification of dance practitioners by the dance masters parallels Boethius's classification of what we now call "musicians" into three categories, the highest of which was the educated musician, who had an intellectual understanding of the discipline, rather than just a considerable skill in the playing of an instrument or in singing.

> How much nobler, then, is the study of music as a rational discipline than as composition and performance! It is as much nobler as the mind is superior to the body: for devoid of reason, one remains in servitude. . . . Just how great the splendor and merit of reason are can be perceived from the fact that those people—the so-called men of physical skill—take their names not from a discipline, but rather from instruments. . . . But a musician is one who has gained knowledge of making music by weighing with the reason, not through the servitude of work, but through the sovereignty of speculation. . . . Thus, there are three classes of those who are engaged in the musical art. The first class consists of those who perform on instruments, the second of those who compose songs, and the third of those who judge instrumental performance and song.[13]

Similarly, as far as Alberti was concerned, the architect had to possess far more than the manual skills of a carpenter:

Before I go any farther, however, I should explain exactly whom I mean by an architect; for it is no carpenter that I would have you compare to the greatest exponents of other disciplines: the carpenter is but an instrument in the hands of the architect. Him I consider the architect, who by sure and wonderful reason and method, knows both how to devise through his own mind and energy, and to realize by construction, whatever can be most beautifully fitted out for the noble needs of man, by the movement of weights and the joining and massing of bodies. To do this he must have an understanding and knowledge of all the highest and most noble disciplines.[14]

For Alberti an architect had to have an intellectual understanding of the process of building, and also of the theoretical principles on which it is based, as well as an education in "the highest and most noble disciplines"—the liberal arts—so that he could create through his ingenuity the buildings appropriate to the "noble needs of man." Filarete in his treatise goes even further than Alberti and lists the humanistic education that he considered necessary for an architect:

In which branches of knowledge, which sciences, should the architect participate? It says that he should know letters, because without letters he cannot be a perfect artist. In addition to this he should know the art of drawing. He should know geometry, astrology, arithmetic, philosophy, music, rhetoric, and medicine. He should also know civil law. He should also be a historian in all these branches of knowledge.[15]

In Alberti's definition of an architect, and in Guglielmo's discussion of the perfect dancer, the necessity of *ingenio* is stressed. *Ingenio*, an inborn talent or creative power, the intellectual vision needed to conceive of the work in the first place, was increasingly claimed by painters, architects, and dance masters as a sign that their art was an expression of intellectual qualities. The association of their work with the gift of *ingenio* also brought it closer to the literary, philosophical, and rhetorical work of the humanists, who saw themselves as the arbiters of the intellectual section of society. In common with those who promoted other arts in the fifteenth century, in their treatises the dance masters were expounding their vision of their art, in which intellectual and physical aspects (*ingenio* and *ars*) were in harmony. The dance masters do discuss the manual, workmanlike aspects of dancing, such as adjusting one's steps to fit the available space, but, as we have seen, they give far more attention to the philosophical basis and fundamental principles of the practice, such as *misura*.

One of the major ways in which Domenico, Guglielmo, and Cornazano were influenced by the humanists can be seen in their passion for eloquent movements. Echoing the humanists' passion for eloquence in the spoken and written text, the dance masters were concerned to produce elegance in their counterpart to poetry and prose: movement of the human body. Thus a large part of the specialized technical vocabulary they developed dealt with descriptions of these elegant movements: *maniera, aiere, ondeggiare, campeggiare, gratia,* and *fantasmata*. Following the rhetorical tradition of Cicero and Quintilian, the humanists, as well as the dance masters, believed that a person's gestures, deportment, facial expressions, and manner of walking were a silent language that carried a rich treasury of meaning. The close relationship between the dance masters and the humanists can be seen in the similarity of their comments on movement, whether while dancing (in the case of Domenico and his colleagues) or while carrying out day-to-day activities (in the case of the humanists). Furthermore both groups shared the belief that a person's character was revealed in deportment and gestures. Both were concerned that movement should always be moderate and the body controlled, seeing movements of the body as reflections of movements of the soul.

The humanists recognized that it was part of the virtuosity and skill of artists that they could render in paint or stone human features that externalized inward emotional and moral states, and could thus move a viewer to rational pleasure upon recognition of those states. So too could dancers move those who saw their performance to sorrow, anger, or laughter: the emotions of the dancers were made visible through the movements of their bodies. Along with painters, sculptors, and architects, dancers had the power to affect the emotions of those who watched, and a responsibility to represent only morally edifying emotions. Since a person watching a dance performance could learn to recognize virtues by observing their physical manifestations, dance could teach ethical behavior.

The dance masters, therefore, had an interest in promoting the moral virtues of the art of dance, and in emphasizing its benefits for society as a whole. The humanists believed that moral lessons could be learned by reading the lives of virtuous public figures and the appropriate classical texts. Therefore their educational program was necessary for the continued good governance of the state and the health of society in general. The dance masters promulgated a similar claim for their art: it too was of benefit to society as a method of teaching moral truths. Dance made people noble in that it helped those who practiced it to cultivate the virtues that bestowed true nobility, in particular prudence and moderation. Furthermore, the choreographies of Domenico and Guglielmo were geometric and ordered, and their patterns imitated the order inherent in both the natural and divine worlds. The shapes around which the choreographies were constructed were those regular geometric figures that represented the cosmos, and that formed the basis of the other arts in fifteenth-century Italy. Through their recognition of these geometric representations of the cosmos men and women could be led into a greater understanding of the nature of God, and encouraged to lead lives of moral virtue.

The dance masters were not the only ones to claim beneficial effects for their art. In his treatise on architecture Alberti claims that the architect and the practice of architecture are essential to the well-being of the state: the architect uses his knowledge to serve society.[16]

> [L]et it be said that the security, dignity, and honor of the republic depend greatly on the architect: it is he who is responsible for our delight, entertainment, and health while at leisure, and our profit and advantage while at work, and in short, that we live in a dignified manner, free from any danger.[17]

Evidence for the influence of humanist thought on the work of the dance masters can also be found in the manner in which the latter discussed the art of dance in their treatises. Domenico, Cornazano, and Guglielmo all borrowed the humanistic discourse on painting and sculpture. Both the humanists and the dance masters were committed to the idea that their art was for an elite, the "informed" group in society, not for the uninformed populace. The latter were incapable of deriving anything but sensual pleasure from a work of art, and were certainly not capable of participating in the intellectual pleasure gained from meditating upon religious scenes or watching performances of virtuous actions. Dance, like painting, was able to enrich and delight the souls only of those who had a true appreciation of it. Furthermore, it was only the informed viewers who could appreciate the subtleties of the form and resist being seduced by the superficialities of matter. The pupil in Guglielmo's dialogue does not belong in this group, as he can understand only the surface requirements of the dance practice, like dancing in time and remembering the correct step sequences.

The final concept which was borrowed by the dance masters from the humanists' writings on painting and sculpture was the opposition between nature and art. Guglielmo explicitly states that dance can be both a natural activity and an art, an activity in which human skill and ingenuity transform an innate behavior or order into a man-made order. The contrast between nature and art, so fundamental to the theoretical discussion of dance, is also found in the choreographies themselves. The twelve steps are divided into the natural, innate steps and the man-made steps, which are used to decorate and ornament the basic natural steps.

The dance practice of the elite in *quattrocento* Italy was tightly woven into the fabric of Italian life and society. As a cultural phenomenon it participated in, and was influenced by, other contemporary artistic practices, intellectual movements, social conditions, and philosophical debates. The intellectual and philosophical framework developed by the dance masters for their art placed dance firmly within the rhetorical tradition of the humanists. The "eloquent body" of the dance master or his noble pupils was a silent exposition of the humanistic literary values of rhetorical eloquence. A picture of life in the Italian courts and republics, from Milan in the north to Naples in the south, is incomplete if it ignores dance. Once dance is seen within the context of the contemporary humanist movement, a much clearer and more comprehensive picture emerges. When dance is considered, *quattrocento* society is revealed as far richer and more complex than previously thought, as ties between what were previously thought of as distinct cultural practices are discovered to be numerous and binding.

As we have seen, the dance masters were strongly influenced by the values and intellectual concerns of the humanists. Their work was also part of fifteenth-century Italian society's response to the changing ideas of the measurement of space. Dance as an art form is necessarily concerned with the movement of bodies not only on a two-dimensional surface—the dance floor—but also in three-dimensional space. The dance masters' concepts of *misura*, *aiere*, *ondeggiare*, and *campeggiare* were all concerned with the movement of the dancer's body in all three dimensions: up and down, as well as sideways, forward, and backward. Through concepts like *aiere* the dance masters were concerned with defining and measuring the space through which the dancers moved. The dance masters' concern with the measuring and proportioning of space ran parallel to developments in other areas of society. By the fourteenth century the medieval Western concept of space as a series of finite and compartmentalized zones was changing, particularly under the influence of Euclidian geometry.[18] By the fifteenth century space was conceived of as continuous: whether on earth or in the heavens, it now had to have the same physical properties and follow the same geometrical rules. Artists, cartographers, scientists, and philosophers all realized that space could be measured and, through the principles of Euclidian geometry, depicted in three dimensions by linear perspective.

Society grew more interested in depicting the spatial relationships between objects or figures, rather than just their physical appearance. This is most vividly illustrated by a comparison between the maps or city plans of the fourteenth century and those of the late fifteenth century. In the former all the houses, walls, and prominent buildings are depicted as squashed together, so crowded that there is no visible space between them. By the late fifteenth century, however, city plans were conceived of and drawn as a "geometric picture of the spatial arrangement of the town."[19] In the fifteenth-century dance treatises the choreographies were notated in the form of written descriptions that were concerned with the spatial arrangements of the dancers and the relationships between them. In fact, given the complexity of many of the dances, the choreographer and author must have had a very clear picture in his mind of those changing spatial arrangements. One might speculate that one impetus for the written description of choreographies in fifteenth-century Italy was the rise in interest in spatial relationships in society in general at this time.

Whether by adapting the humanists' rhetorical theory of eloquence, their mode of discourse on the art of painting, or their concern for the teaching of moral virtue, the dance masters played a vital part in the intellectual and artistic culture that surrounded them. When performing, the dance masters did so under the critical eyes of the elite. Similarly, in other aspects of their professional work, they did not isolate themselves from their social milieu: they were actively engaged with humanist concerns. In constructing a philosophical framework for dance, they marshaled humanistic arguments and values both as a sword in the promulgation of dance as a liberal art, and as a shield in the defense of their status as members of the intellectual elite, possessors of both *ingenio* and *ars*. The influence of humanism in fifteenth-century Italy did not stop with art and music: it had a profound effect upon dance as well.

Appendix 1. Transcription and Translation of MS from Florence, Biblioteca Nazionale Magl. VII 1121, f. 63r–69v

GIOVANNI CARSANIGA

An anonymous poem in terza rima from 1459 in praise of Cosimo de' Medici and his sons and the celebrations made for the visit to Florence of Galeazzo Maria Sforza and the pope.

The visit to Florence in 1459 of the heir to the duchy of Milan and Pope Pius II was an event that resonated throughout Italy. At least two anonymous works describing the festivities have survived: one manuscript, a portion of which is transcribed below, and a second, shorter poem in terza rima of thirty folios in length, found in Florence, Biblioteca Nazionale Magl. XXV 24. (It has been published in *Rerum italicarum scriptores: Raccolta degli storici italiani dal 500 al 1500*, revised and edited by Giosuè Carducci and Vittorio Fiorini, vol. 27, part 1 [Città di Castello, 1907].) Interest in the event has continued to this day, as descriptions of the various *feste* performed in 1459 have found a place in a large number of studies of fifteenth-century Italian cultural history. But in spite of this interest, the poems themselves have not received much scholarly attention in the form of published transcriptions and translations. In 1895 Vittorio Rossi published a transcription of 168 lines (f. 66v line 13 to f. 67r line 20, then f. 67v line 11 to f. 69v line 15) of the poem from Magl. VII 1121, that is, part of the description of the *ballo* in the Mercato Nuovo (Vittorio Rossi, *Un ballo a Firenze nel 1459* [Bergamo: Istituto Italiano d'Arti Grafiche, 1895]). Guglielmo Volpi in 1902 published a short work that described this same manuscript and paraphrased the contents of the entire poem. Included in his paraphrase were brief quotations, usually only a few lines (Guglielmo Volpi, *Le feste di Firenze del 1459: Notizia di un poemetto del secolo xv* [Pistoia, 1902]). In 1995, as part of his translation of the fifteenth-century Italian dance treatises, A. William

Smith included a transcription and translation of the portion of Magl. VII 1121 that described the *ballo*. Once again the translation is only partial, as only selected excerpts—sometimes isolated, individual lines—have been included (A. William Smith, trans., *Fifteenth-Century Dance and Music: Twelve Transcribed Italian Treatises and Collections in the Tradition of Domenico da Piacenza* [Stuyvesant, N.Y.: Pendragon Press, 1995]). Therefore the transcription and translation given here are the first to be published of f. 63r–69v. This section of the poem describes in vivid detail the preparation and setting of the *ballo*, the participants and their luxurious costumes, and the dance itself, together with the associated feast. For precise details on the different types of headdresses, hoods, hats, clothes, and jewelry mentioned in the poem, see Carole Collier Frick, *Dressing Renaissance Florence: Families, Fortunes, and Fine Clothing* (Baltimore: Johns Hopkins University Press, 2002), especially pages 228–30.

The text has been modified by adding punctuation and diacritics; separating words and all proclitics (articles, prepositions, conjunctive pronouns, etc.) from following words; and making conjectural corrections whenever the text does not seem to make sense. The spelling is unchanged, except that ç has been modernized to z, u to v, and y to i. Obscure or untranslatable passages, their attempted translations, and conjectural changes have been placed between [square brackets]. Added words are placed between <chevrons>. The transcription was made from a microfilm of the original manuscript without reference to the earlier, partial transcriptions.

MS from Florence, Biblioteca Nazionale Magl. VII 1121 f. 63r–69v

63r

Et quella sera molto si parloe
della gran giostra & poi a pposar vanno.
& chome l'altro giorno ritornoe
ciaschun levossi & molto allegri stanno
però che 'l giorno in sul merchato nuovo
far si dee il ballo: & già l'ordine danno.
Et chome già ti dissi ora t'approvo

That night people talked a lot
about the great joust; then they went to sleep.
And as the new day dawned
everyone got up, and they were very merry
because on this day in the New Market
a ball is to take place: and they have to already given the order.
And as I told you already, now I can confirm

che 'ntorno è lo stecchato & più riseggi	that there is a fence around, and also seats,
& di sopra le tende anche vi trovo.	and above I also find tents.
Più civi deputar ch'ongniun proveggi	Also citizens have charged everyone to make sure
ch'ongni chosa abbia l'ordine & l'effetto	that everything is in order and fit for the purpose
di ciò che per quel dì si faccia o veggi.	of whatever is being done or seen on the day.
Fessi dal saggio fare un bel palchetto	The wise <organizer> had a beautiful little dais made
in sul qual fosse dengnia residenza	which could be a worthy place
al mangnio chonte [& altissimo]° prefetto.	for the great count* and the pope.†
Et rispondea a quel locho in presenza	And what was inside the market
ciò che d'intorno interno al merchato era	matched that place in appearance;
& fu parato a gran mangnificienza	it was decked with great magnificence
di panni arazzi panchali & spalliera.	with fabrics, tapestries, seat and back padding for the benches.
Di sopra un ciel di panni lochupleti	Above there was a sky canopy of rich cloth
& di dietro & da llato ongni frontiera.	and back and side borders also of this material.
Il pian del palcho era pien di tappeti	The floor of the dais was covered in carpets
& tutti i seggi altissimi & reali	and all the high princely chairs
ch' eran d'intorno splendienti & lieti,	which were around, shining and bright,

63v

Addorni fur di spalliere & panchali,	were adorned with back and seat cushions,
chom'io so che per te chomprender puoi,	as I know you can guess by yourself,
chon ordin che ma' più si fecier tali.	so well laid out that the like was never to be seen.
Tre gradi intorno abe seditoi,	There were three ranks of seats all around,
più alto l'un che l'altro acciò che veggha	one higher than the next, so that both those sitting
chi siede prima & chi sedeua poi.	in the front and in the back could see.
Et per ordine par che si proveggha	And there seemed to be a provision that

° altissimo &
* Galeazzo Maria Sforza
† Dante used Prefetto to mean the Pope in Par. 30, 142.

che 'l primo grado a llato allo stec-
        chato

pe' grandi & dengni cittadini
        s'eleggha,

et l'altro un po' più basso che gli è a
        llato

per donne che non sieno atte a ballare

pel tempo o per grossezza o vedovato.

Et quel dinanzi sol s'è fatto ornare

che le donne & fanciulle da ffar festa

intorno intorno su v'abbino a stare.

Al dirinpetto alla singnioril giesta

sopra dello stecchato, alto si fé

pe' pifferi & tronbone un locho
        assesta.

Io ti prometto sopra la mia fé:

doppo mangiare vi venne tanta giente

che in un'ora ongni chosa s'empié.

Palchetti, tetti, chase, che presente

erano al ballo bel, tutto s'enpieva

senza restarvi voto di niente.

Sì grande il popol d'intorno v'aveva

ch'i' nol so dire a uno migliaio o due,

ma più che venti milia si credeva.

Et sarevene stati molti piùe

se 'l circhuito fosse stato grande

ma picciolo era & per tutto pien fue.

64r

Le bocche & vie per ciaschedune
        bande

furan piene chon tal chalcha ch'io ti
        dicho

che e' vi si ghustò strette vivande;

tal ch'i' son cierto ch'un gran di
        panicho

---

the first rank near the fence

would be for the important and
        worthy citizens,

and the next, a little lower,

for ladies who could not dance

because of their age, pregnancy, or
        widowhood.

Only the front rank has been deco-
        rated

so that women and girls who would
        spread

the festive mood all around should
        occupy it.

Opposite the seignorial coat of arms

above the fence, a place was prepared

high up for the shawm and trombone
        <players>.

I assure you upon my faith:

after lunch so many people came

that in one hour the whole place was
        full.

Scaffoldings, roofs, houses overlooking

the beautiful dance area were
        completely filling up

without any space remaining empty.

So big was the crowd that I cannot
        estimate,

give or take one or two thousand,
        how many there were,

but it was believed there were more
        than 20,000.

And there would have been many
        more

if the circumference <of the
        enclosure> had been large,

but it was small, and everywhere full
        up.

The alleys and roads leading to it on
        every side

were choked by such a crowd that I
        tell you

it was like being in a jam-packed
        eating house;

so that I'm sure that a grain of millet

non sarebbe potuto chader mai
sulle strade d'intorno al locho apricho.

Il preparato fu chome udito <h>ai:

ora tu entendi quel che poi seguie,
ben ch' i' so che 'l vedesti & cierto il
 sai.
Nel primo seggio molti civi gie

& tanto mangniamente & bene ornati
non gli viddi già mai quanto quel die.

Furansi nel bel ballo raunati

sessanta giovinetti, che quaranta
avean veste & giubbon di brocchati.
Mangnificienza mai fu tale o tanta
quanto fu quella di vestir di seta:

& credi a quel che la mia lingua
 chanta.
Festanti, allegri & cholla faccia lieta
erano i giovinetti peregrini
cholla persona a' chostumi decreta.

Figliuoli eran di dengni cittadini
& di gientile & gienerose gieste
& pulcri chome spiriti divini.
Et fu tra lloro più di cinquanta veste

tutte pien di richami d'ariento
a llor funzioni & gientiligie oneste.
Pien di razzi di sole parean dentro
ch'era una chosa ammiranda a vederle
& parmi anchor quando me ne
 rammento.

64v
Et più che cinquanta altre pien di
 perle
pulite equali bianche grosse & tondi

a llor divise richamate ferle.
Questi gharzoni di chostumi fechondi
in quel giorno una volta o due o tre
mutarsi mangni lor vestir giochondi.

Fodere ricche & chon tire dappié

could not have fallen to the ground
on any road surrounding the open
 space.

The preparations were as you've
 heard:
now listen to what followed,
even if I'm sure you saw it and know
 it well.
The first rank of seats was occupied
 by many citizens

who were so beautifully caparisoned
that I have not seen anything like it
 since that day.

In the beautiful dance area sixty
 young people

had gathered together, of whom forty
wore brocade dresses and jackets.
There was never such magnificence
as this, that they were all dressed in
 silk:
believe what my poem tells you.

Festive, joyful, and with a happy face
were the distinguished youth
whose persons were suited to their
 attire.

They were sons of worthy citizens
and of noble and patrician lineage,
and handsome like divine spirits.
They had between them more than
 fifty dresses

all covered in silver embroidery,
fit for their functions and noble status.
They seemed full of sunbeams
so that it was a wondrous thing to see
and even now when I remember it.

And more than fifty other liveries,

embroidered with large white round
 pearls
of equal size, were made for them.
These well-caparisoned young men
changed their lovely grand costumes
on that day once, twice, or three
 times.

They all had rich linings, with lower
 hems

avean tutti, & tanto acchonci bene
che orrevoli sarien emperio o re.

Pareano d'angioletti le lor giene,

ylar, giubilli & pien di festa & risa

chome in sì dengnio locho si chon-
viene.
Et aven tutti le chalze a ddivisa,
di perle & d'ariento richamate,

ciaschuno a ssua gientile & bella
guisa.
Et chosì stando le giovan brighate
aspettavan le donne che venire
dovevan, belle & mangnifiche ornate.

In questo tempo & io vedevo gire

i pifferi e 'l tronbone di tromba torta

nel deputato loro locho salire.
Venti tronbetti stavan per ischorta

nello stecchato sulla bella entrata,

che quando donne giunghano alla
porta
facievan grande & bella stormeggiata.
E' giovan si facieano inchontro a esse
chon reverenzia leggiadra & ornata,
et pel merchato poi givan chon esse

mettendo innanzi a sseder quelle
prima
atte a ffare festa & l'altre andentro
messe.

65r
Ciaschuna donna splendida &
subblima
che in quel giorno venir vido via

in una ora ivi fu. Chonprendi &
stima,
però, che a quattro a ssei ve ne
giungnia,

of Tyrian purple, so well fitting
that they would have done a king or
an emperor proud.
The young men's faces were angel-
like,
full of hilarity, joy, merriment, and
laughter,
as suited such a worthy place.

They all had hose in livery colors,
embroidered with pearls and silver
thread,
each one in the fine insignia of his
noble house.
Thus the young brigade
were waiting for the ladies who had
to come, beautiful and magnificently
adorned.
It was at this time that I saw the
shawm players
arrive with the trombone <trombone
with bent pipe>
and go up to their appointed place.
There was an escort of twenty
trumpet players
by the beautiful doorway to the
enclosure,
who, whenever any ladies came to the
entry,
burst into a loud and striking flourish.
The young people went to meet them
with a charming and elegant bow
and then accompanied them to the
market,
placing in the first row those

who could take a part in the feast, and
the others behind.

Every splendid and sublime woman

whom I saw coming away on that day
was there
at one and the same time. Consider
and understand,
therefore, that they came in groups of
four or six

a otto & dieci: chon ordin sinciero
al bel riseggio ongniuna si mettia.
Venne una squadra da cchasa di Piero,

moglie & chongniate & parenti &
   figliuole
che furan ben cinquanta a ddire il
   vero.
Lustre leggiadre & belle quanto un
   sole
entraron dentro & furon poste tutte
a sseder chome il dato ordine vole.
Fu 'l primo seggio di fanciulle &
   nupte
pien dall'un chapo all'altro intorno
   intorno
che pulcre stelle paren le più brutte.

E vi fu ciento donne chon tanto orno

che di saper ridire non mi rinchoro

la loro mangnificienzia e 'l grande
   addorno.
Ciaschuna avea il dì brocchato d'oro

in mangnificha vesta o in giornea

o in maniche o in altro bel lavoro.

D'alchuna qualità non ve n'avea
sanza brocchato o di sopra o disotto

& chi di sotto & di sopra il tenea.

Egli era il dì per foderare ridotto

& ben tre braccia o più per terra
   andava
strascinando chome un panno rotto.
In orli in gielosie vi si portava

& chi nal chappuccino & chi la chotta

& chi l'extremità tutte n'orlava.

Fuvvi di mangnie veste una gran
   frotta

---

or eight and ten: in the proper order
each one took her beautiful seat.
A group came from the house of
   Piero,
wife, sisters-in-law, parents, and
   daughters:
there must have been fifty of them, to
   tell the truth.
Bright, lovely, as beautiful as the sun,

they came within and were all seated
as the seating plan demanded.
The first row, full from one end to
   the other,
was of unmarried and married ladies,

the ugliest of whom seemed beautiful
   stars.
And there were a hundred ladies so
   adorned
that I cannot be sure to be able to
   describe
their magnificence, and their great
   adornments.
Each one on that day had golden
   brocade
in her marvelous dress, or in her
   robe,
in its sleeves or in other fancy
   needlework.
There was no garment of quality
without brocade, either above or
   below <the belt>,
and some had it both above and
   below.
That day <brocade> was downgraded
   to lining,
and a good three *braccia* or more lay
   on the ground
trailing behind like a ragged cloth.
There was some in hems and face
   covers [?],
some had it in their hood, others in
   the tunic,
and some put it in all the possible
   hems.
There was a surfeit of rich robes

65v

richamate di perle, argienti & ori

che chome 'l sol risplendon
    ciaschun'otta.
Perché son pien di tanti & be' lavori

chon tal somma di perle ricche &
    belle
che memorarne mi danno stupori.

Vediensi tutte le donne & pulzelle

chon molte varie addorne acchon-
    ciature
sopra i chapelli rilucienti & snelle.
<H>an di tante ragion chapellature:
di treccie, di ciocchette & ricci belli
chon ordini chonposti & chon misure.
Chi <h>a sovr'essi balzi & chi chap-
    pelli
chi bovol, chi stregghioni & chi
    mazzocchi,
ghirlande & chorna & chappuccini
    snelli.
Et sopra queste chose cho' miei occhi
vidivi tante perle che in effetto

parea grangniuola che sopr'essi
    fiocchi.
Aveano intorno al chollo, in testa &
    in petto
vezzi, chollane, brocchette & fermagli,

ricchi gioielli in oro puro & netto.
Chonvien per forza che ciaschuno
    abbagli
che sopra loro tenesse gli occhi saldi

perché son pien di gioie & dengni
    intagli.
Sonvi rubini turchiesse & smeraldi

balasci, topazzii, zaffiri, diamanti
preziosi & fini, ricchi senza fraldi.
A mme non par di dir di tanti & tanti

embroidered with pearls, silver, and
    gold,
which shine like the sun at every turn.

Because they are full of so many
    excellent works,
with such a lot of fine rich pearls,

that it astonishes me even to
    remember it.
All the ladies and young girls could be
    seen
with their shiny and sleek hair turned
    into
a variety of ornamental hairstyles.
They have hairdos of so many types:
tresses, bobs, lovely curls,
fashioned with order and measure.
On top some wear veils, and some
    hats,
others chains [?], combs, or head-
    bands,
garlands, horned hats, and small
    hoods.
And on them, with my very eyes,
I saw so many pearls that gave the
    impression
of hailstones that had landed on them.

Round their neck, head, and chest
    they wore
pendants, necklaces, brooches, and
    studs,
rich jewelry in pure fine gold.
Surely any one would necessarily be
    dazzled
who kept his eyes on them for any
    time,
because they are full of jewels and
    fine filigrees.
There are rubies, turquoises, and
    emeralds,
spinels, topazes, sapphires, diamonds
precious and fine, rich with no fakes.
There is no point in talking about so
    many types

velluti & vellutati & alti & bassi

ch' i' non saprei né ti potrei dir
    quanti.
Né so per che chagione io mi chon-
    tassi

66r
martore, zibellini lattizii & vai
o gientili ermellini ch'io nominassi,

che più di ciento & ciento cientinai

di ciaschuna ragione in quelle dame

furon di quelle pelle ch'udito ai.
Quel giorno fu da cchavarsi la fame

di veder belle donne & belle chose

& bene examinar tutte lor trame.
In questa forma le donne vezzose
si stavan tutte dinanzi a ssedere:
in bel meschuglio di fanclulle &
    spose.
La mia gran singnioria venne a vedere
in una chasa a parati balchoni
di panni & di tappeti al mio parere.

Di poi pervenuti alle chonclusioni
il gientil chonte allo stecchato giunse
chon suoi mangni singniori & gran
    chanpioni.
Ciaschun trombetto la sua tromba
    sumse
& a gloria sonando volentieri
in fin che 'l chonte dentro si chon-
    giunse.
Et nell'entrare i gientili schudieri,
giovani belli addorni & peregrini,

si fero inchontro [al martesc' e]*
    guerieri.
Chon dengnie reverenzie & belli
    inchini

---

of velvets and velveteens, with high
    and low pile,
because I would not know nor could I
    say how many.
I don't know why I began counting
    the number

of marten, baby sable, and squirrel
or noble ermine furs, or any other I
    might think of,
as more than a hundred and a
    hundred hundreds
of any type of those furs you have
    heard me mention
were worn by those dames.
That day was when one could satisfy
    one's hunger
for the sight of beautiful women and
    lovely things,
and examine in detail all their guiles.
In this form the coquettish ladies
were all sitting in the first rank:
a lovely mixture of unmarried and
    married women.
My lord came to watch
from a house with balconies adorned
(I believe) with hangings and tapes-
    tries.
Later, toward the end,
the noble count came to the enclosure
with his great lords and great cham-
    pions.
Each trumpter took his instrument

and played flourishes at will
until the count joined the others
    inside.
On entering, his noble equerries,
handsome well-dressed young men of
    rare distinction,
moved forward, with a martial and
    warlike air.
With deferential bows and dutiful
    signs of homage

---

* almãtiste.

verso 'l palchetto bel
   l'acchonpangniaro
cho' suoi seguaci mangni paladini.

Et nell'andare le donne si rizzaro
facciendo reverenzia a sua persona
& quasi sino in terra s'inchinaro
Il singnior mangnio dengnio di
   chorona
cholla berretta in mano la reverenzia

rendea loro quanto potea buona.

66v
Et giunto nella bella residenzia

subitamente a sseder fu posato
in locho ch'ongni chosa gli è in
   presenzia.
Non domandar se fu maravigliato
delle dame parate dengniamente
& quanto egli ebbe lor biltà laudato.

I suoi singniori & tutta la sua giente
si furano a sseder nel palcho assisi,
ciaschun dove lo stato suo chonsente,
tenendo gli occhi fissi ne' bei visi
di quelle donne chon gran dilezzione
che angioli parèn di paradisi.
In questo tempo i pifferi e 'l tronbone

chominciaro a ssonare un salterello
fondato d'arte d'intera ragione.

Allora ongni schudier gientile &
   snello
chi piglia maritata & chi pulzella
& a ddanzar chomincia or questo or
   quello.
Chi passeggia d'intorno & chi saltella,

chi schanbia mano & chi lascia & chi
   'nvita,
& chi in due parti o 'n tre fa danza
   bella.
Due giovinette cholla voglia unita

di gientilezza & chon ridente fronte

they escorted him to the beautiful dais

with the noble members of his
   household in attendance.
As they went by, the ladies got up,
making a curtsey to his person
almost reaching the ground.
The great lord, worthy of a king's
   crown,
with his hat in his hand, returned
   their gesture
of reverence as well as he could.

And, as he reached the beautiful
   stand,
he was at once shown his seat,
placed where he could see everything.

Do not ask if he was astounded
by the worthily attired ladies
and how much he praised their
   beauty.
His lords and all his retinue
sat down on the dais,
each one where his rank allowed,
their eyes fixed with great delight
on the beautiful faces of those ladies
who looked like angels of paradise.
That was the time when the shawms
   and the trombone
began to play a *saltarello*
artistically designed in all its proportions.
Then each noble and nimble squire

took a married lady or a young girl
and began to dance, first one, then
   the other.
Some promenade around, hop, or
   exchange hands,
some take leave from a lady while
   others invite one,
some make up a beautiful dance in
   two or three parts.
Two young girls, united in their courteous
purpose, and with a smiling mien,

& cholla guancia splendida & pulita
andarono a 'nvitare il gientil chonte
facciendogli uno inchino in fino in
    terra
chon reverenzia ornatissime & pronte.

Drizzossi ritto il chapitan di guerra
& rendé loro l'inchino & poi entrò

nel mezzo & danza & nel danzar non
    erra.

Mentre che 'l chonte chon chostor
    danzò

and with their radiant polished face
went to invite the noble count,
showing how ready they were to pay
    formal homage
to him by making a bow down to the
    ground.
The warlike leader stood up straight,
bowing back to them in his turn, then
    made his way
on to the middle of the floor, danced,
    and in dancing did not make a
    mistake.
While the count was dancing with
    these ladies,

67r
huomini & donne ongniun si rizza e
    'nchina
quantunque volte innanzi a llor passò.

Ballato quella danza peregrina

le dame il rimenarono al suo locho

oprando in fargli onore ongni
    dottrina.
Et doppo questo il chonte stette
    pocho
che si rizzò & due dame invitava

le qual ferian la guancia lor di focho.
Pur dengniamente ongniuna l'onorava
messollo in mezzo & ballavan chon
    esso
& nel passare ciaschedun si rizzava.

Danzò anchor chon questo ordine
    appresso
messer Tiberto & gli altri gran sing-
    niori
& ciaschun da due dame in mezzo è
    messo.
Non domandar s'aven giubilli i chori
& se le damigielle miran fiso

veggiendosi da lloro far tanti onori.

every time he passed before any man
    or woman
each one of them would get up and
    bow.
Having danced that characteristic
    dance,
the ladies escorted him back to his
    seat
using every means they knew to do
    him honor.
After that the count did not wait
    much
before he got up and invited two
    ladies
whose cheeks at once turned to fire.
Yet each one worthily honored him,
placing him in between them and
    dancing with him;
and as they passed everyone would
    get up.
Subsequently Messer Tiberto and the
    other great lords
also danced in this manner,

each one placed between two ladies.

Do not ask if they had joyful hearts
and if the young ladies kept a straight
    face, seeing
so much respect being shown to them
    by their partners.

Pareva quel trepudio il paradiso

di gierarchie angieliche chi balla
& era pien ciaschun di gioia & riso.

Ongni gienerazion festante ghalla

sotto il triumfo delle menbra snelle

di quell[o]⁺ a cchi 'l pastore donò la
palla.
Parea il tutto un ciel di rose belle

nel quale il chonte rappresenta un
sole
& le donne e gharzon lucienti stelle.

Quivi si ghode quanto ciaschun vole

sotto le chalde & gloriose insengnie
del gran chupido di biforme prole.

Io credo che lle dame mangnie &
dengnie
il dì faciessero ardere mille fochi

67v
sanza fucile o pietra, zolfo o lengnie.

Usò Venere il dì tutti i suoi giuochi

perché ghalantemente ongniun
festeggia
senza sospetto alchun che nulla
nuochi.
Chi danza chi sollazza & chi
motteggia,
chi è mirato & chi fisso altri guarda

& chi è vagheggiato & chi vagheggia

That joyful dance seemed like a
paradise
of dancing angelic hierarchies,
and everyone was full of joy and
laughter.
People of all ages rejoice and show
their happiness
under the authority of the nimble
body
of the man to whom the pastor gave
the ball.#
The whole seemed like a heaven of
beautiful roses
in which the count represents the sun

and the young boys and girls the
shining stars.
There one enjoys oneself as much as
one wishes
under the warm and glorious banner
of the great Cupid with twofold
progeny.*
I believe that the great and worthy
ladies
made a thousand fires burn on that
day

without tinder-box, flint, sulphur, or
wood.
Venus used all her tricks on that day
because
everyone makes merry in an amorous
disposition
without any thought that anything
might be harmful.
Some dance, others sport, others jest,

some stare at people and others are
stared at,
some are objects of desire, and others
desire.

⁺ diquella acchil
An allusion to the Medici coat of arms,
  showing six balls.
* Probably Piero (Cosimo's son, 1414–69),
  mentioned on 65r, who had two sons,
  Lorenzo and Giuliano.

Quel dì si dette il focho alla bonbarda
in forma tal che non v'era alchun
    petto
nel quale il chor chon gran fiamma
    non arda.
Se 'n paradiso si sta chon diletto,
& puossi in paradiso in terra stare,

il paradiso è questo ch'io t'<h>o
    detto.
Un'ora era durato già il danzare

nel quale amore strinse più d'un nodo

quando la chollazion s'ordinò fare.

Della qual tutto il bello ordine &
    modo
disposto sono di ben volerti dire
chol proprio vero & metti questo in
    sodo.
Inprimamente si vedea venire
per lo stecchato in circhulo sonando

molti tronbetti, & doppo lor seguire
quattro donzelli i quai venien
    portando
un gran bacino d'argiento in man per
    uno.
& doppo loro venieno seguitando
d'argiento pur venti bacini
    ch'ongniuno
pieno di bicchieri & panllin ben
    lavati.
& poi seguivan trenta, che ciaschuno
avea dua vasi in man d'argiento orati
che d'aqqua chiara & pura eran pien
    drento
ch' a uno a uno venieno ordinati.

68r
Seguiva poi chon bello ordinamento
d'amabil zuccheroso & buon treb-
    biano
cinquanta che portavan fiaschi ciento.
Ciaschuno n'avea un alto in ongni
    mano

On that day the big gun was fired
so that there was no breast

in which the heart did not burn with
    a fierce flame.
If to be in paradise is delightful
and it is possible to be in paradise on
    this earth,
then paradise is what I have just
    described to you.
Dancing had been going on already
    for one hour,
during which love tied more than one
    knot,
when the time came arranged for a
    meal.
Of which I am disposed to reveal to
    you
the fine order and manner of service
as it really was, and hold it for true.

At first one saw many trumpeters
walking round the perimeter of the
    enclosure
while playing, followed by
four pages, each carrying

a large silver basin in his hands.

And they were followed by
at least twenty silver basins, each

full of glasses and well-washed linen
    cloths.
Then came thirty <waiters>,
one after the other in order,
each having in his hands two silver-
    gilt vessels
full of clear pure water.

There followed in good order
fifty <attendants> carrying one
    hundred flasks
of good *trebbiano*, sweet and sugary.
Each one held one high in each hand,

& l'ordine seguia sanza intervallo	and they followed one another in procession, without a break,
chon chontenenza & chon un passo piano.	with calm demeanor and slow gait.
Vien poi quaranta giovani del ballo	Then came forty young men, those who had danced,
chon chonfettiere d'argiento dorate	holding silver-gilt confectionery trays
resplendienti chome chiar orpallo [?]*.	shining like bright pinchbeck [?].
Che cholla mano in alto l'\<h\>an portate	They have carried them high with one hand,
tutte [e] quaranta⁺ pien di morselletti	the forty of them all full of little pieces
di pinnocchiato biancho & di zuchate [?].	of white pine-nut nougat and sugar sweets [?].
Di sopra bistie & leoni di chonfetti	On top, confectionery snakes and lions
ritratti chon grand'arte al naturale	portrayed with great art and realism
per man di mastri pratichi & prefetti.	by experienced and proficient masters.
Et chon tal modo subblime & reale	And, while with such a lofty and regal manner
intorno intorno allo stecchato andando	they were going all round the fenced-in area,
l'un dietro all'altro chon ordine equale,	one behind the other in orderly single file,
poi dall'un lato i tronbetti sonando	and the trumpeters were playing on one side,
& intro 'l mezzo i gran bacin posarsi	and the big trays were placed in the middle,
i giovani i bicchieri venien pigliando:	the young men began to take the glasses:
chi mestie vino & chi aqqua fa darsi	some poured out wine, others asked for water,
& dan bere alle donne & chiunque v'era	and offered drinks to the ladies and whoever was there;
& del chonfetto ciaschuno può pigliarsi.	people could help themselves to the confectionery.
Parean proprio una solare spera	Two damsels really looking like
due damigielle che ritte levate	the sphere of the sun rose upright
destre n'andaron dove 'l gran chonte era.	and nimbly went where the great count was.
Et giunte a llui si furano inchinate	Once before him they bowed,
facciendogli una dengnia reverenza	giving him worthy obeisance
chome gientili oneste & chostumate.	as the noble, chaste, and well-mannered ladies they were.
Ferongli poi chon gran mangnificienza	Then, with great magnanimity, they openly showed,

* chome chiā &pāllo
⁺ tutte aquaranta

68v

del vino & del chonfetto alla palese	by touching and tasting, that the wine
chol tocchare & ghustar fedel credenza.	and the confectionery were to be trusted.
Allora il chonte cholle sue man prese	Then the count took with his own hands
chonfetto & vino dalle incharnate rose	wine and confectionery from the two roses made flesh,
& ringraziolle dello atto chortese.	and thanked them for their gracious act.
Le gientil donne angieliche & vezzose	The noble ladies, angel-like and charming,
da llui partiron chon un bello inchino	left him with a graceful bow
& nel suo locho ciaschuna si pose.	and returned each to her seat.
Fatto ongniun chollazione a ssuo domino	After everyone had eaten to their satisfaction,
fiaschi & chonfetto che v'era avanzato	any wine and confectionery left over
si gittò intorno & missesi a bbottino.	were thrown around for people to grab as they pleased.
Quei della chollazione fuor del merchato	Those who had brought in the food took
l'argiento & ongni chosa riportaro	the silverware and everything out of the market
là dove a cciaschedun fu ordinato.	wherever each one of them was told to take it.
E' giovan tutti addorni ritornaro	The young men came back all decked out
chon nuove veste ricche & mangnie molto	in new, rich, and very grand clothes,
e 'n questo tempo i pifferi sonaro.	and the shawms played at this time.
Et ciò sentendo ongni schudiere <h>a tolto	Hearing the music, every squire got hold
chi una donna & chi fanciulla piglia	of a lady or a girl,
perch'al ballare ciaschuno <h>a l'almo volto.	because everyone's mind has turned to dancing.
Si mangniamente il bel danzar s'appiglia	So magnificently this beautiful dance begins
che ciaschun che lo vide o che lo sente	that whoever sees it or hears it
mirabilmente se ne maraviglia.	is struck by wonder and amazement.
Ballò più volte il gran chonte exciellente	The great excellent count danced several times
chon dame che pareano angiolette	with ladies who looked like angels:
che givano a 'nvitarlo & ei chonsente.	they went to invite him and he accepted.
Talvolta invitò il chonte giovinette	On occasions it was the count who invited young girls,
lucienti chome stelle mattutine	bright like the morning stars,

& al ballare in mezzo a llor si mette
and danced among them.

Gli altri singniori & giente peregrine
The other lords and distinguished people

invitar dame & erano invitati
invited the ladies, and were invited

69r

da quelle donne che paiano reine.
by those women who looked like queens.

I gharzoni mangni dengni & tanto ornati
The worthy youths, splendidly dressed,

ch'eran destri & leggier chom'uno ucciello
who were agile and light as birds,

danzavan cholle dame acchonpang-niati.
danced with the accompanying ladies.

Et ballato gran pezza al salterello
And, after dancing the *saltarello* for a long time,

ballaron poi a danza variata
they danced a variety of dances,

chome desiderava questo & quello.
as one or the other desired.

Feron la chi<a>rintana molto ornata
They danced an ornamented version of *Chiarintana*,

& missero amendue gli arrosti in danza
and both *Arrosti*,

chon laura, cho<n> mummia & charbonata
with *Laura*, *Mummia*, and *Carbonata*,

Lionciel, bel riguardo & la speranza
Lioncel, *Bel riguardo*, and *La speranza*,

l'angiola bella & la danza del re
L'angiola bella and *La danza del re*,

& altre assai che nominar m'avanza.
and many others which I omit to mention.

Ma vo' che bene examini da tte
What I want you to keep well in your mind is

che ciò che per ciaschuno si chon-osciea
that every deed each one knew

che fosse dengnio & mangnio vi si fé;
to be worthy and magnificent was done there;

et tutto quel che non vi si faciea
and whatever magnificent or dignified thing

di mangnificha chosa o di dechora
was not done there

non si chongniobbe o far non si potea.
either was not known or was not possible.

Et chonclusive ballossi un'altra ora,
In the end the dances went on for another hour,

& ordinossi un'altra chollazione
and another collation was ordered

chome la prima, & fu più mangnia anchora.
like the first one, but even bigger.

Perché ebbe l'usato ordine & ragione,
Because it had the same order and type of food,

ma doppo le quaranta chonfettiere
but after the forty trays

pien della nominata chonfezzione,

quattro gran zane si potero vedere
dorate & portate alto da schudieri
cholme di pinnocchiati al mio parere.

Quivi è chi empie & chi vota bicchieri

quivi è chi porgie & chi piglia chon-
    fetti
& chosì fassi in tutti que' sentieri.

69v
Et chomo di mangnifici antedetti

fu fatta la credenza al gran singniore
da due dame gientili di lieti aspetti.

I giovan delle zane a gran furore

gittavan qua & là di quel chonfetto

al popol che faciea un gran romore.

Chi 'l gitta alle finestre, chi al
    palchetto,
& chi al tetto, alle femmine e maschi

fin ch'elle furan vote chon effetto.

Et tutti quanti gli avanzati fiaschi
si gittar qua & là chon gran tempesta

acciò che mangniamente ongniun si
    paschi
Chosì finì la mangnificha festa
del gientil ballo che fu sì giulia
ch'alchuna ne fu mai simile a questa.

full of the aforementioned confec-
    tionery,
one could see four big gilded baskets
carried high by the pages,
which I believe were full of pine-nut
    nougat.
There some drained and others filled
    glasses,
some offered and others took sweet-
    meats,
and that was done all over the place.

And, like the magnanimous gesture I
    mentioned before,
two gentlewomen with a smiling face
tasted the food offered to the great
    lord.
The young men carrying the baskets
    threw
in a frenzy here and there pieces of
    confectionery
to the people who made a great
    uproar.
Some threw it at the windows, some
    at the dais,
others at the roof, to women and men
    alike,
until the baskets were effectively
    empty.
And the flasks of wine that were left
were thrown here and there at
    random
so that everyone may have their fill.

Thus ended the magnificent festival
of courtly dance, which was so joyful
that no other feast could ever be
    compared to it.

Appendix 2. The Use of Mensuration Signs as Proportion Signs in the Dance Treatises

In explaining how Domenico uses mensuration symbols and proportion signs, I rely on three assumptions. The first of these is breve equivalence.[1] The second assumption is that factors of two are not notated, which is consistent with the recorded music. For example, the assumption that one breve (or bar) of ₵ has to equal two breves (or bars) of ₵ is confirmed when the music and choreography are put together, as X *tempi* of *quaternaria misura* always coincides with 2X breves' worth of music. The third assumption is that Domenico's description of the proportions is concerned with what is happening at the minima level. Domenico's concern is a practical response to the demands of the dancer, since the three movements of a *doppio* step occur on minima beats.

In the theoretical section of his treatise Domenico often reminds the reader that *bassadanza misura* is the basis of the other three *misure*, whose speeds are derived from it. The appellation given to *bassadanza misura*, that is, major imperfect or ₵, must therefore be the reference point for the other proportions. Domenico then says that *saltarello misura* is major perfect, or ☉. When the sign for major perfect, ☉, is used as a proportion sign after the mensuration of ₵, the proportion of 2:3 (or *sesquialtera*) is produced (assuming breve equivalence), as is shown in figure 8. The ratio of 2:3 between *bassadanza* and *saltarello* is the same ratio that results from the description of *saltarello misura* as two-sixths faster than *bassadanza misura*.

Elsewhere the ratio of *bassadanza* to *piva* is given as 1:2 (or *proportio dupla*). Domenico gives the sign of minor perfect, ○, to *piva*, but the ratio of ₵ to ○ does not give the ratio of 1:2. It is at this point I must assume that Domenico did not notate factors of two. This does not seem unreasonable, as exactly doubling or exactly halving the speed is the easiest proportion for musicians to perform. Support for this assumption, albeit indirect, is found in Bobby Wayne Cox's article on the sign Φ in another manuscript.[2] Cox's argument is well summarized by Eunice Schroeder, who emphasizes Cox's point that "the original use of Φ [was] as a convenient way of writing ₵ in the next higher level of note values in order to avoid flagged semiminims," and "only incidentally does Φ

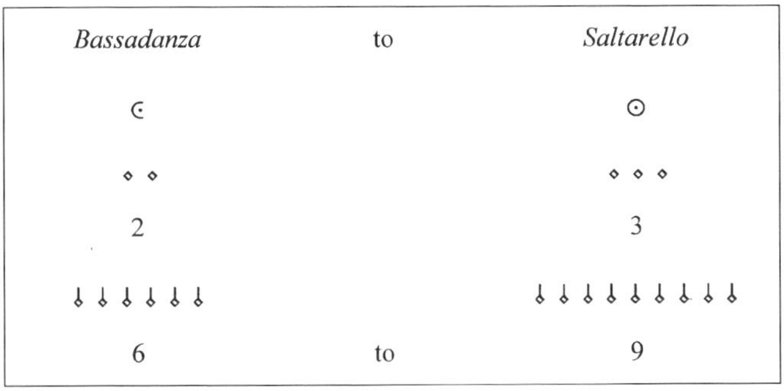

Bassadanza	to	Saltarello
₵		⊙
◇ ◇		◇ ◇ ◇
2		3
♪ ♪ ♪ ♪ ♪ ♪		♪ ♪ ♪ ♪ ♪ ♪ ♪ ♪ ♪
6	to	9

Figure 8. Relationship between *bassadanza* and *saltarello misure*

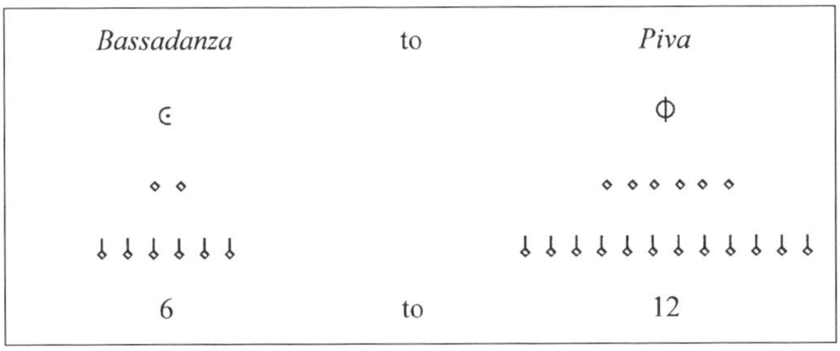

Bassadanza	to	Piva
₵		Φ
◇ ◇		◇ ◇ ◇ ◇ ◇ ◇
♪ ♪ ♪ ♪ ♪ ♪		♪ ♪ ♪ ♪ ♪ ♪ ♪ ♪ ♪ ♪ ♪ ♪
6	to	12

Figure 9. Relationship between *bassadanza* and *piva misure*

appear to mean twice as fast as ○."[3] The point of Cox's argument is the scribes were not portraying *proportio dupla* by the sign Φ, but simply wanted to avoid writing flagged semiminima. Thus, if in one manuscript practice it was not considered especially important to notate *proportio dupla*, then it is easier to assume it was not so important in other manuscript practices as well. This is the case, for instance, in the dance *Rostiboli gioioso* in the *ballo* repertory. The notes for the first three musical sections of this dance are all semibreves, but for the choreography to fit the music, they must all be played at the speed of minima. John Caldwell has also pointed out that it is unnecessary to account for factors of two; since "major prolation in the fifteenth century normally implied augmentation, it is actually unnecessary to assume diminution of the minor perfect mensuration [○] here."[4] Therefore, if one assumes that factors of two were not notated, one breve of ₵ is equal to two breves of ○ (as is shown in figure 9) and *proportio dupla* is achieved on the minima level. Thus the relationship is between ₵ and Φ.

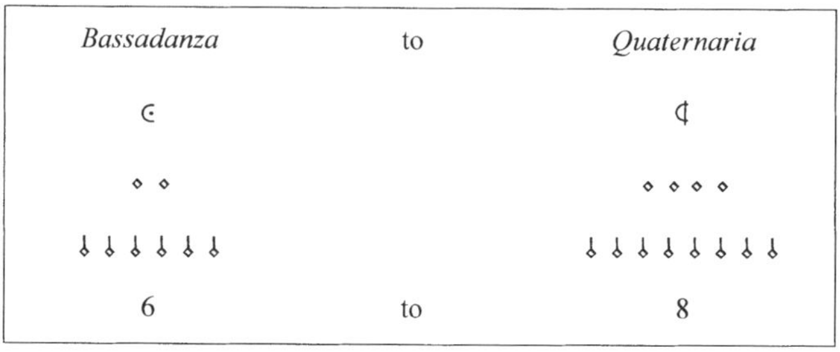

Bassadanza	to	Quaternaria
₵		₵
◇ ◇		◇ ◇ ◇ ◇
♪ ♪ ♪ ♪ ♪ ♪		♪ ♪ ♪ ♪ ♪ ♪ ♪ ♪
6	to	8

Figure 10. Relationship between *bassadanza* and *quaternaria misure*

Domenico describes the relationship between *bassadanza* and *quaternaria misura* as ₵ to C. The ratio of ₵ to C, however, causes the music to slow down, not speed up, as four minima are played in the time of six. But Domenico is quite definite that *quaternaria* is faster than *bassadanza misura*, and so one has to assume that one breve of ₵ is equal to two breves of C; that is, a stroke is missing from the C sign (see figure 10). Once allowance has been made for this factor of two, then the *bassadanza* to *quaternaria* ratio on the minima level is 6:8 or 3:4, another one of the commonly used proportions.

Appendix 3. Floor Track and Music of Anello, Ingrata, Pizochara, and Verçeppe

Dance is a visual as well as a kinetic art, and it is difficult to visualize a series of movements and interactions from a written description. The floor tracks presented in this appendix are provided to help readers, especially those who are not familiar with the repertory, understand the sections of the text in which the dances are discussed. Presenting a floor track of a written choreographic description involves making a large number of decisions in order to resolve the inherent ambiguities of the written text. Each floor track presented here, therefore, is one version of how the written descriptions translate into sequences of floor patterns, and how the steps and the music fit together, rather than a definitive, critical edition.

In the floor tracks the male dancers are represented by odd numbers, female dancers by even numbers. Small black arrowheads indicate the direction a dancer is facing. Dancers' paths and directions of movement are indicated by black lines with arrowheads. Where gray lines occur, they have been used only to help distinguish between two interweaving paths. "L" stands for "left," and "R" for "right." Editorial comments are given in [square brackets].

For a detailed explanation of the steps and their variants found in the fifteenth-century Italian *balli* and *bassadanze*, readers are advised to consult David Wilson's *The Steps Used in Court Dancing in Fifteenth-Century Italy* (Cambridge: Published by the author, 1992). The information given in the dance treatises regarding the steps is not exhaustive, and a great deal is left to individual performers, especially in the area of gesture and bodily movements. Presented below is a simplified interpretation of the fifteenth-century step repertoire. Both the *balli* and the *bassadanze* were made up of sequences of nine basic, or natural, steps and three ornamental, or "man-made," steps. A description of the nine natural steps follows. The three "man-made" steps are not described in the treatises. They occur infrequently in comparison with the natural steps, and are mainly used to embellish the choreography.

(1) *Sempio:* a single step that takes one-half of a breve. *Sempi* are usually in groups of two and normally start on the left foot.

A series of *sempi* always alternates feet, that is, left, right, left, right, etc., as in normal walking. "1 sempio L" means stepping forward on the flat of the left foot, as if walking, while the right foot remains behind. The dancer's weight moves over the left foot as the left foot is advanced, so that the right heel is raised as the *sempio* step progresses. "1 sempio R" would be one step forward on the right foot.

(2) *Doppio:* a double step that takes one breve. In fifteenth-century Italy there were four different types of *doppio: bassadanza doppio, quaternaria doppio, saltarello doppio,* and *piva doppio.* All four involved three paces forward. The difference in performance involved slight turning movements of the shoulders and raising and lowering of the dancer's body. Like *sempi,* a series of *doppi* always alternates feet, and almost always starts on the left foot. Both the *doppi* and *sempi* can be performed forward and backward. "1 doppio L" means stepping forward on the left foot, then on the right foot, then on the left foot again. Conversely, "1 doppio R" means three similar paces, but starting with the right foot.

Bassadanza doppio forward on the left foot

A *bassadanza doppio* begins on the "void," that is, on the upbeat or the sixth minima of the previous breve. At that moment, the dancer bends the knees slightly and begins to move the left foot forward. At this stage the foot is just skimming the floor. On the first minima of the new breve, the left foot lands on the ground ahead. On the second minima, the dancer's body begins to rise, with weight shifting onto the balls of both feet. The left shoulder turns slightly backward, and the right shoulder forward. All these movements are small. The right foot begins to move forward. On the third minima, the dancer steps forward on the ball of the right foot. The left shoulder is still slightly turned behind. On the fourth minima, the dancer steps forward on the flat of the left foot, with both knees slightly bent so that the body is lowered. The shoulders turn back to their starting position, that is, parallel with the torso. The right heel remains slightly raised. On the sixth minima, the dancer starts to move the right foot forward from behind, repeating the sequence on the other side. Now right and left are reversed, so that the right shoulder turns back and the left shoulder forward.

Saltarello doppio forward on the left foot

A *saltarello doppio* also starts on the upbeat. On the sixth minima of the previous breve, the dancer hops on the right foot.

On the first minima of the new breve, the left foot is placed on the floor slightly ahead, with the heel just off the ground. The left shoulder turns slightly backward. A *saltarello doppio* in *saltarello misura* is a quicker step, since one breve of *saltarello misura* takes less time than one breve of *bassadanza misura*. Therefore the turning movements in the *saltarello doppio* cannot be as large as those for a *bassadanza doppio*. On the second minima the right foot begins to move forward, the body rises, and the dancer's weight is shifted onto the balls of both feet. On the third minima, the dancer makes a *very* small leap forward onto the ball of the right foot. On the fourth minima, the dancer takes a step forward with the left foot, placing it flat on the ground. The knees are bent slightly, so the body is lowered. On the sixth minima, the sequence begins on the other side, with a hop on the left foot.

Quaternaria doppio forward on the left foot

This type of *doppio* comprises three steps forward plus an additional short, quick movement at the end of the third step. There are many suggestions in the treatises for this additional movement. There is no preparatory movement, as a *quaternaria doppio* begins on the "full." For *quaternaria doppi* in *quaternaria misura* there are four minima to the breve, and each *quaternaria doppio* in *quaternaria misura* takes two breves' worth of music. On the first minima, the dancer steps forward, placing the left foot flat on the ground. On the third minima, the same step with the right foot. On the fifth, the same with the left again, and on the seventh and eighth minima the dancer does the additional movement.

Piva doppio forward on the left foot

Once again a *piva doppio* is three paces forward. But *piva doppi* in *piva misura* are very fast. Therefore there is no time for the subtle nuances of turning the shoulders or raising and lowering the body. *Piva misura* can have either four or six minima to the breve. Depending on the performer's choice of tempo, *piva doppi* can be so fast that they need to be performed on the balls of the feet. If there are four minima to the breve, on the first the dancer steps forward on the left foot, and on the second minima, on the right. On the third minima, the dancer steps forward on the left again, and then on the fourth minima pauses. If there are six minima to the breve, then the dancer steps forward on the first, third, and fourth minima, and pauses on the fifth and sixth.

(3) *Continenza:* a small step to the side that takes one-half of a breve. *Continenze* are usually performed in pairs, first to the left side, then to the right side.

(4) *Ripresa:* a larger step to the side that takes one breve. *Riprese* are also performed in pairs, one to the left side and one to the right side. They could be also performed all to the same side, in order to travel in that direction. Thus these steps can be done sideways, diagonally forward, or diagonally backward.

(5) *Meza volta:* a half turn, that is, the dancer turns 180 degrees to face the opposite direction. This step can be performed on the up-beat, usually one-half or one minima, by quickly pivoting on the foot bearing the dancer's weight. Alternatively, it can be executed using other steps: for example, one *doppio*, two *sempi*, two *riprese*, or two *continenze*. In these cases the *meza volta* takes the length of time that these steps normally would take.

(6) *Volta tonda:* a full turn, that is, the dancer turns 360 degrees in a complete circle. This turn was executed using a variety of other steps, for example, two *doppi*, two *sempi* and one *ripresa* (this combination was very common in the *bassadanze*) or two *sempi* and one *doppio*.

(7) *Riverenza:* a bow that normally takes one breve. There are two main types: *riverenza* and *riverenza in terra*. In the latter, the back foot is moved as far back as is necessary to allow the bent knee to touch, or almost touch, the ground.

(8) *Salto:* a jump that normally takes one-half of a breve. The treatises do not say how to perform this step; it may be a hop on one foot, or a jump into the air with the dancer's weight starting and ending on both feet, or a leap from one foot to the other. Sometimes in individual cases what is required is clarified by the choreographic context.

(9) *Movimento:* a "step" that takes one-half of a breve. It is found only in the *balli*, not in the *bassadanze*. This step is not explained at all. It is often used in dances as a "dialogue," almost always appearing with the verb *rispondere*, so that the men do a *movimento* and the women "respond" with a second *movimento*. Women can also initiate a sequence of *movimenti*. Cornazano (V, f. 7r–7v) says that the *bassadanze* can have all the nine natural steps except the *movimento*. He then says that the *movimento* provides an occasion in public for a totally decorous signal from the man to the lady, as in *Leonçello* and many other dances.

Anello: a *ballo* for four by Domenico

Figure 11. *Anello:* a *ballo* for four by Domenico

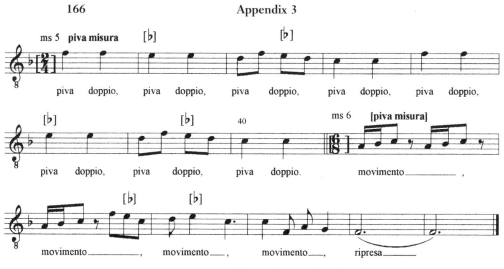

Figure 11. (continued)

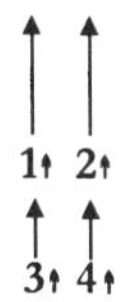

1st couple is 4 passi in front of the 2nd couple. Partners start holding hands.

7 saltarello doppi in piva misura LRLRLRL

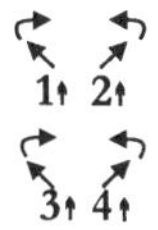

1 saltarello doppio on R in piva misura. Move away from each other to form a square.

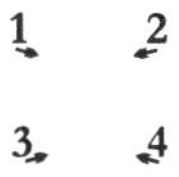

1 movimento – men, then

1 movimento - women

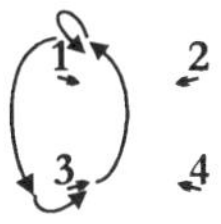

2 saltarello doppi LR [in saltarello misura] and a meza volta to face into the square

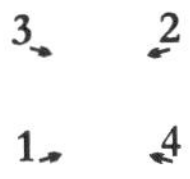

1 movimento – women, then

1 movimento - men

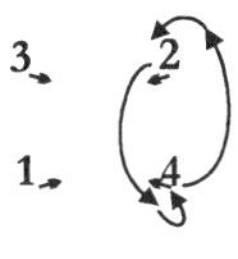

2 saltarello doppi LR [in saltarello misura] and a meza volta to face into the square

Figure 12. Floor track of *Anello*

3   4   1 movimento – men, then

1   2   1 movimento - women

3   4   1 volta tonda in piva misura with 1

1   2   doppio L

3   4   1 movimento – women, then

1   2   1 movimento - men

3   4   1 volta tonda in piva misura with 1

1   2   doppio L

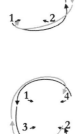
              4 piva doppi LRLR in piva misura

              4 piva doppi LRLR in piva misura

Figure 12. (continued)

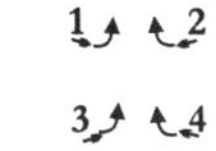

1⌐↗ ↖2   1 movimento – men, then 1

3↗ ↖4   movimento – women, then

                        1 movimento – men, then 1

                        movimento – women

                        [Couples start moving closer to each

                        other with these movimenti].

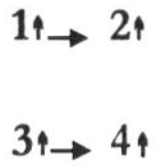

1↑→ 2↑   1 ripresa on R to rejoin women and

3↑→ 4↑   take hands

Figure 12. (continued)

Ingrata: a *ballo* for three by Domenico

Figure 13. *Ingrata:* a *ballo* for three by Domenico

* The ms has ϴ, but as the choreography calls for 16 *tempi* of *bassadanza misura*, what is needed is two more breves of C to complete the 16 *tempi*.

+ The sign 'C3' must indicate a 4:3 ratio, that is, in the last 15 bars, which are 15 breves of *quaternaria misura*. Therefore, instead of a 'normal' *sempio* in *quarternaria misura* (C) that has 4 minima (♪♪♪♪), in these bars there are only 3 minima per *sempio* (♪♪♪ = ♩.). In this transcription a *sempio* takes a dotted crotchet (♩.) rather than a minim (♩).

Figure 13. (continued)

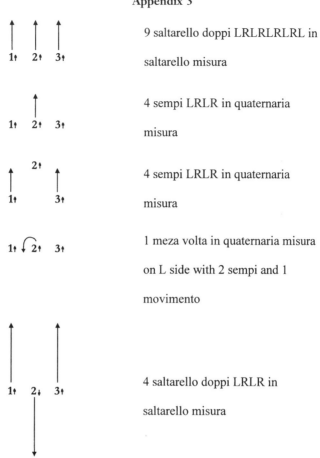

9 saltarello doppi LRLRLRLRL in saltarello misura

4 sempi LRLR in quaternaria misura

4 sempi LRLR in quaternaria misura

1 meza volta in quaternaria misura on L side with 2 sempi and 1 movimento

4 saltarello doppi LRLR in saltarello misura

Figure 14. Floor track of *Ingrata*

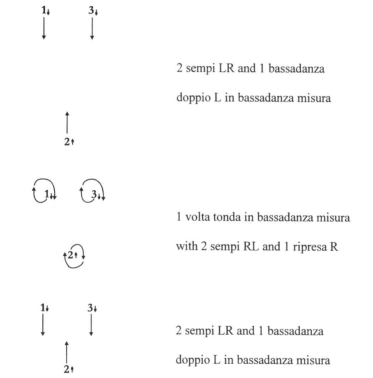

1 meza volta in bassadanza misura

on R side with 2 riprese

2 sempi LR and 1 bassadanza

doppio L in bassadanza misura

1 volta tonda in bassadanza misura

with 2 sempi RL and 1 ripresa R

2 sempi LR and 1 bassadanza

doppio L in bassadanza misura

Figure 14. (continued)

1 volta tonda in bassadanza misura

with 2 sempi RL and 1 ripresa R

4 bassadanza doppi LRLR in

bassadanza misura

1 meza volta in bassadanza misura

on R side with 2 riprese

2 sempi LR and 2 riprese LR in

quaternaria misura

2 sempi LR and 2 riprese LR in

quaternaria misura

2 sempi LR and 2 riprese LR in

quaternaria misura

Figure 14. (continued)

3 piva doppi in quaternaria misura

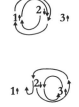 2 piva doppi in quaternaria misura

1↑ 2↑ 3↑   1 movimento in quaternaria misura

– all 3.

Figure 14. (continued)

Pizochara: a *ballo* for eight by Domenico

Figure 15. *Pizochara*: a *ballo* for eight by Domenico

* The repeat indication for musical section 4 is missing in Pd.

Figure 15. (continued)

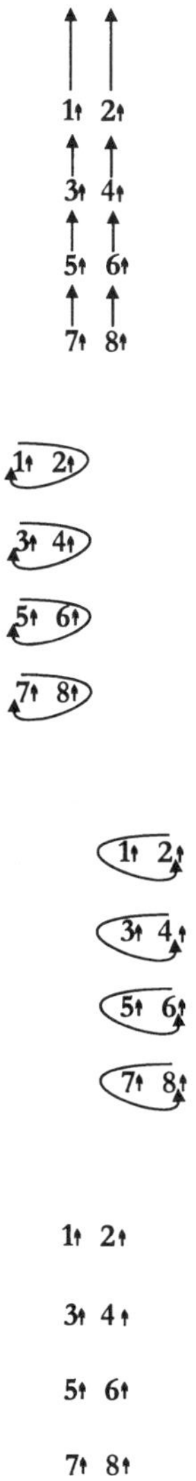

Couples are 3 passi apart. Partners

start holding hands.

12 piva doppi in piva misura

LRLRLRLRLRLR

4 piva doppi LRLR in piva misura

4 piva doppi LRLR in piva misura

1 riverenza with R behind in

bassadanza misura, and touching R

hands with their partners

Figure 16. Floor track of *Pizochara*

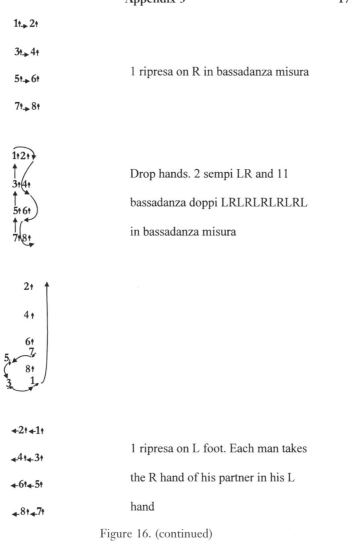

1 ripresa on R in bassadanza misura

Drop hands. 2 sempi LR and 11

bassadanza doppi LRLRLRLRLRL

in bassadanza misura

1 ripresa on L foot. Each man takes

the R hand of his partner in his L

hand

Figure 16. (continued)

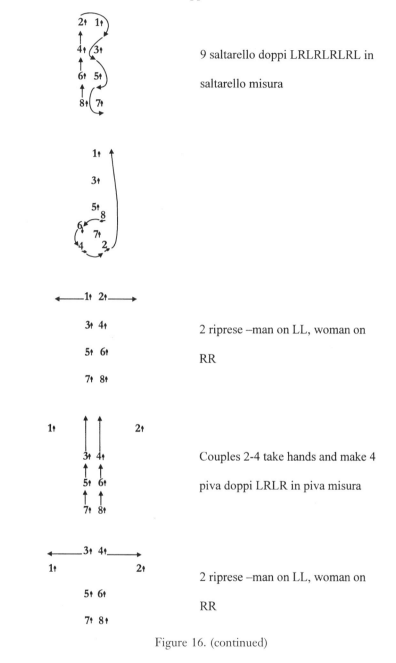

9 saltarello doppi LRLRLRLRL in

saltarello misura

2 riprese –man on LL, woman on

RR

Couples 2-4 take hands and make 4

piva doppi LRLR in piva misura

2 riprese –man on LL, woman on

RR

Figure 16. (continued)

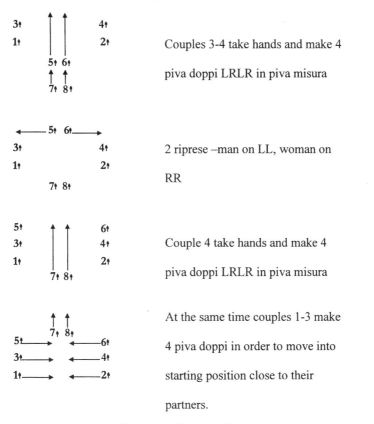

Couples 3-4 take hands and make 4

piva doppi LRLR in piva misura

2 riprese –man on LL, woman on

RR

Couple 4 take hands and make 4

piva doppi LRLR in piva misura

At the same time couples 1-3 make

4 piva doppi in order to move into

starting position close to their

partners.

Figure 16. (continued)

Verçeppe: a *ballo* for five by Domenico

Figure 17. *Verçeppe:* a *ballo* for five by Domenico

Figure 17. (continued)

Appendix 3

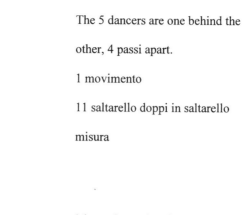

The 5 dancers are one behind the

other, 4 passi apart.

1 movimento

11 saltarello doppi in saltarello

misura

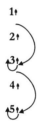

2 bassadanza doppi LR in

bassadanza misura

2 bassadanza doppi – both on L

foot – in bassasanza misura, and 1

ripresa on R

1 volta tonda in bassadanza misura

with 2 sempi RL and 1 ripresa on R

Figure 18. Floor track of *Verçeppe*

2 bassadanza doppi LR in bassadanza misura. 2 bassadanza doppi – both on L foot – in bassasanza misura, and 1 ripresa on R

1 volta tonda in bassadanza misura with 2 sempi RL and 1 ripresa on R

3 quaternaria doppi – all on L foot – in quaternaria misura, and a meza volta to the L

Figure 18. (continued)

3 quaternaria doppi – all on L foot

– in quaternaria misura, and a meza

volta to the L

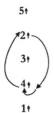

1st man does a meza volta to the L

and 4 saltarello doppi in saltarello

misura, with a salto at the

beginning of the 1st doppio.

3rd man does a salto and then 4

saltarello doppi in saltarello misura

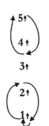

3 bassadanza doppi in bassadanza

misura. 1st woman does RLR and

2nd woman LRL

3 saltarello doppi RLR in saltarello

misura

Figure 18. (continued)

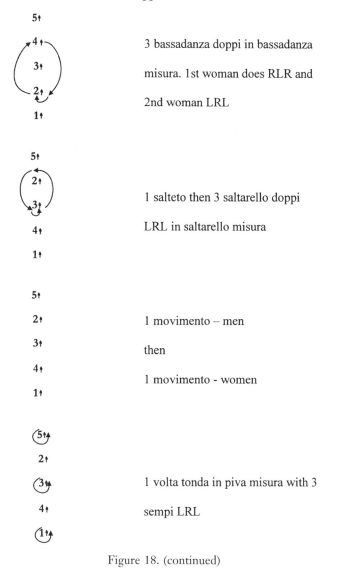

5↑

4↑
3↑
2↑
1↑

3 bassadanza doppi in bassadanza misura. 1st woman does RLR and 2nd woman LRL

5↑
2↑
3↑
4↑
1↑

1 salteto then 3 saltarello doppi LRL in saltarello misura

5↑
2↑
3↑
4↑
1↑

1 movimento – men

then

1 movimento - women

5↑
2↑
3↑
4↑
1↑

1 volta tonda in piva misura with 3 sempi LRL

Figure 18. (continued)

5↑

2↑   1 movimento – women

3↑   then

4↑
                                     1 movimento - men 
1↑

5↑

②↯
                                     1 volta tonda in piva misura with 3
3↑
                                     sempi LRL
④↑↯

1↑

Figure 18. (continued)

Notes

ABBREVIATIONS

Manuscript sources are identified as follows:

V   Antonio Cornazano, *Libro dell'arte del danzare*, Rome, Biblioteca Apostolica Vaticana, Codex Capponiano, 203.

Pd   Domenico da Piacenza, *De arte saltandj & choreas ducendj De la arte di ballare et danzare*, Paris, Bibliothèque Nationale, MS fonds it. 972.

Pa   Guglielmo Ebreo da Pesaro, *Domini Iohannis Ambrosii pisauriensis de pratica seu arte tripudii vulgare opusculum faeliciter incipit*, Paris, Bibliothèque Nationale, MS fonds it. 476.

FN   Guglielmo Ebreo da Pesaro, *Ghuglielmi hebrei pisauriensis De practicha seu arte tripudij vulghare opusculum feliciter incipit*, Florence, Biblioteca Nazionale Centrale, Codex Magliabecchiana-Strozziano XIX 88.

NY   Guglielmo Ebreo da Pesaro, *Ghuglielmi ebrei pisauriensis de praticha seu arte tripudi vulghare opusculum feliciter incipit*, New York, New York Public Library, Dance Collection, *MGZMB-Res. 72-254.

Pg   Guglielmo Ebreo da Pesaro, *Guilielmi Hebraei pisauriensis de practica seu arte tripudii vulgare opusculum incipit*, 1463, Paris, Bibliothèque Nationale, MS fonds it. 973.

FL   Guglielmo Ebreo da Pesaro, *Qui chominca elibro de bali Ghugliemus ebreis pisauriensis de praticha seu arte tipudi volghare opuschulum*, Florence, Biblioteca Medicea-Laurenziana, Codex Antinori, A13.

S   (Guglielmo Ebreo), Siena, Biblioteca Comunale, Codex L. V. 29.

M   (Guglielmo Ebreo), Modena, Biblioteca Estense, Codex Ital. 82, α. J. 94.

INTRODUCTION

1. Baldesdar Castiglione, *The Book of the Courtier,* trans. George Bull (Harmondsworth: Penguin, 1981), pp. 67, 70.

2. Ibid., pp. 67–68.

3. Scholars in other fields, such as art history, have similarly investigated artists' interaction with and participation in the intellectual climate of the day. See Francis Ames-Lewis, *The Intellectual Life of the Early Renaissance Artist* (New Haven: Yale University Press, 2000); and Joanna Woods-Marsden, *Renaissance Self-Portraiture: The Visual Construction of Identity and the Social Status of the Artist* (New Haven: Yale University Press, 1998).

4. Paul Oskar Kristeller, *Renaissance Thought,* vol. 2, *Papers on Humanism and the Arts* (New York: Harper and Row, 1965), pp. 1–2. See also Nicholas Mann, "The Origins of Humanism," in *The Cambridge Companion to Renaissance Humanism,* ed. Jill Kraye (Cambridge: Cambridge University Press, 1996), p. 2; and Charles Trinkaus, *The Scope of Renaissance Humanism* (Ann Arbor: University of Michigan Press, 1983), p. 15.

5. Albert Rabil Jr., ed., *Renaissance Humanism: Foundations, Forms, and Legacy,* 3 vols. (Philadelphia: University of Pennsylvania Press, 1988).

6. For example, Richard Trexler has documented accounts of men and women dancing in single-sex groups in dance competitions in Florence (Richard C. Trexler, *Public Life in Renaissance Florence* [Ithaca: Cornell University Press, 1991], pp. 235–37). For contemporary accounts of single-sex dancing, see Bartolommeo di Michele del Corazza, *Diario Fiorentino, anni 1405–1438,* in *Archivio storico italiano,* 5th series, 14 (1894): pp. 240–98, in particular pp. 255–56, 276; and Vespasiano da Bisticci, *Le vite,* vol. 2, ed. Aulo Greco (Florence: Istituto Nazionale di Studi sul Rinascimento, 1976), pp. 467–99.

7. For more information on improvised dances, see Barbara Sparti, "Improvisation and Embellishment in Popular and Art Dances in Fifteenth- and Sixteenth-Century Italy," in *Improvisation in the Arts of the Middle Ages and the Renaissance,* ed. Timothy J. McGee (Kalamazoo: The Medieval Institute, 2003), pp. 117–44.

8. Lorenzo Lavagnolo was one *maestro di ballo* who taught the children of the Gonzaga, Sforza, and d'Este families. For more details on his career, see Katherine Tucker McGinnis, "Moving in High Circles: Courts, Dance, and Dancing Masters in Italy in the Long Sixteenth Century" (Ph.D. diss., University of North Carolina, 2001), pp. 250–52.

9. Giuseppe Ebreo not only ran a dancing school in Florence, but also was associated with Lorenzo de' Medici. For more details on his activities, see Timothy J. McGee, "Dancing Masters and the Medici Court in the 15th Century," *Studi musicali* 17, no. 2 (1988), pp. 201–24.

10. In 1446 in Florence, for example, a harp player, Mariotto di Bastiano di Francesco, rented a room in order to teach dance (Frank A. D'Accone, "Lorenzo the Magnificent and Music," in *Lorenzo il magnifico e il suo mondo,* ed. Gian Carlo Garfagnini [Florence: Olschki, 1994], p. 263 n. 8).

11. One source of evidence for popular dancing is the sermons written for *Quinquagesima* against carnival amusements, particularly dance. For more information on these sermons and the information they provide about popular dancing in Italy and southern Germany, see Alessandro Arcangeli, "Carnival in Medieval Sermons," in *European Medieval Drama* 1 (1997), pp. 199–209. As Arcangeli notes, the increasing importance of popular dancing at carnival festivities in the fifteenth century is attested to by the large amount of space devoted to dance by the clerical sermon writers (p. 206).

12. Domenico wrote his treatise c. 1440–50, and the other two men acknowledged him as their teacher. Cornazano wrote two versions of his treatise. The first version, now lost, was dedicated to Ippolita Sforza, and the second to Ippolita's half-brother Secondo Sforza in 1465. The presentation version of Guglielmo's treatise is dated 1463.

13. The two major sources for the French *basse danse* tradition are the Brussels manuscript (Bibliothèque Royale de Belgique, MS 9085) and the Toulouze printed edition (*S'ensuit l'art et l'instruction de bien dancer* [Paris: Michel Toulouze, n.d.]). Frederick Crane has argued that the Brussels manuscript was compiled close to 1470 (Frederick Crane, *Materials for the Study of the Fifteenth-Century Basse Danse* [New York: Institute of Mediæval Music, 1968], pp. 6–7), while Daniel Heartz dates the manuscript as c. 1495–1501 (Daniel Heartz, "The Basse Dance: Its Evolution circa 1450 to 1550," *Annales musicologiques* 6 [1958–63], pp. 318–19). The Toulouze source is not dated, but Crane gives its printing as "1496 or a year or two earlier" (Crane, *Materials for Study*, p. 26). For information on the *basse danse* sources, see also David R. Wilson, "Theory and Practice in 15th-Century French Basse Danse," *Historical Dance* 2, no. 3 (1983): 1–2; David R. Wilson, "The Development of the French Basse Danse," *Historical Dance* 2, no. 4 (1984–85): 5–12; and David R. Wilson and Véronique Daniels, "The Basse Dance Handbook," unpublished manuscript.

14. One should note the collection of seven *basses danses* that are recorded on the "reverse of the first flyleaf of a copy of the *Geste des nobles françois* belonging to Jean d'Orleans, Comte d'Angoulême. It is plausibly conjectured that he made these notes at Nancy in 1445" (Wilson, "Development of French Basse Danse," p. 5).

15. Gresley of Drakelow papers, Derbyshire Record Office, D77 box 38, pp. 51–79.

16. As early as 1519 there are records of payment to a Peter Carmelet, named as the king's dancer (Andrew Ashbee, ed., *Records of English Court Music, vol. 7, 1485–1558* [Aldershot: Scolar Press, 1993], pp. 242–43). However, a permanent post of court dancing master (as opposed to just "a dancer") did not appear at the English court until 1575, when Thomas Cardell was "given an annuity of £20 a year" (Peter Holman, *Four and Twenty Fiddlers: The Violin at the English Court, 1540–1690* [Oxford: Clarendon Press, 1993], p. 115).

17. See chap. 1 for a discussion of dance as an aristocratic pastime.

1. DANCE AND SOCIETY

1. Pg, f. 46r–47r. Translation by Giovanni Carsaniga. "Tanto è suave & angelica harmonia / Nel dolce suon di Guglielmo hebreo, / Tanto è nel bel danzar la lizadria. / L'arme faria riporre al Machabeo. / . . . Il suo danzar non è d'industria humana / Ma d'ingegno celeste, & saper divo. / . . . Non son sì destre l'acquile in lor ali / Quanto è l'agilità di Guglielmo: / Le virtue cui si pon creder fatali. / Ma' non fu Hector sì destro solo l'elmo, / Quanto è costui in l'arte sua excellente, / Tra gli altri qual fra gli altri paraschelmo."

Throughout the notes, quotations from primary Italian sources retain their original spelling and punctuation, with certain exceptions: *u* is changed to *v*; accents are added to distinguish "it is" (*è*) from "and" (*e*) and at the end of certain other words, such as *perchè* and *più;* and an apostrophe indicates a missing letter, as in *dell'arte*.

2. Filelfo's poem appears at the end of Guglielmo's treatise on dance, written in 1463 as a presentation copy for Galeazzo Maria Sforza.

3. Nicoletta Guidobaldi, *La musica di Federico: Immagini e suoni alla corte di Urbino* (Florence: Olschki, 1995), p. 92. Pietrobono worked at the court of Ferrara, starting in the reign of Leonello and continuing under Borso and Ercole d'Este. His fame spread throughout Italy, from Ferrara and Milan in the north to Naples in the south, and he was generously rewarded by his patrons. In 1447 a portrait medal was made depicting Pietrobono, and he was praised by humanists such as Antonio Cornazano, Battista Guarino, and Raffaello Maffei, as well as the music theorist Johannes Tinctoris. For the full extent of Pietrobono's enormous reputation during his lifetime, see Lewis Lockwood, *Music in Renaissance Ferrara, 1400–1505: The Creation of a Musical Centre in the Fifteenth Century* (Oxford: Clarendon Press, 1984), pp. 98–108, and Lockwood's article on him, "Pietrobono and the Instrumental Tradition at Ferrara in the Fifteenth Century," *Rivista italiana di musicologia* 10 (1975): 115–33.

4. Michael Baxandall, *Giotto and the Orators: Humanist Observers of Painting in Italy and the Discovery of Pictorial Composition, 1350–1450* (Oxford: Clarendon Press, 1971), p. 16.

5. "[L]o ingegnio sança disciplina o la disciplina sança ingenio non puo fare perfecto artefice" (ibid., p. 16 n. 22, quoting Lorenzo Ghiberti, *Lorenzo Ghibertis Denkwürdigkeiten (I Commentari)*, ed. Julius von Schlosser, 1 [Berlin: J. Bard, 1912], p. 5).

6. Pg, f. 47r. "Molte madonne illustre & eminente / Di mortale ha fatte parer Diane. / Mia figlia Theodora novamente."

7. Pa, f. 74r–74v. "Ancora me atrovai a una gran festa a milano quando venne el ducha de cleves: quando venne el papa a mantoa. El ducha francesco glie fece un grandissimo hononore. E hongne volta era acompagnito dançando con tucta la corte. . . . Ancora me atrovai a una dignissima festa a milano de una madonna todesca [74v] che venne li con cinque donçelle la quale andava a mantoa dal papa." Both these visits were in 1459.

8. For more information on Cornazano's literary production, see chap. 2.

9. P. Farenga, "Cornazano," *Dizionario biografico degli Italiani*, vol. 29 (Rome: Istituto della Enciclopedia Italiana, 1983), p. 128.

10. The date Domenico was knighted is not known, but in his treatise Cornazano refers to Domenico as "cavagliero aurato" (V, f. 28v).

11. Lauro Martines, *Power and Imagination: City-States in Renaissance Italy* (London: Allen Lane, 1980), p. 270.

12. Artur Michel, "The Earliest Dance-Manuals," *Medievalia et humanistica* 3 (1945): 119–20.

13. This information is mentioned by Cornazano in his work *La vita della Vergine Maria*, which he dedicated to Ippolita Sforza in 1457–58. "E si come piu volte io vho provata / porgermi man se vho conducta in ballo / e dare urecchie a chi vi havra insegnata" (quoted in Sharon E. Fermor, "Studies in the Depiction of the Moving Figure in Italian Renaissance Art, Art Criticism, and Dance Theory" [Ph.D. diss., Warburg Institute, University of London, 1990], p. 29).

14. A. William Smith, introduction to *Fifteenth-Century Dance and Music: Twelve Transcribed Italian Treatises and Collections in the Tradition of Domencio da Piacenza*, trans. A. William Smith (Stuyvesant, N.Y.: Pendragon Press, 1995), p. xxi.

15. Even in the matter of a private fitting of a noblewoman's clothes, the issue of physical contact was important. See Carole Collier Frick, *Dressing Re-*

naissance Florence: Families, Fortunes, and Fine Clothing (Baltimore: Johns Hopkins University Press, 2002), pp. 5–6.

16. Frank A. D'Accone, *The Civic Muse: Music and Musicians in Siena during the Middle Ages and the Renaissance* (Chicago: University of Chicago Press, 1997), p. 641.

17. Richard W. Kaeuper and Elspeth Kennedy, *The* Book of Chivalry *of Geoffroi de Charny: Text, Context, and Translation* (Philadelphia: University of Pennsylvania Press, 1996), pp. 113, 115. The original text is given on pp. 112 and 114. "Et toutevoies devroit il sembler que li plus beaux gieux et li plus beaux esbatemens que telles gens qui tel honnour veulent querre devroient faire seroient qu'il ne se doivent point lasser de jouer, de jouster, de parler, de dancer et de chanter en compaignie de dames et de damoiseles ainsi honorablement comme il puet et doit appartenir et en gardant en fait et dit et en tous lieux leur honneur et leurs estas, que toutes bonnes gens d'armes le doivent ainsi faire de droit; . . . Iteulx gieux sont plus beaux et plus honorables et dont plus de biens pueent venir que des gieux des doz dont on puet perdre le sien et son honnour et toute bonne compaignie."

18. Ibid., p. 113.

19. Ibid., pp. 113–15.

20. Giovanni Boccaccio, *The Decameron*, vol. 1, trans. J. M. Rigg (London: Dent, 1930), p. 58.

21. Ibid., pp. 151–52.

22. Christine de Pisan, *The Treasure of the City of Ladies or The Book of the Three Virtues*, trans. Sarah Lawson (London: Penguin, 1987), p. 75.

23. For a summary of the courtly dancing of *caroles* in thirteenth-century France, see Christopher Page, *Voices and Instruments of the Middle Ages: Instrumental Practice and Songs in France, 1100–1300* (Berkeley: University of California Press, 1986), pp. 78–82 and also pp. 154–56. For further information on medieval dance and French dance songs, see Lawrence Earp, "Genre in the Fourteenth-Century French Chanson: The Virelai and the Dance Song," *Musica disciplina* 45 (1991): 123–41; Timothy J. McGee, "Medieval Dances: Matching the Repertory with Grocheio's Descriptions," *Journal of Musicology* 7, no. 4 (1989): 498–517; Timothy J. McGee, *Medieval Instrumental Dances* (Bloomington: Indiana University Press, 1989); Robert Mullally, "Cançon de carole," *Acta musicologica* 58, no. 2 (1986): 224–31; Robert Mullally, "Dance Terminology in the Works of Machaut and Froissart," *Medium ævum* 59, no. 2 (1990): 248–59; Robert Mullally, "Johannes de Grocheo's 'Musica Vulgaris,'" *Music and Letters* 79, no. 1 (1998): 1–26; Christopher Page, *The Owl and the Nightingale: Musical Life and Ideas in France, 1100–1300* (Berkeley: University of California Press, 1989); and John Stevens, *Words and Music in the Middle Ages: Song, Narrative, Dance, and Drama, 1050–1350* (Cambridge: Cambridge University Press, 1986). For a discussion of dancing in *Le roman de la rose*, see Susan W. Maynard, "Dance in the Arts of the Middle Ages" (Ph.D. diss., Florida State University, 1992), pp. 143–50.

24. Dante Alighieri, *The Divine Comedy*, vol. 1, book 1, *Inferno*, trans. Charles S. Singleton (London: Routledge and Kegan Paul, 1971), p. 143. In this case the "dance" of the damned souls is far closer to mad, unstructured, continuous movement than to what occurs in Paradise.

25. Dante Alighieri, *Purgatorio*, trans. W. S. Merwin (New York: Knopf, 2000), p. 97.

26. At this point the dance is performed at first by the three theological virtues of Faith, Hope, and Charity (ibid., p. 289), who are subsequently joined by the female representations of Justice, Prudence, Fortitude, and Temperance (pp. 309–11).

27. For example, canto XXV line 99 and canto XXVIII lines 124–26. For further discussion of dancing in Dante's *Divine Comedy* and how it is a manifestation of divine love, see Maynard, "Dance in the Arts of the Middle Ages," pp. 110–17.

28. Gene Brucker, ed., *Two Memoirs of Renaissance Florence: The Diaries of Buonaccorso Pitti and Gregorio Dati*, trans. Julia Martines (Prospect Heights, Ill.: Waveland Press, 1991), p. 36.

29. Ibid., pp. 36–37.

30. For details of this attitude, see Alessandro Arcangeli, "Dance under Trial: The Moral Debate, 1200–1600," *Dance Research* 12, no. 2 (1994): 129–30. As Jonathan Alexander has pointed out, the Christian church was ambivalent about dance: "[d]ance was often anathematized in the Christian religious context, . . . [b]ut it was also sanctified and incorporated into Christian experience. Its sanctification took place literally and physically in religious ceremonies and festivals" (Jonathan J. G. Alexander, "Dancing in the Streets," *Journal of the Walters Art Gallery* 54 [1996]: 154).

31. Alessandro Arcangeli, *Davide o Salomè? Il dibattito europeo sulla danza nella prima età moderna* (Rome: Viella, 2000), p. 108.

32. See Alexander, "Dancing in the Streets," pp. 147–62, for a discussion of how the images of dance in the fourteenth and fifteenth centuries had different meanings for differing groups of spectators, and "that there . . . [were even] contestations, contradictions, and uncertainties for each spectator" (p. 159).

33. Alan Ryder, *Alfonso the Magnanimous: King of Aragon, Naples, and Sicily, 1396–1458* (Oxford: Clarendon Press, 1990), p. 310.

34. Eileen Southern, "A Prima Ballerina of the Fifteenth Century," in *Music and Context: Essays for John M. Ward*, ed. Anne Dhu Shapiro (Cambridge, Mass.: Department of Music, Harvard University, 1985), p. 192.

35. For a discussion of Lorenzo's association with dancing, see Piero Gargiulo, " 'Leggiadri passi con intellecto attento': Lorenzo teorico di basse danze," in *La musica a Firenze al tempo di Lorenzo il magnifico*, ed. Piero Gargiulo (Florence: Olschki, 1993), pp. 249–55, and for Lorenzo's musical abilities see, in particular, Frank A. D'Accone, "Lorenzo the Magnificent and Music," in *Lorenzo il magnifico e il suo mondo*, ed. Gian Carlo Garfagnini (Florence: Olschki, 1994), pp. 259–90.

36. *Venus* and *Lauro* are found in FN, f. 26r–27v; in FL, f. 26r–27v; and in NY, f. 14r–15r.

37. V, f. 3v bis. "Et a mostrarvi le cose in vivo exempio dico cosi che se Vostra Signoria imitarà la regina delle feste, Madonna La Illustrissima Madonna Beatrice, non potrete mal fare alcuna cosa e per inanimarvi alla leggiadra."

38. V, f. 4r. "Chi vole passare da un mondo a l'altro odi sonare pierobono. Chi vole trovare el cielo aperto provi la liberalità del Ducha Borso. Chi vole vedere el paradiso in terra veggia Madonna Beatrice insu una festa." "Pierobono" is the famous lutenist Pietrobono del Chitarino, mentioned earlier, who worked at Ferrara under Leonello d'Este.

39. Vittorino da Feltre's school, for example, emphasized mathematics, whereas Guarino's school placed a very strong emphasis on language skills.

40. Baxandall, *Giotto and the Orators*, p. 129.

41. Barbara Sparti, introduction to *De pratica seu arte tripudii: On the Practice or Art of Dancing*, by Guglielmo Ebreo, ed. and trans. Barbara Sparti (Oxford: Clarendon Press, 1993), p. 57.

42. "Great concern for physical training was one of the distinctive marks of the educational system . . . of the fourteenth and fifteenth centuries" (Joel Stanislaus Nelson, introduction to *Aeneae Silvii: De liberorum educatione*, by Pope Pius II [Aeneas Silvius Piccolomini], ed. and trans. Joel Stanislaus Nelson [Washington,

D.C.: Catholic University of America Press, 1940], p. 48). In spite of their approval of physical education, the humanist educators were not universally in favor
of dance. There were a few who expressed reservations. Pier Paolo Vergerio admits in his treatise that there is "a certain usefulness" in dancing, because it exercises the body and imparts "great agility." But dancing could also spoil the
character of the young by "corrupting their habits with an excess of vanity" (Pier
Paolo Vergerio, "De ingenuis moribus," in *Educazione umanistica in Italia*, ed. and
trans. Eugenio Garin, 9th ed. [Rome: Laterza, 1975], p. 117).

43. See Arcangeli, *Davide o Salomè?* pp. 111–12 for further discussion of this
point.

44. Pius II (Piccolomini), *De liberorum educatione*, pp. 103–105.

45. Leon Battista Alberti, *The Family in Renaissance Florence*, trans. Renée
Neu Watkins (Columbia: University of South Carolina Press, 1969), p. 63.

46. Ibid., p. 65.

47. Guidobaldi, *La musica di Federico*, p. 87.

48. Cecil H. Clough, review of *De practica seu arte tripudii: On the Practice
or Art of Dancing*, by Guglielmo Ebreo da Pesaro, edited and translated by Barbara
Sparti, *Renaissance Studies* 11, no. 3 (1997): 268.

49. Guidobaldi, *La musica di Federico*, p. 87.

50. Pg, f. 22v.

51. Pa, f. 73v.

52. Pa, f. 77v.

53. Pa, f. 76v.

54. "Le dolce melodie et bel dançare / de belle donne et gioven peligrini:
/ ciascun pareva im paradiso stare" (quoted in Guidobaldi, *La musica di Federico*,
p. 88. Guidobaldi gives the source as the codex Urbinate Latin 692, f. 123r–149r).

55. Bernardino Zambotti, *Diario Ferrarese dall'anno 1476 sino al 1504*, ed.
Giuseppe Pardi, in vol. 24, part 7 of *Rerum italicarum scriptores*, ed. Lodovico
Antonio Muratori, revised by Giosue Carducci and Vittorio Fiorini (Bologna,
1928), p. 23.

56. Ibid., p. 172. "Li scolari lezisti e canonisti feceno una bella festa in Schi-
vanolgio e detteno dexenare a li fioli maschi e femene de lo illustrissimo duca
nostro, a sue spexe, e convocate altre zintildone, feceno ballare tuto il dì sotto la
loza verso il zardino, per darse qualche piacere."

57. Gregory Lubkin, *A Renaissance Court: Milan under Galeazzo Maria
Sforza* (Berkeley: University of California Press, 1994), p. 212.

58. Francis Ames-Lewis, *The Intellectual Life of the Early Renaissance Artist*
(New Haven: Yale University Press, 2000), p. 74.

59. For more details on this school and how the two men organized their
teaching, see Alessandra Veronese, "Una *societas* ebraico-cristiano in *docendo tripudiare sonare ac cantare* nella Firenze del quattrocento," in *Guglielmo Ebreo da
Pesaro e la danza nelle corti italiane del xv secolo*, ed. Maurizio Padovan (Pisa: Pacini,
1990), pp. 51–57, and Katherine Tucker McGinnis, "Moving in High Circles:
Courts, Dance, and Dancing Masters in Italy in the Long Sixteenth Century"
(Ph.D. diss., University of North Carolina, 2001), pp. 229–32.

60. Christiane Klapisch-Zuber, "Le chiavi fiorentine di Barbablù:
L'apprendimento della lettura a Firenze nel XV secolo," *Quaderni storici* 57, no. 3
(1984): 789 n. 68.

61. For further discussion of the status of the Castellani family, see Judith
Bryce, "Performing for Strangers: Women, Dance, and Music in Quattrocento
Florence," *Renaissance Quarterly* 54, no. 4.1 (2001): 1091–92.

62. D'Accone, "Lorenzo the Magnificent," p. 263 n. 8.

63. McGinnis, "Moving in High Circles," p. 232.

64. For details on the lives of these dance masters in the Mariotto family, see D'Accone, *Civic Muse*, pp. 649–51.

65. Ibid., p. 652.

66. For more information on dancing schools in Siena in the sixteenth century, see D'Accone, *Civic Muse*, pp. 652–55.

67. Pa, f. 73r.

68. S, f. 83v. "Ballo di guiglielmo chiamato colonnese in sei facto per Madonna Sveva di chasa colonna."

69. Werner L. Gundersheimer, ed., *Art and Life at the Court of Ercole I d'Este: The* De triumphis religionis *of Giovanni Sabadino degli Arienti* (Geneva: Librairie Droz, 1972), p. 23.

70. Ibid., p. 24.

71. In 1435 Leonello married Margherita Gonzaga, and in 1444 Maria d'Aragona.

72. Guglielmo was also present at this event and he recorded it in his autobiography (Pa, f. 72r).

73. Thus the *ballo* is a dance form in which the sections of the choreography are continually changing speed. But the dance masters did not appear to have any set rules as regards these speed changes, as there is no discernable order in the way the sections of differing speed were used. The *balli* do not conform to any rule such as a slow start, then an increase in speed, then a decrease of speed toward the end of the dance. Each dance is different from all others, with the changes in speed underlying the dramatic aspects of each dance.

74. V, f. 32r.

75. A *doppio*, or double step, consisted of three paces forward, alternating feet.

76. For a catalogue of the floor shapes used in the *balli* and *bassadanze*, see Jennifer Nevile, "The Courtly Dance Manuscripts from Fifteenth-Century Italy" (Ph.D. diss., University of New South Wales, 1992), appendix 3, pp. 311–19.

77. In the fifty-four choreographies that include music, a musical section ends in the middle of a floor shape only eight times.

78. A *riverenza*, or bow, is made by moving the left foot slightly behind the right foot and then bending both knees so that the body is lowered. The left foot is then moved slightly forward, level with the right, as the knees are straightened. A second form of the *riverenza* was the *riverenza in terra*, in which the back leg was extended behind, and the back knee bent so that it touched, or almost touched, the ground.

79. Pd, f. 22v. "et una posada guardandose in lo volto l'uno al'altro."

80. Timothy J. McGee, "Dancing Masters and the Medici Court in the 15th Century," *Studi musicali* 17, no. 2 (1988): 202.

81. Ibid., p. 205; for more information on Bussus, see p. 207. McGee suggests that the author of the letter to Lorenzo was probably the same person as "Phylippo," the author of the *bassadanza Consolata*, that was recorded in the Siena version of Guglielmo's treatise.

82. Ibid., p. 205.

83. V, f. 13r. "Mercantia è ballo appropriato al nome che una sol donna dança con tre homini e dà audientia a tutti gli ne fossero, pure assai come quella che fa mercantia d'amanti."

84. V, f. 17r.

85. Most of the *balli* have only three or four changes of *misura*.

86. "Social dances" are the type of dances performed for enjoyment and entertainment, both after dinner in private apartments and also on more formal occasions. These would include public occasions, such as the *feste* that occurred

in honor of both secular and religious personages. The term "social dance" also refers to dances in which the participants were not disguised or masked, or representing generic types such as nymphs or shepherds. Dances in which the performers, in elaborate costumes, represented figures from Greek mythology, famous people from history, or fabulous animals such as centaurs are not recorded in the dance treatises. For a discussion of the close relationship between social and theatrical dance at this time, see Arcangeli, *Davide o Salomè?* p. 42.

87. Gundersheimer, *Art and Life*, p. 65. A *passo* is "a step, . . . a pace in going, . . . the measure of two foote and a halfe." John Florio, *A Worlde of Wordes* (1598; facsimile ed., Hildesheim: George Olms, 1972), p. 261.

88. These three dances are *Humana, Bialte di chastiglia*, and *Santomera*. Each of them occurs only once in the dance manuscripts, *Humana* in S and the other two in NY.

89. For descriptions of *moresche* in fifteenth-century Italy, see Alessandro Pontremoli and Patrizia La Rocca, *Il ballare lombardo: Teoria e prassi coreutica nella festa di corte del xv secolo* (Milan: Vita e Pensiero, 1987), pp. 219–31.

90. Richard C. Trexler, *Public Life in Renaissance Florence* (Ithaca: Cornell University Press, 1991), pp. 306–18.

91. Ibid., p. 316.

92. For a detailed study of the morris dance in the English records, see John Forrest, *The History of Morris Dancing, 1458–1750* (Toronto: University of Toronto Press, 1999). As Forrest emphasizes, morris dances do not have one origin, nor were they a single phenomenon, as the dance form changed continuously throughout its history (p. 27). Forrest stresses that the early forms of morris were all in courtly or royal contexts, and that their place in court spectacles had its origin in tournaments and courtly disguisings (pp. 60–65).

93. In spite of the implications of its name, there are actually very few recorded examples of Moorish participants in *moresche* (ibid., p. 89). The idea that the morris/*morrisco*/*moresca* was originally a "Moorish" dance from Spain originates in the seventeenth century, and was derived solely from the etymology of the term. See ibid., pp. 5–7, for the reasons behind the enduring popularity of this theory of origin.

94. For further discussion of the *moresca* and an interpretation of its characteristics, see Sparti, introduction to *De Practica*, pp. 53–57; McGinnis, "Moving in High Circles," pp. 171–76; and Forrest, *History of Morris Dancing*, pp. 74–90.

95. Tammaro De Marinis, ed., *Le nozze di Costanzo Sforza e Camilla d'Aragona celebrate a Pesaro nel maggio 1475* (Florence, 1946), p. 38.

96. One example of dancing forming part of the celebration of a military victory is found in Guglielmo's autobiography, where he mentions that he was present in Milan for Francesco Sforza's triumphal entry into the city, and that the "jousts, dancing, and grand festivities lasted for a month." Pa, f. 73v. "E più me atrovai quando el ducha Francesco fece l'intrata de milano e fo facto duca e durò un mese le giostre e lo dançare e le feste grande."

97. D'Accone, *Civic Muse*, p. 646.

98. Patrizia Castelli, " 'Quella città che vedete è Roma': Scena e illusione alla corte dei Montefeltro," in *Federico di Montefeltro: Lo stato, le arti, la cultura*, vol. 2, *Le arti*, ed. Giorgio Cerboni Baiardi, Giorgio Chittolini, and Piero Floriani (Rome: Bulzoni, 1986), pp. 335–36. "Da man dritta ne l'intrare è la credenza da capo con li arzenti suoi solamente che non sono pocho a numero. Da l'altro è il tribunale ornato di veluto cremisi et certe peze de panno d'oro. Da un canto de la sala, da li capitelli de la volta fino a le banche sono tirate peze di veluto cremesci e verdi intorno, et sono compartite in quadri con colonne de ligno depinte; et da questo lato stanno le donne. Da l'altro sono baltresche con li scalini, dove stanno

li homini a vedere, da le quale fin a li capitelli sono pur peze de veluto verde et
alexandrino, tirato fra le colone como è da l'altro lato. El corpo de la sala rimane
netto per ballare. Dal capo de la credenza è fatto un pozzo dove stanno li piffari
et donne che non intervengono in ballo." Castelli is quoting from Alessandro
Luzio and Rodolfo Renier, *Mantova e Urbino: Isabella d'Este e Elisabetta Gonzaga*
(1893; reprint, Bologna: Forni, 1976), p. 19.

99. Fabrizio Cruciani, *Teatro nel Rinascimento: Roma, 1450–1550* (Rome:
Bulzoni, 1983), p. 152.

100. Pa, f. 72r. "Imprima me atrovai alle noççe del marchese Leonello che
tolse la figliola de Re alfonso che un mese durò la corte bandita. E gran giostra
e gran balli foro facte." For a discussion of other wedding celebrations which
Guglielmo attended or was involved with, see Patrizia Castelli, "La kermesse degli
Sforza pesaresi," in *Mesura et arte del danzare*, ed. Patrizia Castelli, Maurizio Mingardi, and Maurizio Padovan (Pesaro: Pucelle, 1987), pp. 13–28.

101. De Marinis, *Le nozze di Costanzo Sforza*, pp. 33–34.

102. Ibid., p. 34. "[I]n questo mezo vene fuora da doi parte quasi come de
due grote de quel monte dui gioueni . . . et danzando a tempo ueneronno fuora
admiratiui, et cum bona maniera."

103. Ibid., p. 34. "[D]icti gioueni, cinque vestiti di alexandrino, et cinque de
verde precixi como quelli dui primi, et havea ciaschun di loro una casata in mano
di zucharo dorata et dipinta, et tendendola cum bono aire feceron una bella mo-
rescha a molti mesure cum degni salti et gesti di corpo." Clothes made from fabric
dyed "alexandrino" blue were highly valued. Their appearance at the *spettacoli* for
the Sforza wedding indicates the luxuriousness of the dancers' costumes. For more
information on clothes and fabrics of fifteenth-century Italy, see Frick, *Dressing
Renaissance Florence*.

104. De Marinis, *Le nozze di Costanzo Sforza*, pp. 34–35.

105. A detailed discussion of all the fundamental principles of the dance
practice, including *maniera*, is found in chap. 3.

106. De Marinis, *Le nozze di Costanzo Sforza*, p. 38.

107. Ibid., p. 45.

108. Ibid. "[E]t danzando a la prefata mesura in algune parte de la piua, tuti
ad un tempo se ingenochiaronno facendo reuerentia: et tuti ad uno tempo se
leuorono, ch'era el più splendido et el più magnifico spectaculo che fosse mai
veduto."

109. Ibid., p. 46.

110. Ibid. "Et facta dicta collatione, el signor prese madona a ballare, cossì
signori et gentil homini, et doctori et caualeri, per la magior parte prexeno una
dona facendose vno longo et gran ballo."

111. For a list of the primary sources that describe this event, see appendix
2 of Gabriele Cazzola's " 'Bentivoli machinatores': Aspetti politici e momenti teatrali di una festa quattrocentesca bolognese," *Biblioteca teatrale* 23–24 (1979): 38.

112. Ibid., p. 31 n. 20. "Dançata che ebbe questa fançuleta, subito al suono
de le tube in la sala apparve un uomo peloso come silvano vestito cum irsuta barba
et lunga, et capilli horrendi cum uno troncho in mano, cum lo quale facendo far
largo a la gente, fu portata artificiosamente una torre de legno bene posta de sotto
la sala oposita a la richa credentia, in la quale torre era la Dea Junone cum due
legiadri giovani, di quali uno presentava la persona del nobilissimo sponso. Posata
la torre, sença indusia venne uno palazo ballando, che proprio parea venisse, non
vedendosi ch'el portasse, in lo quale era Venus cum el faretrato Cupido et cum
due Donne: l'una era grande ale et di bruto viso et questa era la Infamia, l'altra
era de passionato aspecto et vestita de vestimenta piena de infiniti occhij et questa
era la Gelosia; et eranli quatro Imperatori adcompagnati ciascuno da una bellis-

sima donna. Et così decto palazo se posò un poco presso la torre. Di poi similmente ne venne una montagna de bosco circundata, nel cui corpo era a modo una speloncha, dove Diana cum octo nimphe dimorava, et danzando andò a diposare quasi a lato la torre, de l'altro lato. Di poi venne uno saxo anchora danzando, in lo quale era una bella giovane cum octo a fogia moresca vestiti." Cazzola is quoting from the contemporary description by G. S. degli Arienti, *Hymeneo*, MS Parm. 1294, Biblioteca Palatina di Parma, f. 38r–38v.

113. F. Alberto Gallo, "La danza negli spettacoli conviviali del secondo quattrocento," in *Spettacoli conviviali dall'antichità classica alle corti italiane del'400: Atti del convegno di Viterbo, 1982* (Viterbo: Centro di studi sul teatro medioevale e rinascimentale, 1982), pp. 266–67. Gallo also includes the relevant passages from Arienti's account, that is, f. 39v–40r, 42v–43r, and 43v–44r. See p. 267 for Gallo's identification of the hunting song and the song that accompanied Juno's dance.

114. See ibid., pp. 262–63, and D'Accone, *Civic Muse*, pp. 643–44, for more information about this occasion.

115. Clelia Falletti, "Le feste per Eleonora d'Aragona da Napoli a Ferrara (1473)," in *Spettacoli conviviali*, p. 281. For a discussion of all the entertainments offered to Eleonora on her journey from Naples to Ferrara, see pp. 269–89.

116. For two contemporary accounts of the banquet and the final dances (one by Eleonora herself, and one by Bernardino Corio), see Cruciani, *Teatro nel Rinascimento*, pp. 157–64.

117. Vespasiano da Bisticci, *Le vite*, vol. 2, ed. Aulo Greco (Florence: Istituto Nazionale di Studi sul Rinascimento, 1976), p. 478.

118. *Diario Ferrarese dall'anno 1409 sino al 1502 di autori incerti*, ed. Giuseppe Pardi, in vol. 24, part 7 of *Rerum italicarum scriptores*, ed. Muratori, Carducci, and Fiorini, pp. 35, 54.

119. Magl. VII 1121, Biblioteca Nazionale, Florence, f. 64v lines 1–3, 13–14, and f. 65r–65v lines 1–5, 16, 19–21. See appendix 1 for a transcription of the original Italian text.

120. Ibid., f. 66v line 13–67r line 14.

121. Ibid., f. 66v lines 13–15.

122. Ibid., f. 67v line 14.

123. Ibid., f. 69r lines 5–7.

124. Ibid., f. 69r lines 8–13.

125. "Danzare a *bassadanza* e *lioncello* / A doi a doi con l'altre damigelle, / Quale *a la piva* e quale *a saltarello* / E chi a *rostiboli* e chi al *gioioso* / E chi a *la gelosia*, novo modello." These lines are from a sonnet written c. 1454 by Gaugello Gaugelli and contained in the Codex Urbinati 692 in the Vatican Library. They are quoted from Daniel Heartz, "A 15th-Century Ballo: Rôti Bouilli Joyeux," in *Aspects of Medieval and Renaissance Music*, ed. Jan LaRue (New York: Pendragon Press, 1966), p. 373.

126. See Zambotti, *Diario Ferrarese*, pp. 31, 44, 60–61, 72, and 285–86 for records of carnival balls in 1477–80 and 1499.

127. Bartolommeo di Michele del Corazza, *Diario Fiorentino, anni 1405–1438*, in *Archivio storico italiano*, 5th series, vol. 14 (Florence, 1894), p. 276. "[U]na brigata di giovani cittadini feciono una ricca e bella festa di ballare: in su la piazza de'Signori feciono uno isteccato grandissimo. . . . Elessono quattro donne che avessino a giudicateri l'onore delle donne, e stettono a sedere alte come giudicatori; e così elessono chi avesse a giudicare quello de' giovani . . . al figliuolo di Bernardo Gherardi." For a discussion of the Florentine brigades and their involvement in organizing these dancing competitions, see Trexler, *Public Life in Renaissance Florence*, pp. 225–36.

128. Corazza, *Diario Fiorentino*, p. 254. The six hundred ladies at the 1415

dance probably constituted, very roughly, 10 percent of the eligible population, as, according to the 1427 Catasto, Florence had 5,949 females between the ages of eleven and forty, that is, of a danceable age (Giovanni Ciappelli, *Carnevale e quaresima: Comportamenti sociali e cultura a Firenze nel Rinascimento* [Rome: Edizioni di Storia e Letteratura, 1997], p. 153 n. 137).

129. Corazza, *Diario Fiorentino*, pp. 254–56, 276–77.

130. Ciappelli, *Carnevale e quaresima*, p. 143.

131. See *Barriera* (pp. 77v–79v), *Barriera nuova* (pp. 171v–172v), and *Torneo amoroso* (pp. 159v–161r) in Fabritio Caroso's *Il ballarino* (Venice, 1581; facsimile ed., New York: Broude Brothers, 1967); *Barriera* (pp. 139–48) and *Barriera nuova* (pp. 190–93) in Caroso's *Nobiltà di dame* (Venice, 1600; facsimile ed., Bologna: Forni, 1980); and *La barriera* (pp. 122–24), *La battaglia* (pp. 257–63), and *Il torneo amoroso* (pp. 140–43) in Cesare Negri's *Le gratie d'amore* (Milan, 1602; facsimile ed., New York: Broude Brothers, 1969); and the manuscript dance *La battaglia*, in Magl. XIX 31 f. 1r–7r, Biblioteca Nazionale, Florence.

132. Ryder, *Alfonso the Magnanimous*, p. 358. Ryder's quotation is from a letter sent to Barcelona on 23 June 1457, which is printed in J. M. Madurell Marimón, *Mensajeros barceloneses en la corte de Nápoles de Alfonso V de Aragon, 1435–1458* (Barcelona, 1963), p. 590.

133. See also Bryce, "Performing for Strangers," pp. 1080–81.

134. From the eighteenth century onward scholarly interpretations of these dancers have always identified them as female. This interpretation has recently been called into question by Jane Bridgeman, who argues that the figures are male. She bases her conclusion on the fact that all the dancers have short hair (women wore their hair long at this time), the dancers' feet and ankles are clearly visible, in some cases their garments are slit to thigh height, and they are all flat-chested, and, in some cases, pot-bellied (Jane Bridgeman, "Ambrogio Lorenzetti's Dancing 'Maidens': A Case of Mistaken Identity," *Apollo* 133, no. 350 [1991]: 245–51; a list of the works from 1957 to 1988 in which the dancers are seen as female is given on p. 250 n. 2).

135. Chiara Frugoni, *A Distant City: Images of Urban Experience in the Medieval World*, trans. William McCuaig (Princeton: Princeton University Press, 1991), pp. 162–63.

136. Keith Polk, *German Instrumental Music of the Late Middle Ages: Players, Patrons, and Performance Practice* (Cambridge: Cambridge University Press, 1992), p. 11.

137. Martines, *Power and Imagination*, p. 325.

138. The few that are not explicitly choreographed for both men and women do not mention the sex of the performers. There are no dances that are explicitly choreographed for men only or for women only.

139. For a transcription of the dance material from the Derbyshire Record Office, D77 box 38, pp. 51–79, see David Fallows, "The Gresley Dance Collection, *c.* 1500," *RMA Research Chronicle* 29 (1996): 1–20. For a discussion of these dances in their international context, see Jennifer Nevile, "Dance in Early Tudor England: An Italian Connection?" *Early Music* 26, no. 2 (1998): 230–44.

140. Eighty-seven percent of the *balli* and 84 percent of the *bassadanze* fall into this category of two to four performers.

141. "[W]hen men were uncertain as to the precise quality of their sensed humanity, they appealed to the concept of wildness to designate an area of sub-humanity that was characterized by everything they hoped they were not" (Hayden White, *Tropics of Discourse: Essays in Cultural Criticism* [Baltimore: Johns Hopkins University Press, 1978], p. 152).

142. John Gillies, *Shakespeare and the Geography of Difference* (Cambridge: Cambridge University Press, 1994), pp. 8–9.

143. Ibid., p. 25.

144. "Cursedness, or wildness, is identified with the wandering life of the hunter (as against the stable life of the shepherd and farmer), the desert (which is the Wild Man's habitat), linguistic confusion (which is the Wild Man's as well as the barbarian's principal attribute), sin, and physical aberration in both color (blackness) and size" (White, *Tropics of Discourse*, p. 162).

145. Gillies, *Shakespeare and the Geography of Difference*, p. 180.

146. Lionello Puppi, "Nature and Artifice in the Sixteenth-Century Italian Garden," in *The History of Garden Design: The Western Tradition from the Renaissance to the Present Day*, ed. Monique Mosser and Georges Teyssot (London: Thames and Hudson, 1991), p. 47.

147. For a discussion of Altieri's treatise, its context, and its author's political agenda, see Christiane Klapisch-Zuber, "An Ethnology of Marriage in the Age of Humanism," chap. 11 in *Women, Family, and Ritual in Renaissance Italy*, trans. Lydia G. Cochrane (Chicago: University of Chicago Press, 1985), pp. 247–60.

148. Marco Antonio Altieri, *Li nuptiali di Marco Antonio Altieri*, ed. Enrico Narducci (1873; reprint, Rome: Roma nel Rinascimento, 1995), p. 58.

149. Ibid., p. 58. "Li mastri deputati dello ballo mettevano in ordine uno homo et una donna continuatamente, da grado in grado, delli più propinqui et benivoli conioncti."

150. Ibid., p. 59.

151. Ibid., pp. 58–59.

152. Ibid., p. 85.

153. The *Chirintana* is found in the Siena redaction of Guglielmo's treatise, and Fabritio Caroso included the *Chiaranzana* in his 1581 treatise, *Il ballarino*, where it is labeled "anonymous."

154. Caroso, *Il ballarino*, p. 179v.

155. Richard C. Trexler, preface to *The Libro Ceremoniale of the Florentine Republic*, by Francesco Filarete and Angelo Manfidi, ed. Richard C. Trexler (Geneva: Librairie Droz, 1978), p. 9.

156. Timothy J. McGee, "Dinner Music for the Florentine Signoria, 1350–1450," *Speculum* 74, no. 1 (1999), p. 97.

157. Ibid., p. 103.

158. Martines, *Power and Imagination*, p. 325.

159. Trexler, *Public Life in Renaissance Florence*, p. 309.

160. De Marinis, *Le nozze di Costanzo Sforza*, p. 45. "[E]l primo che guidaua el ballo de la colatione presentò el suo castello de zucharo ali S. sposi: et cossì per ordine a ciaschuno signore et imbassiatore et digno gentil homo, fo presentato uno de li dicti castelli, et anche uasi, et anche animali secundo loro conditione et secundo l'arme de li signori et ambassarie et communità."

161. For a more extended discussion of the relationship between ritual and the projection of an image of a ruler's power, see Martines, *Power and Imagination*, pp. 322–26.

162. Trexler, *Libro Ceremoniale*, p. 77. "Non enarro la nobil pompa e lla quantità delle ricche e ornatissime veste con peregrine divise e ricami, e degl'uomini e delle donne, che parve certo a ogniuno universalmente piutòsto cosa angelica che terrena con quanta quantità di perle e nobilissime gioie. E maxime a gl'esterni parve cosa mirabilissima la quantità delle nobili donne, l'ordine de' giovani, el modo del danzare e festeggiare con ogni genere d'onestà e civile allegreza."

163. Trexler, *Public Life in Renaissance Florence*, p. 316.

164. Trexler, *Libro Ceremoniale*, pp. 78, 85. "Prima gli si mandò incontra fuori della città più che tre migle molti de' nostri optimati e cavalieri e altri principali cittadini e giovani. . . . [F]u da grandissimo numero de' nostri preclarissimi cittadini con assai giovani chon ricchi e hornatissimi vestimenti, andatigli sponte incontra, accompagnato piùche otto migla."

165. Magl. VII 1121, f. 67r lines 6–8. See appendix 1 for a transcription of the original Italian text.

166. Ibid., f. 66v lines 7–9.

167. Ibid., f. 65r lines 10–12.

168. Smith, introduction to *Fifteenth-Century Dance and Music*, p. xix. "[C]on summa riverentia et honesta toltomi in mezo, mi fecero ballare, preso pero da loro si per la destra como per la sinistra mano. Et in quello ponto, tuti li miei anchora se miseno a ballare . . . ma fornita la squadra mia, chi havesse visto levare quatro di quelle damiselle et volgersi verso il tribunale, et con reverente et degno modo, et a doe a doe accostarse a li prefati ambasatori del duca di Borgognia che erano doy già bene attempati, et farli levare a ballare."

169. Ryder, *Alfonso the Magnanimous*, p. 397.

170. James Hankins, "The 'Baron Thesis' after Forty Years and Some Recent Studies of Leonardo Bruni," *Journal of the History of Ideas* 56, no. 2 (1995): 310.

171. Ibid., pp. 309–18.

172. Trexler, *Public Life in Renaissance Florence*, p. 161.

173. "Marrying well" could mean either contracting an alliance with a rich family, or contracting one with an old family with an established lineage.

174. Magl. VII 1121, f. 66r lines 6–11. See appendix 1 for a transcription of the original Italian text.

175. Ibid., f. 67r lines 18, 20, 30–31, and f. 67v line 1.

176. Ibid., f. 67v lines 5–10.

177. For an examination of images of circle dances that represent courtship and the social harmony of marriage, see Alexander, "Dancing in the Streets," pp. 147–50.

178. While the fifteenth-century Italian dance masters do not discuss this aspect of the dance directly in their treatises, later dance masters were not so reticent. Antonius Arena, whose immensely popular treatise was written for his fellow students at the University of Avignon and was published at least forty-two times between 1529 and 1770, stressed this benefit of dancing: "So then, you who desire to caress the girls and kiss them long and sweetly, must learn the correct way to dance: a thousand joys flow from the dance" (John Guthrie and Marino Zorzi, trans., "Rules of Dancing: Antonius Arena," *Dance Research* 4, no. 2 [1986]: 9). The French canon Arbeau is quite blunt as to the necessity of dance partners' being able to "inspect" each other during the course of a dance. For Arbeau this practice was one of the benefits dance gave to a well-ordered society; that is, inspection revealed whether "lovers are in good health and sound of limb . . . [or] if they are shapely or emit an unpleasant odour as of bad meat" (Thoinot Arbeau, *Orchesography* [1589; trans. Mary Stewart Evans, 1948; reprint, New York: Dover, 1967], p. 12).

179. The *riverenza* was the bow, while the *continenza* and the *ripresa* steps were performed to the side, often in pairs, first to the left and then to the right or vice versa. The *continenza* covered a smaller distance than did the *ripresa*. For a detailed examination of these steps and ways of performing them, see David R. Wilson, *The Steps Used in Court Dancing in Fifteenth-Century Italy* (Cambridge: published by the author, 1992), pp. 18–26, 61–72.

180. Cornazano says that while the *movimento* is not found in the *bassadanze*,

it does provide an occasion in public for a totally decorous signal from the man to the lady, as in *Leonçello* and many other dances. V, f. 7r–7v. "Ne la bassadanza possono essere tutti gli nove naturali excepto el movimento che non si mette senno in ballitti et non e tempo perfecto ma scusa in publico da lhomo alla donna uno honestissimo rechiamo come e in leoncello et in molti altri."

181. Twenty-six percent of the *balli* have three different social events, while 34 percent have four.

182. Only 5 percent of the *balli* have six different social events.

183. The majority of the *balli* comprise three to seven social events, with 9 percent of them having ten and 8 percent having eleven to sixteen.

184. "Opening sequence" occurs in 85 percent of the *balli*, "inspection" in 70 percent, and "formal greeting" in 50 percent.

185. Of the 85 percent of the *balli* which begin with an "opening sequence," almost a third of them have a "chase" as their second situation, while a second third have an "inspection." Similarly, among the remaining 15 percent of the *balli* which begin with a "formal greeting," the second social event is usually an "opening sequence" (41 percent), "inspection," or "chase" (28 percent each).

186. The endings of the *balli* are variable, and the only pattern I have been able to discover is in the six *balli* choreographed by Guglielmo that are found in multiple versions of his treatise, and the three *balli* that occur only in Pa, two of which are also by Guglielmo. Seven out of these nine dances end with either a *volta tonda* or a backward *doppio* and then a *volta tonda*. None of the *balli* which occur only in one version in either S or NY end in this way, nor do any of the *balli* choreographed by Domenico.

187. Only 16 percent of the *balli* contain a sequence of movements in which two different social events happen simultaneously.

2. THE DANCE TREATISES AND HUMANIST IDEALS

1. Ann Harding, *An Investigation into the Use and Meaning of Medieval German Dancing Terms* (Göppingen: Alfred Kümmerle, 1973), p. 5.

2. Ibid., p. 52.

3. Henry Holland Carter, *A Dictionary of Middle English Musical Terms* (1961; reprint, New York: Kraus Reprint Corporation, 1968).

4. Eric Stanley, "Dance, Dancers, and Dancing in Anglo-Saxon England," *Dance Research* 9, no. 2 (1991), p. 18. The lack of a specific dance vocabulary in earlier English literature is confirmed by Stanley's conclusion that while "the words that might mean dancing, or might be connected with dancing, in the texts in which they survive, provide no little measure of textual and semantic difficulty," they provide "hardly any firm information about dance, dancers and dancing in Anglo-Saxon England" (p. 29).

5. Jennifer Nevile, "Dance in Early Tudor England: An Italian Connection?" *Early Music* 26, no. 2 (1998): 232–34.

6. Robert Mullally, "Dance Terminology in the Works of Machaut and Froissart," *Medium ævum* 59, no. 2 (1990): 248–59. For a discussion of the passage in Adam de la Halle's play *Robin et Marion* (c. 1283) that appears to refer to dance

patterns or dance steps, see John Stevens, *Words and Music in the Middle Ages: Song, Narrative, Dance, and Drama, 1050–1350* (Cambridge: Cambridge University Press, 1986), pp. 175–77.

7. Jeannine Horowitz, "Les danses cléricales dans les églises au Moyen Age," *Le Moyen Age: Revue d'histoire et de philologie* 95, no. 2 (1989): 285.

8. In 1434 Bruni wrote *La vita di Dante* and *La vita del Petrarca*, both in the vernacular. For examples of the Italian works of Palmieri, Cornazano, and Alberti, see below.

9. Eugenio Garin, "Introduction: Dance in the Renaissance," trans. David Thompson and Alan F. Nagel, in *The Three Crowns of Florence: Humanist Assessments of Dante, Petrarca, and Boccaccio*, ed. and trans. David Thompson and Alan F. Nagel (New York: Harper and Row, 1972), p. xvii.

10. Colucio Salutati, "In Quest of Dante," in ibid., p. 14.

11. Leonardo Bruni, "Life of Dante," in ibid., p. 71. While Bruni admired Petrarch's Latin writings, he also praised his Italian writings (Leonardo Bruni, "Comparison of Dante and Petrarca," in ibid., p. 83).

12. Matteo Palmieri, *Vita civile*, ed. Gino Belloni (Florence: Sansoni, 1982), pp. 5–6. "Altri ne sono composti in lingua volgare, pochi da elevati ingegni. Il primo et sopra a ogni altro dignissimo è il nostro Dante poeta: costui in ogni parte tanto excelle qualunche altro volgare, che non si degna assimigliarsi a essi, però che fuor della lingua poco si truova drieto a sommi poeti latini."

13. Cristoforo Landino, "Commentary on the Commedia," in Thompson and Nagel, *Three Crowns of Florence*, pp. 126–27.

14. Ibid., p. 128.

15. Martin Kemp, introduction to *On Painting (De pictura)*, by Leon Battista Alberti, ed. Cecil Grayson (London: Penguin, 1991), p. 19.

16. Leon Battista Alberti, *The Family in Renaissance Florence*, trans. Renée Neu Watkins (Columbia: University of South Carolina Press, 1969), p. 153.

17. Palmieri, *Vita civile*, p. 5.

18. P. Farenga, "Cornazano," in *Dizionario biografico degli Italiani*, vol. 29 (Rome: Istituto della Enciclopedia Italiana, 1983), p. 126.

19. *De excellentium vivorum principibus*, Cornazano's biographical account of famous men from Adam to Charlemagne, was written in a Latin version in elegiac couplets, and in Italian in *terzine*.

20. One such poem, *Florentinae urbis laudes*, was written in 1464 to celebrate the alliance between Florence and Milan. Its four chapters are in Italian, preceded by a Latin preface.

21. Joanna Woods-Marsden, *Renaissance Self-Portraiture: The Visual Construction of Identity and the Social Status of the Artist* (New Haven: Yale University Press, 1998), p. 79.

22. These later works include *On the Unhappiness of Princes* and *On Nobility* (1440), *Against Hypocrisy* (1447–48), and *On the Misery of the Human Condition* (1455).

23. Pg, f. 4r. "Ma qual di questi o altri chi se fusse prima origine o principio di tal scienza fu di singular laude & memoria digno. La qual arte intra le sette non è la minore annumerata anzi come scienza liberale se mostra sublime et alta & da dover seguire come l'altre dignissima."

24. Pg, f. 4r. "et quasi al humana natura più che alchuna dell'altre aptissima & conforme: Impero che da quattro concordanti & principal voci formata & composta alle nostre quattro principal compositioni correspondente porge ascoltando a tutti nostri sensi singular conforto quasi si chome ella fusse di nostri spiriti naturalissimo cibo."

25. For an extended discussion of the Pythagorean tetrad and its cosmolog-

ical implications, see S. K. Heninger Jr., *The Cosmographical Glass: Renaissance Diagrams of the Universe* (San Marino, Calif.: The Huntington Library, 1977), pp. 99–106. The information in this paragraph is taken from here.

26. The creation of the world is discussed by Plato in the *Timaeus*, where he also explains why the number of elements had to equal four.

> God in the beginning of creation made the body of the universe to consist of fire and earth. But two things cannot be rightly put together without a third; there must be some bond of union between them. . . . If the universal frame had been created a surface only and having no depth, a single mean would have sufficed to bind together itself and the other terms, but now, as the world must be solid, and solid bodies are always compacted not by one mean but by two, God placed water and air in the mean between fire and earth, and made them to have the same proportion so far as was possible. . . . And for these reasons, and out of such elements which are in number four, the body of the world was created, and it was harmonized by proportion (Plato, *Timaeus*, in *The Collected Dialogues of Plato, Including the Letters*, ed. Edith Hamilton and Huntington Cairns [Princeton: Princeton University Press, 1963], pp. 1163–64 [31b–32c]).

For further discussion of the numerical basis of the cosmos as discussed in the *Timaeus*, see chap. 4.

27. Pg, f. 15r. "Appresso per havere più piena cognitione & intelligenza delle preditte cose è da notare, si chome di sopra nel proemio habiamo fatto mentione, chel suono overo canto è principalmente fundato & firmato in quattro voci principali le qual sonno concordante & conforme alle quattro nostre elementale compositioni per la qual concordanza havemo l'essere e 'l sustentamento del nostro vivere per tal modo & in tal misura che quando per alchuno accidente mancha in noi una di queste quattro sustanze principale chiamate elementi de li quali siamo composti et formati: subito mancharia la propia vita."

28. Pg, f. 5r. "& chome anchora fece il glorioso re David: il quale più volte collo suo amoroso & sancto psalterio & agionto insieme il tribulato populo con festevole & honesto danzare: & col harmonia del dolce canto commovea lirato & potente idio a piatosa & suavissima pace."

29. Pg, f. 5v–6r. "Le qual cose ci mostrano la grande excellenza & suprema dignitate d'essa scienza dalla qual l'arte giocunda e 'l dolce effetto del danzare è naturalmente proceduto. La qual virtute del danzare non è altro che una actione demostrativa di fuori di movimenti spiritali: Li quali si hanno a concordare colle misurate et perfette consonanze d'essa harmonia: che per lo nostro audito alle parti intellective & ai sensi cordiali con diletto descende: dove poi si genera certi dolci commovimenti: i quali chome contra sua natura richiusi si sforzano quanto possano di uscire fuori: & farsi in atto manifesti. [6r] Il qual atto da essa dolcezza & melodia tirato alle parti exteriori colla propia persona danzando si dimostra quello quasi con la voce & col harmonia congionto & concordante che dal accordato et dolce canto, overo dall'ascoltante et misurato suono."

30. The reason for these appeals to ancient authorities was that the humanists were not interested in providing an objective, thorough, disinterested, and scholarly dissection of the philosophical, moral, and theological program of their favored Latin and Greek authors, and, through such a careful study of their writings, greater insight into the world of ancient Greece and Rome. Rather, the humanists were interested in supporting and enhancing the utility of the classical texts, and in ensuring their continuing success and popularity. Since the early humanists formed the group promoting non-Christian literature as the basis for their new program of aristocratic education in a Christian society, they had to work hard to "defend the virtue and wisdom of the ancient pagan authors" (James

Hankins, *Plato in the Italian Renaissance*, vol. 1 [Leiden: E. J. Brill, 1990], p. 14). It was up to the humanists to promote and foster the idea that the ancient Greek and Latin writings were "compatible with Christian belief and mores" (ibid., p. 14), as it was in their interest to do so. The status, position, and income of the humanists were dependent upon their ability to interpret and promote the values and authority of the classical texts.

31. Pope Pius II (Aeneas Silvius Piccolomini), *Aeneae Silvii: De liberorum educatione*, ed. and trans. Joel Stanislaus Nelson (Washington, D.C.: Catholic University of America Press, 1940), p. 91.

32. Ibid., p. 93.

33. Ibid., p. 93.

34. Ibid., p. 95.

35. Leonardo Bruni, *De studiis et litteris liber*, in *Educazione umanistica in Italia*, ed. and trans. Eugenio Garin, 9th ed. (Rome: Laterza, 1975), p. 41.

36. Alberti, *On Painting (De pictura)*, p. 60.

37. Michael Baxandall, *Giotto and the Orators: Humanist Observers of Painting in Italy and the Discovery of Pictorial Composition, 1350–1450* (Oxford: Clarendon Press, 1971), p. 58. The 1579 English translation of Petrarch's discussion of art from his work *De remediis utriusque fortunae* appears on pp. 53–58.

38. V, f. 12v. "Vegniromo a quelli balli et bassedanze che son fora del vulgo fabricati per sale signorile e da esser sol dançati per dignissime Madonne et non plebeie."

39. V, f. 5r. "Questa quantunche presso gli precessori nostri fosse principale sono a dançare suso hoggidì per gl'ingiegni assuttigliati in più fiorite cose è abiecta e vilipesa da persone magnifice e da bon dançatori."

40. Pg, f. 23r–23v.

41. Ibid. "Perche acchade el più delle volte [che] alchuni vedendosi un pocho introdutti in esso danzare prosumere coll animo dishonesto [23v] dissoluto & corretto esser prosumptuosi & temerari oltra il dovere et questi son quegli che di arte dignissima la fanno ritornar vile & dishonesta."

42. For a detailed study of the moral debates concerning dance from the medieval period to the eighteenth century, see Alessandro Arcangeli, *Davide o Salomè? Il dibattito europeo sulla danza nella prima età moderna* (Rome: Viella, 2000).

43. Pg, f. 18v–19r. "[P]ensa da te stesso quanto essa sia malvagia & ria perché da lei ne descendeno infiniti mali & sollicitudine: di che ogni dì ne vediamo aperta experienza & non puoi ancora negare che liei non sia mezana & inducitrice alla voluptate: la cui mediante ne pervengono grandissimi homicidij discordie & nimicicie: le qual summamente dispiaceno non solo a idio ma agli mortali. . . . [19r] Quanto alla secunda parte che da liei ne descendano molti homicidij peccati et altri mali questo no[n] niegho & cio quando tal arte e fatta et exercitata da huomini dissoluti mechanici plebei et voluptuosi. Alli quali se bene havete inteso & attentamente letto di sopra gliela prohibischo et nieghо. Ma quando è exercitata da huomini ge[n]tili, virtuosi, & honesti, dico essa scienza & arte essere buona et virtuosa et di commendatione & laude digna."

44. Baxandall, *Giotto and the Orators*, pp. 60–61.

45. Ibid., p. 62.

46. Quoted in ibid., p. 62, from *Historia ragusii*, Venice, Biblioteca Querini-Stampalia, MS IX.II, fol. 80v.

47. Pg, f. 20r. "Non habiando voi la vera intelligenza & cognitione della particularitate & sottilità dell'arte preditta: le qual manchando non è possibile cognoscere quello in la perfectione dessa si richiede: Per tanto niente del vostro dire mi maraviglio: al quale brevemente rispondo che gli è di necessita a voler essere l'arte perfetta ci siano tutte le sei prescritte cose: senza le qual la scienza

non varebbe nulla: et maxime la memoria & misura le qual servino non solamente in quest' arte: ma in tutte l'arte liberali."

48. V, f. 6r–6v. "Nella bassadanza . . . [t]alhor tacere un tempo e starlo morto non è brutto, ma entrare poi nel seguente con aeroso modo: quasi come persona che susciti da morte a vita. In questo Misser Domenichino vostro bon servitore e mio maestro ha havuto evidentissimo giudicio dicendo che 'l dançare specialmente di misura larga vole essere simile ad ombra phantasmatica nella quale similitudine ad explicarla se intendono molte cose che non si sanno dire. [6v] Tacciano adonche gli mastri di baghatelle et frappatori di pedi, ché sol questa maniera è signorile, et extracta la bassadanza di questa una si cambia in vili movimenti & perde la proprietà sua naturale."

49. Baxandall, *Giotto and the Orators*, p. 60.

50. Pg, f. 23r. "Vogli adoncha tu che intendi mostrarla sforzarti compiacere agli animi di coloro [che] la gustano et negarla a quegli per la incapacità & ineptitudine loro la biasmano & ripruovano."

51. Pg, f. 6v–7r. "Ma aliena in tutto & mortal inimicha di vitiosi & mechanici plebei: i quali le più volte con animo corrotto & colla scelerata mente la fano di arte liberale & virtuosa scienza [7r] adultera & servile: et molte volte anchora alle lor inhoneste concupiscenze sotto specie di honestate la inducono mezana per poter cautamente al effetto dalchuna sua voluptate danzando pervenire."

52. Pg, f. 19r–19v. "Ma quando è exercitata da huomini ge[n]tili, virtuosi, & honesti, dico essa scienza & arte essere buona et virtuosa et di commendatione & laude digna. Et più [19v] che non solamente gli huomini virtuosi & honesti fa tornare gentili & pellegrini: ma anchora quegli sonno male acostumati & di vil conditione nati, fa divenir gentili & d'assai."

53. Baxandall, *Giotto and the Orators*, p. 55.

54. Marcus Fabius Quintilian, *The Institutio oratoria of Quintilian*, vol. 1, trans. H. E. Butler (London: Heineman, 1920), p. 345 [II.xvii.41].

55. Ibid., p. 349 [II.xix.1].

56. Ibid., p. 349 [II.xix.3].

57. For further discussion of memory, see chap. 3.

58. [Cicero], *Ad C. Herennium: De ratione dicendi (Rhetorica ad herennium)*, trans. Harry Caplan (London: Heinemann, 1954), p. 207 [III.xvi.28].

59. This paragraph offers a very brief summary of the information given in Robert Black, *Humanism and Education in Medieval and Renaissance Italy: Tradition and Innovation in Latin Schools from the Twelfth to the Fifteenth Century* (Cambridge: Cambridge University Press, 2001), pp. 345–48. See pp. 346–47 for a detailed list of the many ways *ordo naturalis* could be turned into *ordo artificialis.*

60. Pg, f. 18v–19r. "Brevemente quanto al mio parvolino ingegno sera possibile responderò a quello [che] voi contra lo exercitio & arte del ballare dicite. Et prima io dico et confermo essa scienza essere sollenne & virtuosa chome di sopra [19r] havete più diffusamente veduto provandovi per una vera ragione quella essere cosa naturale & accidentale si chome di sotto intenderite: Et quanto alla prima parte di danzare senza suono: Respondo che siando in un ballo otto o diece persone et ballando quelle coi passi concordatamente & misuratamente insieme senza suono è cosa naturale et sonando doppo il sonatore & misurando et concordando quelli ballano i lor passi col ditto suono è accidentale essendo tal scienza di danzare cosa naturale et accidentale adoncha è perfetta & meritamente commendativa."

61. [Cicero], *Rhetorica ad herennium*, p. 207 [III.xvi.29].

62. Pd, f. 2v. "lui dice che dodice motti sono in loperare de questa arte de li quali ne cava nove naturalli e tri acidentalli . . . il soptoscripti sono tutti naturali cioe sempio dopio reprexa continentia reverentia mezavolta voltatonda movimento

salto . . . li tri per accidentia sono li soptoscripti frapamento scorsa ecambiamente
quisti tri se acquistano per accidentia perche non sono neccessarij segondo natura."

63. V, f. 6v. "El dançare contiene inse nove movimenti naturali et corporei
et tre accidentali. Gli naturali sono sempi doppi riprese continentie contrapassi
movimenti voltetonde meçovolte e scambij. Gli accidentali so[no] trascorse frap-
pamenti et piçigamenti."

64. For an extended discussion of how human ingenuity could transform
dance from a natural activity to an art through the practices of ornamentation and
improvisation, see Jennifer Nevile, "Disorder in Order: Improvisation in Italian
Choreographed Dances of the Fifteenth and Sixteenth Centuries," in *Improvisation
in the Arts of the Middle Ages and the Renaissance*, ed. Timothy J. McGee (Kalamazoo: The Medieval Institute, 2003), pp. 145–69.

3 . ELOQUENT MOVEMENT — ELOQUENT PROSE

1. "The Glory of the Latin Language," excerpt from Valla's *Elegantiae
linguae latinae*, translated by Mary Martin McLaughlin, in *The Portable Renaissance
Reader*, ed. James Bruce Ross and Mary Martin McLaughlin (New York: Viking
Press, 1953), pp. 131–32.

2. Lauro Martines, *Power and Imagination: City-States in Renaissance Italy*
(London: Allen Lane, 1980), p. 267. Martines is quoting Patrizi's *De institutione
reipublicae*.

3. Anthony Grafton and Lisa Jardine, *From Humanism to the Humanities:
Education and the Liberal Arts in Fifteenth-and Sixteenth-Century Europe* (Cambridge, Mass.: Harvard University Press, 1986), p. 11.

4. Ibid., p. 12.

5. Ibid., pp. 23–24.

6. Pope Pius II (Aeneas Silvius Piccolomini), *Aeneae Silvii: De liberorum
educatione*, ed. and trans. Joel Stanislaus Nelson (Washington, D.C.: Catholic University of America Press, 1940), p. 137, my italics.

7. John Florio, *A Worlde of Wordes* (1598; facsimile ed., Hildesheim:
George Olms, 1972), pp. 228, 215, 8.

8. V, f. 8v–9r. "Anchora nel dançare non solamente [9r] s'observa la misura
degli soni, ma una misura la quale non è musicale, ançi fore di tutte quelle, che
è un misurare l'aere nel levamento dell'ondeggiare cioè che sempre s'alçi a un
modo che altrimenti si romperia misura. L'ondeggiare non è altro che uno alçamento tardo di tutta la persona et l'abassamento presto."

9. Pd, f. 2r. "L'è un altra mexura la quale è composta, cum la gratia de la
mainera, de el deportamento de tutta la persona la quale è deseperada de le mexure
muxichale dicte di sopra. Questa mexura el tereno è mexura legiera e questa è
quella che fa tenire el mezo del tuo motto dal capo a li piedi el quale non è ní
tropo ní poco e fate fugire li extremi segondo ha dicto lui qui di sopra."

10. Pd, f. 1v. "Sempre operando el fondamento de la causa cioè mexura la
qualle e tardeza ricoperada cum presteza."

11. Pg, f. 13r. "E nota che tutte queste pruove overo experienze consisteno
ad intendere perfettamente la misura sopra la quale è fundata tutta l'arte preditta
del danzare."

12. Pg, f. 5v. "Le qual cose ci mostrano la grande excellenze & suprema dignitate d'essa scienza dalla qual l'arte giocunda e 'l dolce effetto del danzare è naturalmente proceduto."

13. Pg, f. 5v.

14. These ratios are the same as those of the octave (1:2), the fifth (2:3), and the fourth (3:4), which were also held to be beautiful and harmonious. For a detailed discussion of the ratios between the four *misure*, see chap. 4.

15. Pd, f. 4v. "Io sono piva per nome chiamata e de le misure son la piu trista per che da gli villani sono adoperata." Cornazano also repeats Domenico's opinion of the *piva*: "La piva . . . ballo è da villa origine di tutti gli altri el suon suo controvato ne lavena per gli pastori" (V, f. 10v). "Questa [the *piva*] quantunche presso gli precessori nostri fosse principale sono a dançare suso hoggidì per gl'ingiegni assuttigliati in più fiorite cose è abiecta e vilipesa da persone magnifice e da bon dançatori" (V, f. 5r).

16. Pd, f. 4v. "Io sono bassadança de le mesure regina e merito di portare corona. [E]t in l'operare de mi poche genti hano ragione e chi in dançare o in sonare ben di me sadopra força che da li cieli sia data l'opra."

17. Michael Baxandall, *Giotto and the Orators: Humanist Observers of Painting in Italy and the Discovery of Pictorial Composition, 1350–1450* (Oxford: Clarendon Press, 1971), pp. 129–31.

18. The boundary between grammar and rhetoric was never clear-cut. Grammar was taught at the school, or pre-university level, and was primarily concerned with writing grammatical Latin (W. Keith Percival, "Grammar and Rhetoric in the Renaissance," in *Renaissance Eloquence: Studies in the Theory and Practice of Renaissance Rhetoric*, ed. James J. Murphy [Berkeley: University of California Press, 1983], p. 324). The study of grammar was also seen as the first step in the study of literature. "Grammarians, therefore, pursued many problems that lay outside the limits of grammar proper, specifically the study of poetic meters (metrics), the study of the types and categories of poetic composition (poetics), and composition itself, both prose and verse. . . . They remained the teachers of composition throughout the Renaissance and beyond" (ibid., p. 306). Composition was also part of the study of rhetoric, where the advanced student would learn how to construct not just error-free Latin prose, but elegant compositions in Latin, in which all the techniques and resources discussed in the rhetorical treatises would be utilized. For a detailed account of the teaching of grammar in fifteenth-century Italy, see Robert Black, *Humanism and Education in Medieval and Renaissance Italy: Tradition and Innovation in Latin Schools from the Twelfth to the Fifteenth Century* (Cambridge: Cambridge University Press, 2001), pp. 331–65. As Black concludes, the first stages of rhetoric were part of the normal curriculum of the grammar schools. "In Quattrocento Italy, it is clear that grammar was learned first, almost entirely divorced from stylistics and rhetoric. . . . Once this basic grammar was mastered, the pupil's Latin was then gradually purified at the end of the syllabus through the study of stylistics and introductory rhetoric" (ibid., p. 364).

19. Leon Battista Alberti, *On Painting (De pictura)*, ed. and trans. Cecil Grayson (London: Penguin, 1991), p. 71.

20. While the dance masters did not adopt Alberti's model of composition, they did talk about how to compose a dance in their treatises; see Pg, f. 14r–15r.

21. V, f. 3r bis. "Diversità di cose è di sapere dançare dançe insieme differentiate e non sempre mai farne una medesma e così havere passi . . . di diverse guise e quello che s'è facto una fiata nol fare la siconda successivamente."

22. Marcus Fabius Quintilian, *The Institutio oratoria of Quintilian*, vol. 4, trans. H. E. Butler (London: Heinemann, 1922), pp. 265–67 [XI.iii.43].

23. Marcus Tullius Cicero, *Cicero on the Ideal Orator,* trans. James M. May and Jakob Wisse (New York: Oxford University Press, 2001), p. 233 [III.32], my italics.

24. Quintilian, *Institutio oratoria,* vol. 1, pp. 293–95 [II.xiii.8–9 and 11].

25. Michael Baxandall, *Painting and Experience in Fifteenth-Century Italy: A Primer in the Social History of Pictorial Style* (Oxford: Oxford University Press, 1972), pp. 133–35.

26. Alberti, *On Painting (De pictura),* p. 75.

27. James Hankins, *Plato in the Italian Renaissance,* vol. 1 (Leiden: E. J. Brill, 1990), p. 7.

28. Lorenzo Valla, preface to book 4 of *Elegantiae linguae latinae,* in *Renaissance Debates on Rhetoric,* ed. and trans. Wayne A. Rebhorn (Ithaca: Cornell University Press, 2000), p. 40.

29. The first comprehensive treatise on rhetoric written by a humanist appeared in 1435 (Baxandall, *Giotto and the Orators,* p. 138). Before this date the humanists relied on the Latin rhetorical treatises of Cicero and Quintilian and especially the anonymous Latin treatise *Rhetorica ad herennium,* which until the sixteenth century was believed to have been written by Cicero. For a detailed account of the use of these sources in fifteenth-century Italy, see John O. Ward, "Renaissance Commentators on Ciceronian Rhetoric," in Murphy, *Renaissance Eloquence,* pp. 126–73.

30. Mary E. Hazard, *Elizabethan Silent Language* (Lincoln: University of Nebraska Press, 2000), p. 5.

31. Quintilian, *Institutio oratoria,* vol. 4, p. 243 [XI.iii.1].

32. Cicero, *Ideal Orator,* p. 294 [III.222].

33. Quintilian, *Institutio oratoria,* vol. 4, p. 279 [XI.iii.65–66].

34. By the sixteenth century the term *maniera* was widely used in Italy to signify the "good style" that was seen in the "elegance, poise, and refinement in the deportment of courtiers" (Maria Rika Maniates, *Mannerism in Italian Music and Culture, 1530–1630* [Chapel Hill: University of North Carolina Press, 1979], p. 12).

35. Pd, f. 1v. "E nota che questa agilitade e mainera per niuno modo vole essere adoperata per li estremi: Ma tenire el mezo del tuo movimento che non sia ni tropo ni poco ma cum tanta suavitade che pari una gondola che da dui rimi spinta sia per quelle undicelle quando el mare fa quieta segondo sua natura. Alçando le dicte undicelle cum tardeza e asbasandosse cum presteza. Sempre operando el fondamento de la causa cioè mexura la qualle e tardeza ricoperada cum presteza." Once again Domenico is referring to "measure" in the Aristotelian sense of avoiding extremes.

36. V, f. 9r. "L'ondeggiare non è altro che uno alçamento tardo di tutta la persona et l'abbassamento presto."

37. V, f. 3v. "Maniera è che recordandovi el ballo et passeggiando con misura dovete dare aptitudine a le cose che facite campeggiando & ondeggiando colla persona secondo el pede che mouite."

38. For example, if a left *sempio* is performed the dancer will turn his or her body to the left so that the right shoulder comes forward, while stepping forward with the left foot. For further discussion of *campeggiare,* see Mark Franko, *The Dancing Body in Renaissance Choreography (c. 1416–1589)* (Birmingham, Ala.: Summa Publications, 1986), pp. 59–61.

39. Pg, f. 10v. "Anchora nell'arte preditta del danzare bigiogna all'adornamento et perfectione di quella un altro atto overamente regula chiamata mainiera. la quale bigiogna se adopri insieme con l'altre sue parti chome di sopra e ditto. Et questo s'intende che quando alchuno nell'arte del danzare facesse un

sempio overo un doppio che quello secondo accade l'adorni & umbregi con bella mainiera: cioè che dal pie che lui porta il passo sempio o doppio infino ch'el tempo misurato dura tutto se volti in quel lato colla persona & col pie sinistro o col diritto col quale lui habia a fare il ditto atto adornato & umbregiato dalla ditta regula chiamata mainiera."

40. Pg, f. 10r. "[*Aiere*] è un atto de aieroso presenza et rilevato movimento colla propia persona mostrando con destreza nel danzare un dolce & humanissimo rilevamento. . . . perché tenendoli bassi senza rilievo & senza aiere mostraria imperfetto & fuori di sua natura il danzare né pareria ai circonstanti degno di gratia & di vera laude."

41. V, f. 3r bis. "Aere el dançare è in tanto che oltre ch'abbiati le predicte gratie dovete havere un altra gratia tal di movimenti che rendati piacere a gli occhi di chi sta a guardarvi e quelli oprare sopra tucto con iocondita di vista e allegramente."

42. The word *gratia* was also used in fifteenth-century descriptions of dancing, including in letters. For examples of this usage in contemporary documents, see Sharon Fermor, "Studies in the Depiction of the Moving Figure in Italian Renaissance Art, Art Criticism, and Dance Theory" (Ph.D. diss., Warburg Institute, University of London, 1990), pp. 130–31.

43. My statement that *quaternaria doppi* did not involve any rising and falling movements of the body is based on the fact that neither Domenico, Guglielmo, nor Cornazano in their descriptions of this step mentions any such movements.

44. See V, f. 5v.

45. Quintilian, *Institutio oratoria*, vol. 1, p. 293 [II.xiii.8–9].

46. Pd, f. 2r.

47. V, f. 6r–6v.

48. V, f. 6r. "In questo Misser Domenichino vostro bon servitore e mio maestro ha havuto evidentissimo giudicio dicendo che 'l dançare specialmente di misura larga vole essere simile ad ombra phantasmatica nella quale similitudine ad explicarla se intendono molte cose che non si sanno dire."

49. Pd, f. 2r. "[F]acendo requia a cadauno tempo che pari haver veduto lo capo di meduxa come dice el poeta cioè che facto el motto sij tutto di piedra in quello instante et in instante mitti ale como falcone."

50. Mark Franko elaborates on this idea in his article "The Notion of 'Fantasmata' in Fifteenth-Century Italian Dance Treatises," *Dance Research Annual* 16 (1987), pp. 68–86.

51. Florio, *Worlde of Wordes*, p. 125.

52. The translation from Latin is by Deirdre Stone. "Phantasma est, quando qui vix dormire coepit, et adhuc se vigilare aestimat, aspicere videtur irruentes in se, vel passim vagantes formas discrepantes et varias, laetas vel turbulentas. In hoc genere est ephialtes." *Liber de spritu et anima*, chap. 25, in *Patrologiae cursus completus . . . Series latina*, vol. 40, ed. J.-P. Migne (Paris: 1887), p. 798.

53. For examples of humanist writers who discuss this subject, see Fermor, "Studies in the Depiction of the Moving Figure," pp. 67–69.

54. Matteo Palmieri, *Vita civile*, ed. Gino Belloni (Florence: Sansoni, 1982), pp. 95–97. "Seguita dire quello che ne' movimenti e riposi del corpo si convenga. . . . Ogni moto e qualunque stato del corpo, il quale si disforma dal naturale uso et pare a vedere brutto si de' fuggire. . . . Spesso adviene che per piccoli cenni si conosce maximi vitii e dàssi inditii veri di quello sente l'animo nostro, come per elevato guatare si significa arrogantia; pel dimesso, humilità, per ristrignersi in su il lato, dolore. . . . In nello andare si de' considerare l'età e il grado: non andare intero, né muovere i passi tardi, rari e con tanta gravità che si paia pomposo et

simile alle processioni delle degnità sacerdotali; non si de' e' spandere i vestimenti et andare gonfiato et tondo, siché apaia non capere per la via. . . . Non vuole però anche l'andare essere sì presto significhi leggereza, et dimonstri non essere in ella persona constanzia, ma ogni movimento si riferisca a una ordinata verecundia, in nella quale s'osservi la propria degnità, avendo sempre la natura per nostra maestra et guida."

55. Pius II (Piccolomini), *De liberorum educatione*, pp. 103–105.

56. Carlo Marsuppini, "Poem on Nobility," in *Knowledge, Goodness and Power: The Debate over Nobility among Quattrocento Italian Humanists*, ed. and trans. Albert Rabil Jr. (Binghamton, N.Y.: Medieval and Renaissance Texts and Studies, 1991), p. 103, my italics.

57. Pg, f. 16v–17r.

58. Quintilian, *Institutio oratoria*, vol. 4, p. 281 [XI.iii.68–69].

59. By Domenico's time all of Aristotle's works had been known to the medieval West through Latin translations for more than a century.

60. Pd, f. 1r. "L'operante argumenta in lo 2° delheticha contra di questo dicendo lui che tutte le cosse se corompono e guastase se le sono conducte e menate ind[i]verse cioè per le operatione extreme: E la mezanitade conserva."

61. Pd, f. 2r. "[A]domque fuçando li extremi e malitia donque è questa virtu, façando ricordo che Aristotle in lo 2 lauda l'autropelia la quale del mezo tene la virtu fuçando li estremi de lo forstiero campestre e di quello che è guigolatore e ministro."

62. Aristotle, *The Nicomachean Ethics*, rev. ed., trans. J. A. K. Thomson, rev. Hugh Tredennick (London: Penguin, 1976), pp. 100–101.

63. Ibid., p. 104.

64. Quintilian, *Institutio oratoria*, vol. 4, p. 271 [XI.iii.52–53].

65. Ibid., vol. 1, p. 185 [I.xi.2–3]. It is interesting to note that in the last sentence of this passage is found the origin of Castiglione's concept of *sprezzatura:* the concealment of the effort involved in producing elegant and graceful movements.

66. Alberti discusses this at length in book 2 of his treatise on painting. Here he states very clearly several times that "movements of the soul are made known by movements of the body" (Leon Battista Alberti, *On Painting [Della pittura]*, trans. John R. Spencer [London: Routledge and Kegan Paul, 1956], p. 77).

67. Pg, f. 5v. "La qual virtute del danzare non è altro che una actione demonstrativa di fuori di movimenti spirituali: Li quali si hanno a concordare colle misurate et perfette consonanze d'essa harmonia: che per lo nostro audito alle parti intellective & ai sensi cordiali con diletto descende: dove poi si genera certi dolci commovimenti: i quali chome contra sua natura richiusi si sforzano quanto possano di uscire fuori: & farsi in atto manifesti."

68. Baxandall, *Giotto and the Orators*, p. 83.

69. Ibid., p. 82.

70. Alberti, *On Painting (Della pittura)*, p. 77.

71. Even though Guglielmo devoted an entire chapter to the behavior and demeanor expected of young women of gentle birth, which he said had to be more moderate and virtuous than that of young men, he was not excusing a low level of behavior from the latter. They still were expected to be courteous and virtuous.

72. Pg, f. 19r–19v. "Ma quando è exercitata da huomini ge[n]tili, virtuosi, & honesti, dico essa scienza & arte essere buona et virtuosa et di commendatione & laude digna. Et più [19v] che non solamente gli huomini virtuosi & honesti fa tornare gentili & pellegrini: ma anchora quegli sonno male acostumati & di vil

conditione nati, fa divenir gentili & d'assai: La qual da apertamente a cognoscere la qualità di tutti."

73. In Poggio Bracciolini's dialogue all the different contemporary ideas on nobility are outlined. See Poggio Bracciolini, "On Nobility," in *Knowledge, Goodness, and Power: The Debate over Nobility among Quattrocento Italian Humanists*, ed. and trans. Albert Rabil Jr. (Binghamton, N.Y.: Medieval and Renaissance Texts and Studies, 1991), pp. 67–73.

74. Marsuppini, "Poem on Nobility," in Rabil, *Knowledge, Goodness, and Power*, p. 109.

75. Bracciolini, "On Nobility," p. 83.

76. Ibid., p. 74.

77. Platina (Bartolomeo Sacchi), "On True Nobility," in Rabil, *Knowledge, Goodness, and Power*, p. 281.

78. Cristoforo Landino, "On True Nobility," in Rabil, *Knowledge, Goodness, and Power*, pp. 228–31, and Platina, "On True Nobility," pp. 291–97.

79. In the 1450s Platina worked as the tutor to the Gonzaga children at the court at Mantua. His charges would have certainly included the marquis of Mantua's eldest son, Federico, the same person whose wedding Guglielmo attended in 1463 (Pa, f. 76r). Although Guglielmo does not state whether he was engaged professionally for these celebrations, his presence indicates a degree of contact between himself and Federico that might have allowed the exchange of intellectual ideas.

80. Palmieri, *Vita civile*, p. 67. Palmieri's positioning of memory as part of prudence follows Cicero. "Virtue has four parts: wisdom [*prudentia*], justice, courage, temperance. Wisdom [or prudence] is the knowledge of what is good, what is bad and what is neither good nor bad. Its parts are memory, intelligence, and foresight. Memory is the faculty by which the mind recalls what has happened" (Cicero, *De inventione*, trans. H. M. Hubbell [London: Heinemann, 1949], p. 327 [II.liii.159–60]).

81. Palmieri, *Vita civile*, p. 67.

82. Platina, "On True Nobility," p. 294.

83. Memory was one of the five parts of rhetoric: "The speaker, then, should possess the faculties of Invention, Arrangement, Style, Memory, and Delivery.... Memory is the firm retention in the mind of the matter, words, and arrangement" ([Cicero], *Ad C. Herennium: De ratione dicendi (Rhetorica ad Herennium)*, trans. Harry Caplan [London: Heinemann, 1954], p. 7 [I.ii.3]). The same five-part division is also found in Cicero's *De inventione*, p. 21 [I.vii.9] and *De oratore* (*Ideal Orator*, pp. 218–21 [II.350–60]), and in Quintilian's *Institutio oratoria*, pp. 383 and 387 [III.iii.1 and III.iii.10]. Major studies of the place of memory in the classical art of rhetoric, and its survival and development through the Middle Ages until the sixteenth century, include Frances A. Yates, *The Art of Memory* (1966; reprint, London: Pimlico, 1992) and Mary J. Carruthers, *The Book of Memory: A Study of Memory in Medieval Culture* (Cambridge: Cambridge University Press, 1990). See Harry Caplan, "Memoria: Treasure-House of Eloquence," in *Of Eloquence: Studies in Ancient and Medieval Rhetoric*, by Harry Caplan, ed. Anne King and Helen North (Ithaca: Cornell University Press, 1970), pp. 196–246, for a wider discussion of the importance of memory in Greek and Roman culture, education, and religion, not just the art of rhetoric. For an extraordinary detailed study of the use of the classical rhetorical treatises, including the place of memory, in the intellectual and cultural life of Western Europe up until the end of the fifteenth century, see John O. Ward, *Ciceronian Rhetoric in Treatise, Scholion, and Commentary* (Turnhout, Belgium: Brepols, 1995).

84. *Partire di terreno* or *mesura da terreno* was the ability to judge correctly

and apportion the size of the dance space during the course of a dance. These dances were performed in many different-sized spaces, from specially constructed platforms in the middle of the main piazza to the central space in the grand *sale* of the houses of the nobility. The dancers had to adjust the length of their steps so that the dance fitted into the available space, and do so in such a manner that this adjustment was not noticeable. For example, it was only unskilled dancers who, halfway through a forward sequence of five *doppi*, would suddenly find themselves about to fall over the legs of those seated around the edge of the room, forcing them to perform the fourth and fifth *doppi* on the spot, knee to knee with the onlookers. Furthermore, a man had to adjust his steps to those of his partner. It was not considered graceful to indulge in large, expansive steps even when dancing in a large space, if one's partner was unable to keep up. Many of the floor plans of the *balli* and *bassadanze* were primarily long and forward-moving. The disproportionate length of the floor plans presented an added challenge to the performers in adapting their steps to the available space.

85. For Guglielmo, the final principle of the art of dance is *movimento corporeo* (bodily movement), which is the summation of all the other essential principles he has described, in that in it every perfection and virtue of the dance is demonstrated. (Pg, f. 11r, "In questa sexta & ultima parte si denota un atto necessario & conclusivo chiamato movimento corporeo: nel quale apertamente si dimostra in atto & in apparenza tutta la perfectione dell'arte & virtute del danzare.")

86. Pg, f. 19v. "[H]abiamo inteso che in volere havere quella perfettamente se gli richiede sei cose principali: ciò è misura, memoria, partir di terreno, aiere, mainiera, et movimento corporeo, et maximamente la memoria et misura."

87. Pg, f. 20r.

88. Pg, f. 8v. "[È] di bisogno in questo secundo luogho havere una perfetta memoria: ciò è una constante attentione raducendosi alla mente le parti necessarie ad essa memoria havendo i sentimenti a se tutti racolti & ben attenti al misurato et concordato suono. Imperoche se quello in alchun modo si mutasse overo allargasse o astringesse che colui che fusse nel danzare introdutto non remanesse per pocha avertenza o per manchamento di memoria schernito."

89. Pd, f. 1v.

90. [Cicero], *Rhetorica ad herennium*, p. 205 [III.xvi.28].

91. Cicero, *Ideal Orator*, p. 61 [I.18]. As Ward demonstrates in *Ciceronian Rhetoric*, rhetoric and the Latin rhetorical treatises, especially *Rhetorica ad herennium*, continued to be used in education and in the business and political life of Western Europe until the end of the fifteenth century, with Italian vernacular treatises appearing in the thirteenth century. (See also James J. Murphy, *Rhetoric in the Middle Ages: A History of Rhetorical Theory from St. Augustine to the Renaissance* [Berkeley: University of California Press, 1974], pp. 112–15.) In addition, Guarino Guarini lectured on the rhetorical treatises while teaching at Ferrara (in the same period when Domenico was resident in Ferrara), and Guarino's commentary on *Rhetorica ad Herennium* was widely circulated, as it survives in more manuscripts "than any other medieval commentary" (John O. Ward, "From Antiquity to the Renaissance: Glosses and Commentaries on Cicero's *Rhetorica*," in *Medieval Eloquence: Studies in the Theory and Practice of Medieval Rhetoric*, ed. James J. Murphy [Berkeley: University of California Press, 1978], p. 40).

92. Pd, f. 2v. "[M]a non sapiamo noi che la mexura è parte de prudentia et è ne le arte liberale? No[i] sapiamo che la memoria è madre de la prudentia la quale se acquista per lunga experientia."

93. Platina, "On True Nobility," p. 296.

94. See, for example, Pd, f. 1v, and Pg, f. 10r.

95. Pg, f. 23r–23v.

96. Platina, "On True Nobility," p. 296, my italics.

97. Thomas Elyot, *The Book Named the Governor*, ed. S. E. Lehmberg (1531; London: Dent, 1962).

98. Ibid., p. 79.

99. Prudence represented the knowledge of things men and women ought to desire and of things they ought to avoid.

100. Elyot, *Book Named the Governor*, pp. 79–80.

101. Ibid., pp. 80–81.

102. Ibid., pp. 81–82.

103. Ibid., p. 83.

104. Ibid., pp. 85–87.

105. Pd, f. 2r–2v.

106. Alberti, *On Painting (De pictura)*, p. 80.

107. Fermor, "Studies in the Depiction of the Moving Figure," pp. 100–101.

108. Baldesdar Castiglione, *The Book of the Courtier*, trans. George Bull (Harmondsworth: Penguin, 1981), pp. 67–68.

109. Alberti, *On Painting (De pictura)*, p. 79.

110. Pa, f. 31r–31v. "Nota che uno che dançasse con uno vestimento lungho ell' è di bisogno de ballare con gravità & ballare con un altra forma che non se fa de ballare con uno vestito corto, perché dançando como che gisse con uno vestito corto non dirria bono. E bisognia che tucti li suoi giesti & movimenti siano gravi & tanto suave tanto quanto che he debito che porta, & per forma che quella turcha o panno longho che porta indosso, non savia a gire movendo troppo in qua & in là. E siati acorti che bisognia grande actetudine & gran misura & gran tempo a dançare con esso a uno panno longo, ché con lo corto arichiede dançare un poco più gagliardo. Sappiate chi dança con uno vestito [31v] corto bisognia de dançare in altra forma che quella dello longo. Li se arichiede de fare salti & volte tonde & fioregiare con misura & con tempo & a quello abito del vestire corto sta bene affare questo . . . Ancora siate avisati che bisogna altra discriccione de dançare con una mantellina corta . . . e la cagione sie che la mantellina piglia vento ch' è como tu dai un salto o una volta la mantellina se arimove ell' è di bisogno che a certi gesti & a certi movimenti & a certi tempi tu piglie la tua mantellina per un lato e a certi tempi se piglia per tucti doi li lati."

111. V, f. 6v–7v. "De tutti gli naturali nella piva non se ne fanno senno uno cioè el doppio che è [7r] prestissimo per la misura stretta . . . Ne la bassadança possono [7v] essere tutti gli nove naturali excepto el movimento."

112. Pg, f. 8v. "[P]ortando la sua persona libera colli gesti suoi alla ditta misura et secondo il suono concordante."

113. Quintilian, *Institutio oratoria*, vol. 4, p. 279 [XI.iii.65].

114. Ibid., p. 281 [XI.iii.69].

115. Alberti, *On Painting (De pictura)*, p. 77.

116. Ibid., p. 73.

117. Ibid., p. 80.

118. Pg, f. 11r–12r. "Le qual cose sonno molto più facili & suave a chi dal summo cielo ha la sua natura & complexione gentile a cio disposta & ben proportionata colla sua persona libera sana & expedita senza alchuno manchamento di suoi membri: ma giovene formoso destro legiero & di gratia bene dottato: in cui tutte le predicte parti si possano con più longa delectatione liberamente exercitando dimostrare. . . . [11v] Veduto di sopra & pienamente inteso quanto sia il principale fundamento, elle parti necessarie & appertinenti all'arte predicta del danzare senza le quale chom' è ditto: non può alchuno di quella havere perfetta scienza né seria tra gli humani intelligenti di laude degna riputata. Hora bigiogna

notare alchun altre particelle summamente necessarie: per le qual più facilmente
alla practicha si divegna. . . . [12r] però che servando bene le ditte misure & quelle
sapendo ben partire et mettere in atto: è segno di buona intelligenza et principio
della vera practicha alla quale fa di bigiogno con queste prove overo experienze
se stesso misurando pervenire, le qual danno la via all'uso della perfectione
dell'arte preditta se ben saranno chome segue execute."

119. Quintilian, *Institutio oratoria*, vol. 1, p. 297 [II.xiii.15].
120. Ibid., p. 223 [II.iii.11–12].
121. Ibid., p. 345 [II.xvii.43].
122. Baxandall, *Giotto and the Orators*, p. 65.
123. Alberti, *On Painting (De pictura)*, p. 89.
124. Ibid., pp. 93–94.

4. DANCE AND THE INTELLECT

1. Pope Pius II (Aeneas Silvius Piccolomini), *Aeneae Silvii: De liberorum
educatione*, ed. and trans. Joel Stanislaus Nelson (Washington, D.C.: Catholic University of America Press, 1940), p. 121.

2. For a summary of the transmission of these ideas, see Ann E. Moyer,
Musica Scientia: Musical Scholarship in the Italian Renaissance (Ithaca: Cornell University Press, 1992), pp. 24–35.

3. S. K. Heninger Jr., *Touches of Sweet Harmony: Pythagorean Cosmology and
Renaissance Poetics* (San Marino, Calif.: The Huntington Library, 1974), p. 71.

4. Ibid., p. 76.
5. Ibid., p. 76.
6. Ibid., pp. 79, 84.
7. Ibid., p. 95.

8. Plato, *Timaeus*, in *The Collected Dialogues of Plato Including the Letters*, ed.
Edith Hamilton and Huntington Cairns (Princeton: Princeton University Press,
1963), pp. 1165–66 [34c–36e]. For an exegesis of this passage, see Francis Mac-
Donald Cornford, *Plato's Cosmology: The* Timaeus *of Plato Translated with a Running
Commentary* (London: Routledge and Kegan Paul, 1948), pp. 66–72.

9. Plato, *Timaeus*, pp. 1170–72 [41d–44b].
10. Ibid., p. 1175 [47c–47e].

11. Alison White, "Boethius in the Medieval Quadrivium," in *Boethius: His
Life, Thought, and Influence*, ed. Margaret Gibson (Oxford: Blackwell, 1981),
p. 163.

12. Anicus Manius Severinus Boethius, *Fundamentals of Music*, trans. Calvin
M. Bower, ed. Claude V. Palisca (New Haven: Yale University Press, 1989), p. 2.

13. Ibid., p. 4.
14. Ibid., pp. 5–6.
15. Ibid., p. 7.
16. Ibid., pp. 9–10.
17. Pg, f. 3v–4v.

18. Pg, f. 4v. "per li quali se comprende di quella essere alla nostra natura
& alla compositione delli quatro elementi grandemente colligata."

19. Pg, f. 7v. "Qualuncha virtuosamente la scienza & arte del danzare con
lieto animo & colla mente sincera & ben disposta seguir vuole: bisogna che prima
con fermo cuore & con speculante mente & consideratione intenda in generale

che cosa sia danzare ella vera definitione che altro non è, che un atto demostrativo concordante alla misurata melodia d'alchuna voce overo suono."

20. Boethius, *Fundamentals of Music*, p. 8, my italics.

21. Domenico does not explicitly say why there are four *misure* in the *balli* (as opposed to three or five, etc.). I argue that Domenico chose the number four because then dance became another manifestation of the Pythagorean tetrad.

22. Much ink has been spilt in dance scholars' arguments over the meaning of Domenico's explanation of the four *misure*. The main contributors to this debate are Véronique Daniels and Eugen Dombois, "Die Temporelationen im Ballo des Quattrocento," *Basler Jahrbuch für historische Musikpraxis* 14 (1990): 181–247; Barbara Sparti, introduction to *De practica seu arte tripudii: On the Practice or Art of Dancing*, by Guglielmo Ebreo da Persaro, ed. and trans. Barbara Sparti (Oxford: Clarendon Press, 1993), pp. 64–69; and three articles in *Terpsichore, 1450–1900: Proceedings of the International Dance Conference, Ghent, April 2000*, ed. Barbara Ravelhofer (Ghent: Institute for Historical Dance Practice, 2000): John Caldwell, "Some Observations on the Four *Misure*," pp. 9–10; Jadwiga Nowaczek, "The Misery with the *Misure*—A Practical Approach," pp. 7–8; and Jennifer Nevile, "The Four *Misure* in Fifteenth-Century Italian Dance," pp. 1–6. I argue here that although the dance treatises' different descriptions of the *misure* describe the same phenomenon in different ways, they are mutually consistent.

23. Pd, f. 3r–3v. "[N]Ota epriegoti vogli aprire virtu de lo intelecto adintendere che cossa è mexura de motto etiandio como sono compositi li motti sopra le mexure.... E sopra a questa mexura zeneralle sene cava quatro particulare. La prima la quale è più larga dele altre Se chiama per nome Bassedanza . . . La 2ª mexura se chiama quadernaria . . . la quale per distantia de tempo è più strecta [3v] de la bassadanza uno sesto. La 3ª mexura se chiama per nome Saltarello . . . e questa mexura per distantia de tempo è più strecta de la quadernaria uno altro sesto che vene ad esser uno terzo più strecta de la bassadanza: La 4ª et ultima mexura se chiama per lo vulgo piva . . . Questa calla del saltarello per distantia de temp uno sesto. Siche adonque questa mexura ultima dicta piva vene ad esser più strecta de la bassadanza tri sesti . . . In queste quatro mexure consiste el motto del danzadore e del sonatore: più largo e più presto."

24. The practice of using mensuration signs as proportion signs was not unknown in early fifteenth-century music. For a detailed discussion of this subject, see the following works by Anna Maria Busse Berger: "The Relationship of Perfect and Imperfect Time in Italian Theory of the Renaissance," *Early Music History* 5 (1985): 1–28; "The Origin and Early History of Proportion Signs," *Journal of the American Musicological Society* 41, no. 3 (1988): 403–33; and *Mensuration and Proportion Signs: Origins and Evolution* (Oxford: Clarendon Press, 1993), in particular pp. 168–78.

25. P. Farenga, "Cornazano," *Dizionario biografico degli Italiani*, vol. 29 (Rome: Istituto della Enciclopedia Italiana, 1983), p. 123.

26. Paul F. Grendler, *The Universities of the Italian Renaissance* (Baltimore: Johns Hopkins University Press, 2002), p. 226.

27. Pg, f. 13v. The same passage appears in Pa, f. 19v; FL, f. 13v; S, f. 15r; and M, f. 9v. FN, f. 12r only lists "*perfect maggiore et perfecto minore e quaternario*," while NY, f. 5r gives the four *misure* as "*perfetto maggiore e perfetto minore e perfetto minore e quadernario.*"

28. See S, f. 30v, and M, f. 19r.

29. NY, f. 32v. "Basadanza si bala per perfeto maggiore o altri dichono inperfeto magore e salterelo perfeto magore e piva quadernaria inperfeto magore."

30. See Berger, "Origin and Early History of Proportion Signs," pp. 420-21.

31. "We may begin with the fact that the standard 'perfect major' of mensural

music simply does not occur in the tunes recorded in the Italian manuals. Guglielmo seemingly uses the name, appropriately enough, to indicate the longest of the four dance *misure* . . . i.e. it is the greater of the two 'perfect' measures, understanding 'perfect' here to refer to the level of the semibreve in major prolation" (Caldwell, "Observations of the Four *Misure*," p. 9).

32. Ibid., p. 10.

5. ORDER AND VIRTUE

1. Samuel Y. Edgerton Jr., *The Heritage of Giotto's Geometry: Art and Science on the Eve of the Scientific Revolution* (Ithaca: Cornell University Press, 1991), pp. 160, 163 n. 15.

2. Leonardo Bruni, "Panegyric to the City of Florence," trans. Benjamin G. Kohl, in *The Earthly Republic: Italian Humanists on Government and Society*, ed. Benjamin G. Kohl and Ronald G. Witt (Manchester: Manchester University Press, 1978), pp. 144–45.

3. The circle of castles around Florence served as the first line of defence in case of an enemy attack.

4. Hans Baron, *From Petrarch to Leonardo Bruni: Studies in Humanistic and Political Literature* (Chicago: University of Chicago Press, 1968), p. 157.

5. Bruni, "Panegyric to Florence," p. 137.

6. Ibid., p. 158.

7. Ibid., pp. 168–69.

8. Ibid., p. 169.

9. Leon Battista Alberti, *On the Art of Building in Ten Books*, trans. Joseph Rykwert, Neil Leach, and Robert Tavernor (Cambridge, Mass.: MIT Press, 1988), p. 191 [7.i].

10. Ibid., p. 303 [9.v]. See pp. 421–22 for a full explanation of the complex term *concinnitas*.

11. Ibid., p. 305 [9.v].

12. Ibid.

13. Ibid., p. 306 [9.vi].

14. Ibid., p. 220 [7.x]. For a discussion of how Alberti himself followed these rules in the inlaid marble designs on the wall of the tomb he constructed for the Florentine merchant Giovanni Rucellai, see Joan Gadol, *Leon Battista Alberti: Universal Man of the Early Renaissance* (Chicago: University of Chicago Press, 1969), pp. 124–26.

15. Alberti, *On the Art of Building*, p. 196 [7.iv]. For further discussion of this point, see Rudolf Wittkower, *Architectural Principles in the Age of Humanism*, 4th ed. (London: Academy Editions, 1988), pp. 16–22.

16. Alberti, *On the Art of Building*, p. 302 [9.v].

17. Ibid., p. 312 [9.viii]. For a discussion of Alberti's understanding of the Platonic theory of human beings' desire for the beautiful and the good, and how this was expressed in his treatise on architecture, see John Onians, "Alberti and ΦΙΛΑΡΕΤΗ: A Study in Their Sources," *Journal of the Warburg and Courtauld Institutes* 34 (1971): 96–114.

18. For a more extensive discussion of how an architect's design affects the citizens of a city and their civic behavior, see Carroll William Westfall, "Society,

Beauty, and the Humanist Architect in Alberti's *De re aedficatoria*," *Studies in the Renaissance* 16 (1969): 61–79, and Westfall, *In This Most Perfect Paradise: Alberti, Nicholas V, and the Invention of Conscious Urban Planning in Rome, 1447–55* (University Park: Pennsylvania State University Press, 1974), especially pp. 57–62.

19. S. K. Heninger Jr., *The Cosmographical Glass: Renaissance Diagrams of the Universe* (San Marino, Calif.: The Huntington Library, 1977), p. 143.

20. Ibid.

21. Claudia Lazzaro, *The Italian Renaissance Garden: From the Conventions of Planting, Design, and Ornament to the Grand Gardens of Sixteenth-Century Central Italy* (New Haven: Yale University Press, 1990), p. 38.

22. Construction of the Medici villa at Castello began in 1537 (ibid., p. 326). Lorenzo de' Medici started work on the villa at Poggio in the fifteenth century, but Duke Cosimo I made additions from 1545 (ibid., p. 43). The Villa Lante at Bagnaia was laid out in 1568, the Villa d'Este at Tivoli begun in 1560, and the Villa Farnese at Caprarola begun in the 1570s (ibid., p. 34). L'Ambrogiana was begun after 1587 (ibid., p. 70), while Petraia was renovated by Ferdinando de' Medici from 1591 to 1597 (ibid., p. 84).

23. David R. Coffin, *Gardens and Gardening in Papal Rome* (Princeton: Princeton University Press, 1991).

24. Alberti, *On the Art of Building*, p. 300 [9.iv].

25. Lazzaro, *Italian Renaissance Garden*, p. 44.

26. Ibid., p. 8.

27. The "problem" of squaring the circle, that is, changing a circle into a square, had occupied mathematicians since the time of Pythagoras. The circle, with no beginning or end, symbolized perfection and the deity, and the square symbolized the physical world. Therefore, the "problem" of squaring the circle was a problem of how to change the divine into earthly material. For more details, see S. K. Heninger Jr., *Touches of Sweet Harmony: Pythagorean Cosmology and Renaissance Poetics* (San Marino, Calif.: The Huntington Library, 1974), p. 111.

28. Lazzaro, *Italian Renaissance Garden*, p. 80.

29. For an extended discussion of the principles shared by choreographic design and the grand gardens in Italy, particularly in the sixteenth and early seventeenth centuries, see Jennifer Nevile, "Dance and the Garden: Moving and Static Choreography in Renaissance Europe," *Renaissance Quarterly* 52, no. 3 (1999): 805–36.

30. Dances for three could be for either two men and one woman, or two women and one man, with the lone woman or man always standing between the other two performers.

31. NY, f. 36r–36v.

32. The one exception to the continuance of the triangular shape is the eight *piva doppi*, during which the three dancers interweave in a zig-zag hay.

33. Heninger Jr., *Touches of Sweet Harmony*, p. 151.

34. Janet Levarie Smarr, "The Pyramid and the Circle: Ovid's 'Banquet of Sense,'" *Philological Quarterly* 63, no. 3 (1984): 372.

35. Pd, f. 16r. "Anello a balo e va homini dui e done doe . . . e in co de diti tienpi li homeni lasa le done rimanendo in quadro." In this instance, the instructions explicitly mention the figure which the dancers must form.

CONCLUSION

1. Cornazano says that Domenico is "the king of the art, my only master and compatriot . . . [and] through his perfect and most illustrious virtue, a Knight of the Golden Spur." V, f. 28v, "lo re dell'arte mio solo maestro et compatriota misser dominichino da piacença cavagliero aurato per la sua perfecta et famosissima virtute." Guglielmo calls himself the "most devoted disciple and ardent imitator of the most worthy knight messer Domenico da Ferrara." FN, f. 5v, "divotissimo disciepolo et fervente imitatore del dignissimo chavaliere messer domenicho da ferrara."

2. Joseph Rykwert, "Theory as Rhetoric: Leon Battista Alberti in Theory and in Practice," in *Paper Palaces: The Rise of the Renaissance Architectural Treatise*, ed. Vaughan Hart with Peter Hicks (New Haven: Yale University Press, 1998), p. 34.

3. John O. Ward, "Renaissance Commentators on Ciceronian Rhetoric," in *Renaissance Eloquence: Studies in the Theory and Practice of Renaissance Rhetoric*, ed. James J. Murphy (Berkeley: University of California Press, 1983), p. 131.

4. It was Leonello d'Este who, in 1442, expanded the University of Ferrara into a full teaching university. Paul F. Grendler, *The Universities of the Italian Renaissance* (Baltimore: Johns Hopkins University Press, 2002), p. 100.

5. Grendler, *Universities of the Italian Renaissance*, p. 395. In 1416–17 Bruni published a translation of Aristotle's *Nicomachean Ethics*, a work that would have been known in the humanist circles of Ferrara.

6. For a discussion of Filarete's idealized vision of the place of the architect in Italian society through his placement and design of the architect's house in Sforzinda, see Joanna Woods-Marsden, *Renaissance Self-Portraiture: The Visual Construction of Identity and the Social Status of the Artist* (New Haven: Yale University Press, 1998), pp. 83–84.

7. S. K. Heninger Jr., *Touches of Sweet Harmony: Pythagorean Cosmology and Renaissance Poetics* (San Marino, Calif.: The Huntington Library, 1974), p. 76.

8. Caroline van Eck, "Architecture, Language, and Rhetoric in Alberti's *De re aedificatoria*," in *Architecture and Language: Constructing Identity in European Architecture, c. 1000–c. 1650*, ed. Georgia Clarke and Paul Crossley (Cambridge: Cambridge University Press, 2000), p. 81.

9. Leon Battista Alberti, *On the Art of Building in Ten Books*, trans. Joseph Rykwert, Neil Leach, and Robert Tavernor (Cambridge, Mass.: MIT Press, 1988), p. 305 [9.v]. The "outline" is the ratio of the dimensions of an object—length, breadth, and width.

10. Filarete, *Filarete's Treatise on Architecture, Being the Treatise by Antonio di Piero Averlino, Known as Filarete*, trans. John R. Spencer (New Haven: Yale University Press, 1965), vol. 1, p. 16 [2, f. 8r].

11. Ibid., vol. 1, p. 5 [1, f. 2r].

12. John R. Spencer, introduction to *Treatise on Architecture*, by Filarete, vol. 1, p. xxii.

13. Anicus Manius Severinus Boethius, *Fundamentals of Music*, trans. Calvin M. Bower, ed. Claude V. Palisca (New Haven: Yale University Press, 1989), pp. 50–51.

14. Alberti, *On the Art of Building*, p. 3 [prologue].

15. Filarete, *Treatise on Architecture*, p. 198 [15, f. 113r]. Filarete then goes on to explain why the architect must know all these things (pp. 198–99).

16. Christine Smith argues that for Alberti the architect "may be raised to the status of [a] moral exemplar," as his activity "bridges the gap between the active and contemplative lives" (Christine Smith, *Architecture in the Culture of Early*

Humanism: Ethics, Aesthetics, and Eloquence, 1400–1470 [New York: Oxford University Press, 1992], p. 18).

17. Alberti, *On the Art of Building*, p. 5 (prologue).

18. Samuel Y. Edgerton Jr., *The Heritage of Giotto's Geometry: Art and Science on the Eve of the Scientific Revolution* (Ithaca: Cornell University Press, 1991), p. 16. The remainder of this paragraph is a very condensed summary of Edgerton's argument, particularly that found on pp. 16–22.

19. Joan Gadol, *Leon Battista Alberti: Universal Man of the Early Renaissance* (Chicago: University of Chicago Press, 1969), p. 180. See pp. 157–95 for an extended discussion of the change in cartography due to the change in the conceptualization of space, and the role that Alberti played in this change.

A P P E N D I X   2

1. For a discussion of breve equivalence in fifteenth-century music and fifteenth-century theoretical writing, see Anna Maria Busse Berger, *Mensuration and Proportion Signs: Origins and Evolution* (Oxford: Clarendon Press, 1993).

2. Bobby Wayne Cox, " 'Pseudo-augmentation' in the Manuscript Bologna, Civico Museo Bibliografico Musicale, Q 15 (BL)," *Journal of Musicology* 1, no. 4 (1982): 419–48.

3. Eunice Schroeder, "The Stroke Comes Full Circle: ₵ and ₵ in Writings on Music, ca. 1450–1540" *Musica disciplina* 36 (1982): 121.

4. John Caldwell, "Some Observations on the Four *Misure*," in *Terpsichore, 1450–1900: Proceedings of the International Dance Conference, Ghent, April 2000*, ed. Barbara Ravelhofer (Ghent: Institute for Historical Dance Practice, 2000), p. 10.

Bibliography

MANUSCRIPTS

Brussels, Bibliothèque Royale de Belgique, MS 9085.

Cornazano, Antonio. *Libro dell'arte del danzare.* Rome, Biblioteca Apostolica Vaticana, Codex Capponiano, 203.

Domenico da Piacenza. *De arte saltandj & choreas ducendj De la arte di ballare et danzare.* Paris, Bibliothèque Nationale, MS fonds it. 972.

Florence, Biblioteca Nazionale, Magl. VII 1121 and Magl. XIX 31.

Florence, Biblioteca Nazionale Centrale, Codex Palatini.

Foligno, Seminario Vescovile, Biblioteca Jacobilli, MS D.I.42.

Gresley of Drakelow papers. Derbyshire Record Office, D77 box 38, pp. 51–79.

(Guglielmo Ebreo). Modena, Biblioteca Estense, Codex Ital. 82, α. J. 94.

(Guglielmo Ebreo). Siena, Biblioteca Comunale, Codex L. V. 29.

Guglielmo Ebreo da Pesaro. *Domini Iohannis Ambrosii pisauriensis de pratica seu arte tripudii vulgare opusculum faeliciter incipit.* Paris, Bibliothèque Nationale, MS fonds it. 476.

Guglielmo Ebreo da Pesaro. *Ghuglielmi ebrei pisauriensis de praticha seu arte tripudi vulghare opusculum feliciter incipit.* New York, New York Public Library, Dance Collection, *MGZMB-Res. 72-254.

Guglielmo Ebreo da Pesaro. *Ghuglielmi hebraei pisauriensis De praticha seu arte tripudij vulghare opusculum feliciter incipit.* Florence, Biblioteca Nazionale Centrale, Codex Magliabecchiana-Strozziano XIX 88.

Guglielmo Ebreo da Pesaro. *Guilielmi Hebraei pisauriensis de pratica seu arte tripudii vulgare opusculum incipit.* 1463. Paris, Bibliothèque Nationale, MS fonds it. 973.

Guglielmo Ebreo da Pesaro. *Qui chominca elibro de bali Ghugliemus ebreis pisauriensis de praticha seu arte tipudi volghare opuschulum.* Florence, Biblioteca Medicea-Laurenziana, Codex Antinori, A13.

Nuremberg, Germanisches Nationalmuseum, MS 8842/GS 1589.

Il Papa, New York Public Library, *MGZMB-Res. 72-254.

PRINTED WORKS

Aiken, Jane Andrews. "Leon Battista Alberti's System of Human Proportions." *Journal of the Warburg and Courtauld Institutes* 43 (1980): 68–96.

Alberti, Leon Battista. *The Family in Renaissance Florence.* (Translation of *I libri della famiglia.*) Translated and with an introduction by Renée Neu Watkins. Columbia: University of South Carolina Press, 1969.

———. *On Painting.* (Translation of *De pictura.*) Edited and translated by Cecil Grayson, with an introduction and notes by Martin Kemp. London: Penguin, 1991.

———. *On Painting.* (Translation of *Della pittura.*) Translated by John R. Spencer. London: Routledge and Kegan Paul, 1956.

———. *On the Art of Building in Ten Books.* (Translation of *De re aedificatoria.*) Translated by Joseph Rykwert, Neil Leach, and Robert Tavernor. Cambridge, Mass.: MIT Press, 1988.

Alexander, Jonathan J. G. "Dancing in the Streets." *Journal of the Walters Art Gallery* 54 (1996): 147–62.

Alighieri, Dante. *The Divine Comedy.* Vol. 1, book 1, *Inferno.* Translated with commentary by Charles S. Singleton. London: Routledge and Kegan Paul, 1971.

———. *The Divine Comedy.* Vol. 3, book 1, *Paradiso.* Translated with commentary by Charles S. Singleton. Princeton: Princeton University Press, 1975.

———. *Purgatorio.* Verse translation by W. S. Merwin. New York: Knopf, 2000.

Altieri, Marco Antonio. *Li nuptiali di Marco Antonio Altieri.* Edited by Enrico Narducci. 1873. Reprint, Rome: Roma nel Rinascimento, 1995.

Ames-Lewis, Francis. *The Intellectual Life of the Early Renaissance Artist.* New Haven: Yale University Press, 2000.

Ames-Lewis, Francis, and Mary Rogers, eds. *Concepts of Beauty in Renaissance Art.* Aldershot: Ashgate, 1998.

Arbeau, Thoinot. *Orchesography.* 1589. Translated by Mary Stewart Evans, 1948. Reprint, with an introduction and notes by Julia Sutton, New York: Dover Publications, 1967.

Arcangeli, Alessandro. "Carnival in Medieval Sermons." *European Medieval Drama* 1 (1997): 199–209.

———. "Dance and Punishment." *Dance Research* 10, no. 2 (1992): 30–42.

———. "Dance under Trial: The Moral Debate, 1200–1600." *Dance Research* 12, no. 2 (1994): 127–55.

———. *Davide o Salomè? Il dibattito europeo sulla danza nella prima età moderna.* Rome: Viella, 2000.

Aristotle. *The Nicomachean Ethics.* Rev. ed. Translated by J. A. K. Thomson, revised by Hugh Tredennick. London: Penguin, 1976.

Ashbee, Andrew, ed. *Records of English Court Music, vol. 7, 1485–1558.* Aldershot: Scolar Press, 1993.

Baldassarri, Stefano U., and Arielle Saiber, eds. *Images of Quattrocento Florence: Selected Writings in Literature, History, and Art.* New Haven: Yale University Press, 2000.

Baron, Hans. *From Petrarch to Leonardo Bruni: Studies in Humanistic and Political Literature.* Chicago: University of Chicago Press, 1968.

Battista, Eugenio. "*Natura Artificiosa* to *Natura Artificialis.*" In *The Italian Garden,* edited by David R. Coffin, pp. 3–36. Washington, D.C.: Dumbarton Oaks, 1972.

Baxandall, Michael. *Giotto and the Orators: Humanist Observers of Painting in Italy and the Discovery of Pictorial Composition, 1350–1450.* Oxford: Clarendon Press, 1971.

———. *Painting and Experience in Fifteenth-Century Italy: A Primer in the Social History of Pictorial Style.* Oxford: Oxford University Press, 1972.

Berger, Anna Maria Busse. "Cut Signs in Fifteenth-Century Musical Practice." In *Music in Renaissance Cities and Courts: Studies in Honor of Lewis Lockwood,* edited by Jessie Ann Owens and Anthony M. Cummings, pp. 101–12. Warren, Mich.: Harmonie Park Press, 1997.

———. *Mensuration and Proportion Signs: Origins and Evolution.* Oxford: Clarendon Press, 1993.

———. "Musical Proportions and Arithmetic in the Late Middle Ages and Renaissance." *Musica disciplina* 44 (1990): 89–118.

———. "The Myth of *diminutio per tertiam partem.*" *Journal of Musicology* 8, no. 3 (1990): 398–426.

———. "The Origin and Early History of Proportion Signs." *Journal of the American Musicological Society* 41, no. 3 (1988): 403–33.

———. "The Relationship of Perfect and Imperfect Time in Italian Theory of the Renaissance." *Early Music History* 5 (1985): 1–28.

Berghaus, Günter. "Neoplatonic and Pythagorean Notions of World Harmony and Unity and Their Influence on Renaissance Dance Theory." *Dance Research* 10, no. 2 (1992): 43–70.

Bernheimer, Richard. *Wild Men in the Middle Ages: A Study in Art, Sentiment, and Demonology.* New York: Octagon Books, 1970.

Bisticci, Vespasiano da. *Le vite.* 2 vols. Edited by Aulo Greco. Florence: Istituto Nazionale di Studi sul Rinascimento, 1976.

Black, Robert. *Humanism and Education in Medieval and Renaissance Italy: Tradition and Innovation in Latin Schools from the Twelfth to the Fifteenth Century.* Cambridge: Cambridge University Press, 2001.

Boccaccio, Giovanni. *The Decameron.* 2 vols. Translated by J. M. Rigg. London: Dent, 1930.

Boethius, Anicius Manlius Severinus. *Fundamentals of Music.* (Translation of *De institutione musica.*) Translated and with an introduction by Calvin M. Bower, edited by Claude V. Palisca. New Haven: Yale University Press, 1989.

Borsi, Franco. *Leon Battista Alberti.* Translated by Rudolf G. Carpanini. New York: Harper and Row, 1977.

Boudon, Françoise. "Garden History and Cartography." In *The History of Garden Design: The Western Tradition from the Renaissance to the Present Day*, edited by Monique Mosser and Georges Teyssot, pp. 125–34. London: Thames and Hudson, 1991.

Bracciolini, Poggio. "On Nobility." In *Knowledge, Goodness, and Power: The Debate over Nobility among Quattrocento Italian Humanists*, translated, edited, and with an introduction by Albert Rabil Jr., pp. 63–89. Binghamton, N.Y.: Medieval and Renaissance Texts and Studies, 1991.

Brainard, Ingrid. "The Art of Courtly Dancing in Transition: Nurnberg, Germ. Nat. Mus. MS 8842, a Hitherto Unknown German Dance Source." In *Crossroads of Medieval Civilization: The City of Regensburg and Its Intellectual Milieu*, edited by Edelgard E. DuBruck and Karl Heinz Göller, pp. 61–79. Detroit: Michigan Consortium for Medieval and Early Modern Studies, 1984.

———. "An Exotic Court Dance and Dance Spectacle of the Renaissance: *La Moresca.*" In *Report of the Twelfth IMS Congress, Berkeley, 1977*, edited by Daniel Heartz and Bonnie Wade, pp. 715–29. Kassel: Barenreiter, 1981.

———. "Mesura et arte del danzare: The Guglielmo Ebreo Conference at Pesaro, July 1987." *Dance Chronicle* 11, no. 1 (1988): 116–20.

———. "Pattern, Imagery, and Drama in the Choreographic Work of Domenico da Piacenza." In *Guglielmo Ebreo da Pesaro e la danza nelle corti italiane del xv secolo*, edited by Maurizio Padovan, pp. 85–96. Pisa: Pacini, 1990.

———. "The Role of the Dancing Master in Fifteenth-Century Courtly Society." *Fifteenth-Century Studies* 2 (1979): 21–44.

———. "Sir John Davies' *Orchestra* as a Dance Historical Source." In *Songs of the Dove and the Nightingale: Sacred and Secular Music, c. 900–c. 1600*, edited by Greta Mary Hair and Robyn E. Smith, pp. 176–212. Sydney: Currency Press, 1994.

Bremmer, Jan, and Herman Roodenburg, eds. *A Cultural History of Gesture from Antiquity to the Present Day.* Cambridge: Polity Press, 1991.

Bridgeman, Jane. "Ambrogio Lorenzetti's Dancing 'Maidens': A Case of Mistaken Identity." *Apollo* 133, no. 350 (1991): 245–51.

Brown, Alison. *The Medici in Florence: The Exercise and Language of Power.* Perth: University of Western Australia Press; Florence: Olschki, 1992.

Brown, Howard Mayer. "A Cook's Tour of Ferrara in 1529." *Rivista italiana di musicologia* 10 (1975): 216–41.

Brown, Richard Gordon. "The Politics of Magnificence in Ferrara, 1450–1505." Ph.D. diss., University of Edinburgh, 1982.

Brucker, Gene. "Florentine Voices from the *Catasto*, 1427–1480." *I Tatti Studies: Essays in the Renaissance* 5 (1993): 11–32.

———, ed. *Two Memoirs of Renaissance Florence: The Diaries of Buonaccorso Pitti and Gregorio Dati.* Translated by Julia Martines. Prospect Heights, Ill.: Waveland Press, 1991.

Bruni, Leonardo. "Comparison of Dante and Petrarch." In *The Three Crowns of Florence: Humanist Assessments of Dante, Petrarca, and Boccaccio,* edited and translated by David Thompson and Alan F. Nagel, pp. 81–83. New York: Harper and Row, 1972.

———. "De studiis et litteris liber." In *Educazione umanistica in Italia,* edited and translated by Eugenio Garin, pp. 35–44. 9th edition. Rome: Laterza, 1975.

———. *The History of the Florentine People.* Vol. 1. Edited and translated by James Hankins. Cambridge, Mass.: Harvard University Press, 2001.

———. *The Humanism of Leonardo Bruni: Selected Texts.* Translations and introductions by Gordon Griffiths, James Hankins, and David Thompson. Binghamton, N.Y.: Medieval and Renaissance Texts and Studies, 1987.

———. "Life of Dante." In *The Three Crowns of Florence: Humanist Assessments of Dante, Petrarca, and Boccaccio,* edited and translated by David Thompson and Alan F. Nagel, pp. 57–73. New York: Harper and Row, 1972.

———. "Panegyric to the City of Florence." In *The Earthly Republic: Italian Humanists on Government and Society,* edited and translated by Benjamin G. Kohl and Ronald G. Witt, pp. 135–75. Manchester: Manchester University Press, 1978.

———. "Selected Letters of Leonardo Bruni." Translated by Alissa Rubin. *Allegorica* 6, no. 1 (1981): 21–63.

Bryce, Judith. "Performing for Strangers: Women, Dance, and Music in Quattrocento Florence." *Renaissance Quarterly* 54, no. 4.1 (2001): 1074–1107.

Burke, Peter. *The Art of Conversation.* Cambridge: Polity Press, 1993.

———. *The European Renaissance: Centres and Peripheries.* Oxford: Blackwell, 1998.

———. *The Fortunes of the* Courtier: *The European Reception of Castiglione's* Cortegiano. Cambridge: Polity Press, 1995.

———. *The Historical Anthropology of Early Modern Italy: Essays on Perception and Communication.* Cambridge: Cambridge University Press, 1987.

———. "The Uses of Italy." In *The Renaissance in National Context,* edited by Roy Porter and Mikuláš Teich, pp. 6–20. Cambridge: Cambridge University Press, 1992.

———. *Varieties of Cultural History.* Cambridge: Polity Press, 1997.

Caldwell, John. "The *De institutione arithmetica* and the *De institutione musica.*" In *Boethius: His Life, Thought, and Influence,* edited by Margaret Gibson, pp. 135–54. Oxford: Blackwell, 1981.

———. "Some Observations on the Four *Misure.*" In *Terpsichore, 1450–1900: Proceedings of the International Dance Conference, Ghent, April 2000,* edited by Barbara Ravelhofer, pp. 9–10. Ghent: Institute for Historical Dance Practice, 2000.

———. "Two Polyphonic *istampite* from the 14th Century." *Early Music* 18, no. 3 (1990): 371–80.

Caplan, Harry. "Memoria: Treasure-House of Eloquence." In *Of Eloquence: Studies in Ancient and Mediaeval Rhetoric,* by Harry Caplan, edited by Anne King and Helen North, pp. 196–246. Ithaca: Cornell University Press, 1970.

Caroso, Fabritio. *Il ballarino.* Venice, 1581. Facsimile edition, New York: Broude Brothers, 1967.

———. *Nobiltà di dame.* Venice, 1600. Facsimile edition, Bologna: Forni, 1980.

Carpeggiani, Paolo. "Labyrinths in the Gardens of the Renaissance." In *The History of Garden Design: The Western Tradition from the Renaissance to the Present Day,* edited by Monique Mosser and Georges Teyssot, pp. 84–87. London: Thames and Hudson, 1991.

Carruthers, Mary J. *The Book of Memory: A Study of Memory in Medieval Culture.* Cambridge: Cambridge University Press, 1990.

Carter, Françoise. "Celestial Dance: A Search for Perfection." *Dance Research* 5, no. 2 (1987): 3–17.

———. "Dance as a Moral Exercise." In *Guglielmo Ebreo da Pesaro e la danza nelle corti italiane del xv secolo,* edited by Maurizio Padovan, pp. 169–79. Pisa: Pacini, 1990.

———. "Number Symbolism and Renaissance Choreography." *Dance Research* 10, no. 1 (1992): 21–39.

Carter, Henry Holland. *A Dictionary of Middle English Musical Terms.* 1961. Reprint, New York: Kraus Reprint Corporation, 1968.

Casini-Ropa, Eugenia. "Il banchetto di Bergonzio Botta per le nozze di Isabella d'Aragona e Gian Galeazzo Sforza nel 1489: Quando la storiografia si sostituisce alla storia." In *Spettacoli conviviali dall'antichità classica alle corti italiane del'400: Atti del convegno di Viterbo, 1982,* pp. 291–306. Viterbo: Centro di studi sul teatro medioevale e rinascimentale, 1982.

Castelli, Patrizia. "La kermesse degli Sforza pesaresi." In *Mesura et arte del danzare,* edited by Patrizia Castelli, Maurizio Mingardi, and Maurizio Padovan, pp. 13–33. Pesaro: Pucelle, 1987.

———. "Il moto aristotelico e la 'licita scienta': Guglielmo Ebreo e la speculazione sulla danza nel xv secolo." In *Mesura et arte del danzare,* edited by Patrizia Castelli, Maurizio Mingardi, and Maurizio Padovan, pp. 35–57. Pesaro: Pucelle, 1987.

———. " 'Quella città che vedete è Roma': Scena e illusione alla corte dei Montefeltro." In *Federico di Montefeltro: Lo stato, le arti, la cultura,* vol. 2, *Le arti,* edited by Giorgio Cerboni Baiardi, Giorgio Chittolini, and Piero Floriani, pp. 331–48. Rome: Bulzoni, 1986.

Castelli, Patrizia, Maurizio Mingardi, and Maurizio Padovan, eds. *Mesura et arte del danzare.* Pesaro: Pucelle, 1987.

Castiglione, Baldesdar. *The Book of the Courtier.* Translated by George Bull. Harmondsworth: Penguin, 1981.

Cazzola, Gabriele. " 'Bentivoli machinatores': Aspetti politici e momenti teatrali di una festa quattrocentesca bolognese." *Biblioteca teatrale* 23–24 (1979): 14–38.

Celi, Claudia. "I balli del cardinale Riario: Tra memoria del teatro e teatro della memoria." *Danza italiana* 3 (1985): 91–102.

———. " 'Talhor tacere un tempo e starlo morto' . . . il moto in potenza e in atto." In *Guglielmo Ebreo da Pesaro e la danza nelle corti italiane del xv secolo,* edited by Maurizio Padovan, pp. 153–58. Pisa: Pacini, 1990.

Ciappelli, Giovanni. *Carnevale e quaresima: Comportamenti sociali e cultura a Firenze nel Rinascimento.* Rome: Edizioni di Storia e Letteratura, 1997.

[Cicero]. *Ad C. Herennium: De ratione dicendi (Rhetorica ad herennium).* With an English translation by Harry Caplan. London: Heinemann, 1954.

Cicero, Marcus Tullius. *Cicero on the Ideal Orator.* (Translation of *De oratore.*) Translated with an introduction and notes by James M. May and Jakob Wisse. New York: Oxford University Press, 2001.

———. *De inventione; De optimo genere oratorum; Topica.* With an English translation by H. M. Hubbell. London: Heinemann, 1949.

Clarke, Georgia, and Paul Crossley, eds. *Architecture and Language: Constructing Identity in European Architecture, c. 1000–c. 1650.* Cambridge: Cambridge University Press, 2000.

Clough, Cecil H. Review of *De practica seu arte tripudii: On the Practice or Art of Dancing,* by Guglielmo Ebreo da Pesaro, edited and translated by Barbara Sparti. *Renaissance Studies* 11, no. 3 (1997): 241–69.

Coffin, David R. *Gardens and Gardening in Papal Rome.* Princeton: Princeton University Press, 1991.

———. "The 'Lex Hortorum' and Access to Gardens of Latium during the Renaissance." *Journal of Garden History* 2, no. 3 (1982): 201–32.

Comito, Terry. "The Humanist Garden." In *The History of Garden Design: The Western Tradition from the Renaissance to the Present Day,* edited by Monique Mosser and Georges Teyssot, pp. 37–46. London: Thames and Hudson, 1991.

———. *The Idea of the Garden in the Renaissance.* Hassocks, Sussex: Harvester Press, 1979.

Corazza, Bartolommeo di Michele del. *Diario Fiorentino, anni 1405–1438.* In *Archivio storico italiano,* 5th series, vol. 14 (Florence, 1894): 240–98.

Cornford, Francis MacDonald. *Plato's Cosmology: The* Timaeus *of Plato Translated with a Running Commentary.* London: Routledge and Kegan Paul, 1948.

Cox, Bobby Wayne. " 'Pseudo-augmentation' in the Manuscript Bologna, Civico Museo Bibliografico Musicale, Q 15 (BL)." *Journal of Musicology* 1, no. 4 (1982): 419–48.

Crane, Frederick. *Materials for the Study of the Fifteenth-Century Basse Danse.* New York: Institute of Mediæval Music, 1968.

Cruciani, Fabrizio. "Per lo studio del teatro rinascimentale: La festa." *Biblioteca Teatrale* 5 (1972): 1–16.

———. "Il teatro e la festa." In *Il teatro italiano nel Rinascimento,* edited by Fabrizio Cruciani and Daniele Seragnoli, pp. 31–52. Bologna: Il Mulino, 1987.

———. *Teatro nel Rinascimento: Roma, 1450–1550.* Rome: Bulzoni, 1983.

Cruciani, Fabrizio, and Daniele Seragnoli, eds. *Il teatro italiano nel Rinascimento.* Bologna: Il Mulino, 1987.

Cruickshank, Diana. "Doppii suxo uno piede or Contrapassi in Quadernaria Misura." *Historical Dance* 3, no. 1 (1992): 11–13.

———. " 'E poi se piglieno per mano'—A Brief Study of Hand-Holds in 15th- and 16th-Century Portraits." *Historical Dance* 2, no. 5 (1986–87): 17–19.

———. "The Passo Doppio in 15th-Century Balli and Basse Danze: Some Possibilities of Interpretation." In *Dance and Research: An Interdisciplinary Approach,* edited by Clairette Brack and Irina Wuyts, pp. 29–39. Louvain: Peeters Press, 1991.

———. "Rooted in the Renaissance: A Study of Basic Step Structure and Its Development from Early Renaissance Manuscripts to the Early Baroque Period." In *On Common Ground (Proceedings of D.H.D.S. Conference, 24 February 1996),* pp. 68–77. Dolmetsch Historical Dance Society, 1996.

D'Accone, Frank A. *The Civic Muse: Music and Musicians in Siena during the Middle Ages and the Renaissance.* Chicago: University of Chicago Press, 1997.

———. "Lorenzo the Magnificent and Music." In *Lorenzo il magnifico e il suo mondo,* edited by Gian Carlo Garfagnini, pp. 259–90. Florence: Olschki, 1994.

Daniels, Véronique, and Eugen Dombois. "Die Temporelationen im Ballo des Quattrocento." *Basler Jahrbuch für historische Musikpraxis* 14 (1990): 181–247.

Davies, Sir John. *Orchestra, or A Poem of Dancing.* 1594. Edited by E. M. W. Tillyard. London: Chatto and Windus, 1945.

Daye, Anne. "Towards a Choreographic Description of the Fifteenth-Century Italian Bassa Danza." In *Guglielmo Ebreo da Pesaro e la danza nelle corti italiane del xv secolo,* edited by Maurizio Padovan, pp. 97–110. Pisa: Pacini, 1990.

De Marinis, Tammaro, ed. *Le nozze di Costanzo Sforza e Camilla d'Aragona celebrate a Pesaro nel maggio 1475.* Florence, 1946.

Diario Ferrarese dall'anno 1409 sino al 1502 di autori incerti. Edited by Giuseppe Pardi. In *Rerum italicarum scriptores* 24, part 7 (1928): 1–368.

Earp, Lawrence. "Genre in the Fourteenth-Century French Chanson: The Virelai and the Dance Song." *Musica disciplina* 45 (1991): 123–41.

Eco, Umberto. *Beauty in the Middle Ages.* Translated by Hugh Bredin. New Haven: Yale University Press, 1986.

Edgerton, Samuel Y., Jr. *The Heritage of Giotto's Geometry: Art and Science on the Eve of the Scientific Revolution.* Ithaca: Cornell University Press, 1991.

Elias, Norbett. *The Court Society.* Translated by Edmund Jephcott. Oxford: Blackwell, 1983.

Elyot, Thomas. *The Book Named the Governor.* 1531. Edited with an introduction by S. E. Lehmberg. London: Dent, 1962.

Falletti, Clelia. "Le feste per Eleonora d'Aragona da Napoli a Ferrara (1473)." In *Spettacoli conviviali dall'antichità classica alle corti italiane del'400: Atti del convegno di Viterbo, 1982,* pp. 269–89. Viterbo: Centro di studi sul teatro medioevale e rinascimentale, 1982.

Fallows, David. "The Gresley Dance Collection, *c.* 1500." *RMA Research Chronicle* 29 (1996): 1–20.

———. *Songs and Musicians in the Fifteenth Century.* Aldershot: Variorum, 1996.

Farenga, P. "Cornazano." In *Dizionario biografico degli Italiani.* Vol. 29. Rome: Istituto della Enciclopedia Italiana, 1983, pp. 123–32.

Fermor, Sharon. "Movement and Gender in Sixteenth-Century Italian Painting." In *The Body Imaged: The Human Form and Visual Culture since the Renaissance,* edited by Kathleen Adler and Marcia Pointon, pp. 129–45. Cambridge: Cambridge University Press, 1993.

———. "On the Question of Pictorial 'Evidence' for Fifteenth-Century Dance Technique." *Dance Research* 5, no. 2 (1987): 18–32.

———. "Poetry in Motion: Beauty in Movement and the Renaissance Concept of Leggiadria." In *Concepts of Beauty in Renaissance Art,* edited by Francis Ames-Lewis and Mary Rogers, pp. 124–33. Aldershot: Ashgate, 1998.

———. "Studies in the Depiction of the Moving Figure in Italian Renaissance Art, Art Criticism, and Dance Theory." Ph.D. diss., Warburg Institute, University of London, 1990.

Ferrari-Barassi, Elena. "La tradizione della Moresca e uno sconosciuto ballo del Cinque-Seicento." In *La moresca nell'area mediterranea,* edited by Roberto Lorenzetti, pp. 55–78. Bologna: Forni, 1991.

Field, Arthur. *The Origins of the Platonic Academy of Florence.* Princeton: Princeton University Press, 1988.

Filarete (Antonio di Piero Averlino). *Filarete's Treatise on Architecture, Being the*

Treatise by Antonio di Piero Averlino, Known as Filarete. Translated with an introduction and notes by John R. Spencer. 2 vols. New Haven: Yale University Press, 1965.

Florio, John. *A Worlde of Wordes.* 1598. Facsimile edition, Hildesheim: George Olms, 1972.

Forrest, John. *The History of Morris Dancing, 1458–1750.* Toronto: University of Toronto Press, 1999.

Francalanci, Andrea. "The 'Copia di M° Giorgio e del giudeo di ballare basse danze e balletti' As Found in the New York Public Library." *Basler Jahrbuch für historische Musikpraxis* 14 (1990): 87–179.

———. "La ricostruzione delle danze del'400 italiano attraverso un metodo di studio comparato della fonti." *Danza italiana* 3 (1985): 55–76.

Franko, Mark. *The Dancing Body in Renaissance Choreography (c. 1416–1589).* Birmingham, Ala.: Summa Publications, 1986.

———. "The Notion of 'Fantasmata' in Fifteenth-Century Italian Dance Treatises." *Dance Research Annual* 16 (1987): 68–86.

———. "Renaissance Conduct Literature and the Basse Danse: The Kinesis of Grace." In *Persons in Groups: Social Behavior as Identity Formation in Medieval and Renaissance Europe*, edited by Richard C. Trexler, pp. 55–66. Binghamton, N.Y.: Medieval and Renaissance Texts and Studies, 1985.

Frick, Carole Collier. *Dressing Renaissance Florence: Families, Fortunes, and Fine Clothing.* Baltimore: Johns Hopkins University Press, 2002.

Frugoni, Chiara. *A Distant City: Images of Urban Experience in the Medieval World.* Translated by William McCuaig. Princeton: Princeton University Press, 1991.

Gadol, Joan. *Leon Battista Alberti: Universal Man of the Early Renaissance.* Chicago: University of Chicago Press, 1969.

Galli, Quirino. "Una danzografia in un protocollo notarile a Montefiascone nella seconda metà del xv secolo." In *Arte e accademia: Ricerche studi attività '89*, pp. 121–43. Viterbo: Accademia di Belle Arti "Lorenzo da Viterbo," 1989.

Gallo, F. Alberto. "L'autobiografia artistica di Giovanni Ambrosio (Guglielmo Ebreo) da Pesaro." *Studi musicali* 12, no. 2 (1983): 189–202.

———. "Il 'ballare lombardo' (circa 1435–1475)." *Studi musicali* 8 (1979): 61–84.

———. "La danza negli spettacoli conviviali del secondo quattrocento." In *Spettacoli conviviali dall'antichità classica alle corti italiane del'400: Atti del convegno di Viterbo, 1982*, pp. 261–67. Viterbo: Centro di studi sul teatro medioevale e rinascimentale, 1982.

Gargiulo, Piero. " 'Leggiadri passi con intellecto attento': Lorenzo teorico di basse danze." In *La musica a Firenze al tempo di Lorenzo il magnifico*, edited by Piero Gargiulo, pp. 249–55. Florence: Olschki, 1993.

———, ed. *La danza italiana tra Cinque e Seicento: Studi per Fabrizio Caroso da Sermoneta.* Rome: Bardi, 1997.

Garin, Eugenio, ed. and trans. *Educazione umanistica in Italia.* 9th edition. Rome: Laterza, 1975.

Ghiberti, Lorenzo. *Lorenzo Ghibertis Denkwürdigkeiten (I commentari).* Edited by Julius von Schlosser. Berlin: J. Bard, 1912. Quoted in *Giotto and the Orators: Humanist Observers of Painting in Italy and the Discovery of Pictorial Composition, 1350–1450*, by Michael Baxandall (Oxford: Clarendon Press, 1971), p. 16 n. 22.

Gibson, Margaret, ed. *Boethius: His Life, Thought, and Influence.* Oxford: Blackwell, 1981.

Gillies, John. *Shakespeare and the Geography of Difference.* Cambridge: Cambridge University Press, 1994.

Grafton, Anthony. *Leon Battista Alberti: Master Builder of the Italian Renaissance.* London: Penguin, 2002.

Grafton, Anthony, and Lisa Jardine. *From Humanism to the Humanities: Education and the Liberal Arts in Fifteenth- and Sixteenth-Century Europe.* Cambridge, Mass.: Harvard University Press, 1986.

Gray, Hanna H. "Renaissance Humanism: The Pursuit of Eloquence." *Journal of the History of Ideas* 24 (1963): 497–514.

Grendler, Paul F. *The Universities of the Italian Renaissance.* Baltimore: Johns Hopkins University Press, 2002.

Guglielmo Ebreo da Pesaro. *De pratica seu arte tripudii: On the Practice or Art of Dancing.* Edited and translated by Barbara Sparti. Oxford: Clarendon Press, 1993.

Guidobaldi, Nicoletta. *La musica di Federico: Immagini e suoni alla corte di Urbino.* Florence: Olschki, 1995.

Gundersheimer, Werner L. "Clarity and Ambiguity in Renaissance Gesture: The Case of Borso d'Este." *Journal of Medieval and Renaissance Studies* 23, no. 1 (1993): 1–17.

———. "Popular Spectacle and the Theatre in Renaissance Ferrara." In *Il teatro italiano del Rinascimento*, edited by Maristella de Panizza Lorch, pp. 25–33. Milan: Edizioni de Comunità, 1980.

———, ed. *Art and Life at the Court of Ercole I d'Este: The* De triumphis religionis *of Giovanni Sabadino degli Arienti.* Geneva: Librairie Droz, 1972.

Guthrie, John, and Marino Zorzi, trans. "Rules of Dancing: Antonius Arena." *Dance Research* 4, no. 2 (1986): 3–53.

Hanawalt, Barbara A., and Kathryn L. Reyerson, eds. *City and Spectacle in Medieval Europe.* Minneapolis: University of Minnesota Press, 1994.

Hankins, James. "The 'Baron Thesis' after Forty Years and Some Recent Studies of Leonardo Bruni." *Journal of the History of Ideas* 56, no. 2 (1995): 309–38.

———. "Lorenzo de' Medici as a Patron of Philosophy." *Rinascimento* 34 (1994): 15–35.

———. *Plato in the Italian Renaissance.* 2 vols. Leiden: E. J. Brill, 1990.

———, ed. *Renaissance Civic Humanism: Reappraisals and Reflections.* Cambridge: Cambridge University Press, 2000.

Harding, Ann. *An Investigation into the Use and Meaning of Medieval German Dancing Terms.* Göppingen: Alfred Kümmerle, 1973.

Hart, Vaughan, with Peter Hicks, eds. *Paper Palaces: The Rise of the Renaissance Architectural Treatise.* New Haven: Yale University Press, 1998.

Hazard, Mary E. *Elizabethan Silent Language.* Lincoln: University of Nebraska Press, 2000.

Heartz, Daniel. "The Basse Dance: Its Evolution circa 1450 to 1550." *Annales musicologiques* 6 (1958–63): 287–340.

———. "A 15th-Century Ballo: Rôti Bouilli Joyeux." In *Aspects of Medieval and Renaissance Music*, edited by Jan LaRue, pp. 359–75. New York: Pendragon Press, 1966.

Heninger, S. K., Jr. *The Cosmographical Glass: Renaissance Diagrams of the Universe.* San Marino, Calif.: The Huntington Library, 1977.

———. *Touches of Sweet Harmony: Pythagorean Cosmology and Renaissance Poetics.* San Marino, Calif.: The Huntington Library, 1974.

Hersey, G. L. *Pythagorean Palaces: Magic and Architecture in the Italian Renaissance.* Ithaca: Cornell University Press, 1976.

Hollingsworth, Mary. "The Architect in Fifteenth-Century Florence." *Art History* 7, no. 4 (1984): 385–410.

Holman, Peter. *Four and Twenty Fiddlers: The Violin at the English Court, 1540–1690.* Oxford: Clarendon Press, 1993.

Horowitz, Jeannine. "Les danses cléricales dans les églises au Moyen Age." *Le Moyen Age: Revue d'histoire et de philologie* 95, no. 2 (1989): 279–92.

Hunt, John Dixon, ed. *The Italian Garden: Art, Design, and Culture.* Cambridge: Cambridge University Press, 1996.

Jacks, Philip, and William Caferro. *The Spinelli of Florence: Fortunes of a Renaissance Merchant Family.* University Park: Pennsylvania State University Press, 2000.

Jardine, Lisa. *Worldly Goods: A New History of the Renaissance.* London: Macmillan, 1996.

Kaeuper, Richard W., and Elspeth Kennedy. *The* Book of Chivalry *of Geoffroi de Charny: Text, Context, and Translation.* Philadelphia: University of Pennsylvania Press, 1996.

Kemp, Martin. Introduction to *De pictura* (On painting), by Leon Battista Alberti, edited and translated by Cecil Grayson, pp. 1–29. London: Penguin, 1991.

King, Margaret L. *Venetian Humanism in an Age of Patrician Dominance.* Princeton: Princeton University Press, 1986.

Klapisch-Zuber, Christiane. "Le chiavi fiorentine di Barbablù: L'apprendimento della lettura a Firenze nel xv secolo." *Quaderni storici* 57, no. 3 (1984): 765–92.

————. *Women, Family, and Ritual in Renaissance Italy.* Translated by Lydia G. Cochrane. Chicago: University of Chicago Press, 1985.

Kohl, Benjamin G., and Ronald G. Witt, eds. and trans. *The Earthly Republic: Italian Humanists on Government and Society.* Manchester: Manchester University Press, 1978.

Kolsky, Stephen. "Graceful Performances: The Social and Political Context of Music and Dance in the *Cortegiano*." *Italian Studies* 53 (1998): 1–19.

Kraye, Jill, ed. *The Cambridge Companion to Renaissance Humanism.* Cambridge: Cambridge University Press, 1996.

Kristeller, Paul Oskar. *Renaissance Thought.* Vol. 2, *Papers on Humanism and the Arts.* New York: Harper and Row, 1965.

————. *Renaissance Thought and Its Sources.* Edited by Michael Mooney. New York: Columbia University Press, 1979.

Landino, Cristoforo. "Commentary on the Commedia." In *The Three Crowns of Florence: Humanist Assessments of Dante, Petrarca, and Boccaccio,* edited and translated by David Thompson and Alan F. Nagel, pp. 110–31. New York: Harper and Row, 1972.

————. "On True Nobility." In *Knowledge, Goodness, and Power: The Debate over Nobility among Quattrocento Italian Humanists,* edited, translated, and with an introduction by Albert Rabil Jr., pp. 190–260. Binghamton, N.Y.: Medieval and Renaissance Texts and Studies, 1991.

Lazzaro, Claudia. *The Italian Renaissance Garden: From the Conventions of Planting, Design, and Ornament to the Grand Gardens of Sixteenth-Century Central Italy.* New Haven: Yale University Press, 1990.

Liber de spiritu et anima. In *Patrologiae cursus completus . . . Series latina.* Vol. 40. Edited by J.-P. Migne, pp. 779–831. Paris, 1887.

Lo Monaco, Lauro, and Sergio Vinciguerra. "Il passo doppio in Guglielmo e Domenico: Problemi di mensurazione." In *Guglielmo Ebreo da Pesaro e la danza nelle corti italiane del xv secolo,* edited by Maurizio Padovan, pp. 127–36. Pisa: Pacini, 1990.

Lockwood, Lewis. "Music and Popular Religious Spectacle at Ferrara under Ercole I d'Este." In *Il teatro italiano del Rinascimento,* edited by Maristella de Panizza Lorch, pp. 571–82. Milan: Edizioni de Comunità, 1980.

————. *Music in Renaissance Ferrara, 1400–1505: The Creation of a Musical Centre in the Fifteenth Century.* Oxford: Clarendon Press, 1984.

————. "Pietrobono and the Instrumental Tradition at Ferrara in the Fifteenth Century." *Rivista italiana di musicologia* 10 (1975): 115–33.

Lorenzetti, Roberto, ed. *La moresca nell'area mediterranea.* Bologna: Forni, 1991.

Lubkin, Gregory. *A Renaissance Court: Milan under Galeazzo Maria Sforza.* Berkeley: University of California Press, 1994.

Luzio, Alessandro, and Rodolfo Renier. *Mantova e Urbino: Isabella d'Este e Elisabetta Gonzaga.* 1893. Reprint, Bologna: Forni, 1976. Quoted in Patrizia Castelli, " 'Quella città che vedete è Roma': Scena e illusione alla corte dei Montefeltro," in *Federico di Montefeltro: Lo stato, le arti, la cultura,* vol. 2, *Le arti,* ed. Giorgio Cerboni Baiardi, Giorgio Chittolini, and Piero Floriani (Rome: Bulzoni, 1986), pp. 335–36.

Maniates, Maria Rika. *Mannerism in Italian Music and Culture, 1530–1630.* Chapel Hill: University of North Carolina Press, 1979.

Mann, Nicholas. "The Origins of Humanism." In *The Cambridge Companion to Renaissance Humanism,* edited by Jill Kraye, pp. 1–19. Cambridge: Cambridge University Press, 1996.

Marimón, J. M. Madurell. *Mensajeros barceloneses en la corte de Nápoles de Alfonso V de Aragon, 1435–1458.* Barcelona, 1963.

Marrocco, W. Thomas, and Maire-Laure Merveille. "Antonius Arena: Master of Law and Dance of the Renaissance." *Studi musicali* 18, no. 1 (1989): 19–48.

Marsuppini, Carlo. "Poem on Nobility." In *Knowledge, Goodness, and Power: The Debate over Nobility among Quattrocento Italian Humanists,* edited, translated, and with an introduction by Albert Rabil Jr., pp. 102–109. Binghamton, N.Y.: Medieval and Renaissance Texts and Studies, 1991.

Martin, John. "Inventing Sincerity, Refashioning Prudence: The Discovery of the Individual in Renaissance Europe." *American Historical Review* 102, no. 5 (1997): 1309–42.

Martines, Lauro. *Power and Imagination: City-States in Renaissance Italy.* London: Allen Lane, 1980.

————. "The Protean Face of Renaissance Humanism." *Modern Language Quarterly* 51, no. 2 (1990): 105–21.

————. *The Social World of the Florentine Humanists, 1390–1460.* London: Routledge and Kegan Paul, 1963.

————. *Strong Words: Writing and Social Strain in the Italian Renaissance.* Baltimore: Johns Hopkins University Press, 2001.

Mas i Garcia, Carles. "Baixa Dansa in the Kingdom of Catalonia and Aragon in the 15th Century." *Historical Dance* 3, no. 1 (1992): 15–23.

Maynard, Susan W. "Dance in the Arts of the Middle Ages." Ph.D. diss., Florida State University, 1992.

McGee, Timothy J. "*Dança amorosa:* A Newly-Discovered Medieval Dance Pair." In *Beyond the Moon: Festschrift Luther Dittmer,* edited by Bryan Gillingham and Paul Merkley, pp. 295–306. Ottawa: The Institute of Mediaeval Music, 1990.

————. "Dancing Masters and the Medici Court in the 15th Century." *Studi musicali* 17, no. 2 (1988): 201–24.

————. "Dinner Music for the Florentine Signoria, 1350–1450." *Speculum* 74, no. 1 (1999): 95–114.

————. "Giovanni Cellini, piffero di Firenze." *Rivista italiana di musicologia* 32, no. 2 (1997): 201–21.

————. "Medieval Dances: Matching the Repertory with Grocheio's Descriptions." *Journal of Musicology* 7, no. 4 (1989): 498–517.

————. *Medieval Instrumental Dances.* Bloomington: Indiana University Press, 1989.

————. "Misleading Iconography: The Case of the 'Adimari Wedding Cassone.' " *Imago Musicae* 11–12 (1992–95): 139–57.

————, ed. *Improvisation in the Arts of the Middle Ages and the Renaissance.* Kalamazoo: The Medieval Institute, 2003.

McGinnis, Katherine Tucker. "Moving in High Circles: Courts, Dance, and Dancing Masters in Italy in the Long Sixteenth Century." Ph.D. diss., University of North Carolina, 2001.

Merkley, Paul A., and Lora L. M. Merkley. *Music and Patronage in the Sforza Court.* Turnhout: Brepols, 1999.

Michel, Artur. "The Earliest Dance-Manuals." *Medievalia et humanistica* 3 (1945): 117–31.

Miller, James L. *Measures of Wisdom: The Cosmic Dance in Classical and Christian Antiquity.* Toronto: University of Toronto Press, 1986.

————. "The Philosophical Background of Renaissance Dance." *York Dance Review,* no. 5 (1976): 3–15.

Milner, Christine. "The Pattern of the Dance in Ambrogio Lorenzetti's Peaceful City." *Bullettino senese di storia patria* 99 (1994): 232–48.

Mingardi, Maurizio. "Gli strumenti musicali nella danza del xiv e xv secolo." In *Mesura et arte del danzare,* edited by Patrizia Castelli, Maurizio Mingardi, and Maurizio Padovan, pp. 113–55. Pesaro: Pucelle, 1987.

Mitchell, Bonner. "Les intermèdes au service de l'état." In *Les fêtes de la renaissance,* vol. 3, edited by Jean Jacquot, pp. 117–31. Paris: Editions du Centre National de la Recherche Scientifique, 1975.

————. *The Majesty of the State: Triumphal Progresses of Foreign Sovereigns in Renaissance Italy (1494–1600).* Florence: Olschki, 1986.

————. "The Triumphal Entry as a Theatrical Genre in the Cinquecento." *Forum italicum* 14, no. 3 (1980): 409–25.

Mosser, Monique, and Georges Teyssot, eds. *The History of Garden Design: The Western Tradition from the Renaissance to the Present Day.* London: Thames and Hudson, 1991.

Moyer, Ann E. *Musica Scientia: Musical Scholarship in the Italian Renaissance.* Ithaca: Cornell University Press, 1992.

Mullally, Robert. "Cançon de carole." *Acta musicologica* 58, no. 2 (1986): 224–31.

————. "Dance Terminology in the Works of Machaut and Froissart." *Medium ævum* 59, no. 2 (1990): 248–59.

————. "The Editions of Antonius Arena's *Ad Suos Compagnones Studiantes.*" *Gutenberg-Jahrbuch* (1979): 146–57.

————. "Houes Danses." *Neophilologus* 76, no. 1 (1992): 29–34.

————. "Johannes de Grocheo's 'Musica Vulgaris.' " *Music and Letters* 79, no. 1 (1998): 1–26.

Murphy, James J. *Rhetoric in the Middle Ages: A History of Rhetorical Theory from St. Augustine to the Renaissance.* Berkeley: University of California Press, 1974.

————, ed. *Medieval Eloquence: Studies in the Theory and Practice of Medieval Rhetoric.* Berkeley: University of California Press, 1978.

————, ed. *Renaissance Eloquence: Studies in the Theory and Practice of Renaissance Rhetoric.* Berkeley: University of California Press, 1983.

Negri, Cesare. *Le gratie d'amore.* Milan, 1602. Facsimile edition, New York: Broude Brothers, 1969.

Nelson, Joel Stanislaus. Introduction to *Aeneae Silvii: De liberorum educatione,* by Pope Pius II (Aeneas Silvius Piccolomini), edited and translated by Joel Stanislaus Nelson, pp. 3–84. Washington, D.C.: Catholic University of America Press, 1940.

Nevile, Jennifer. " 'Certain Sweet Movements': The Development of the Concept of Grace in 15th-Century Italian Dance and Painting." *Dance Research* 9, no. 1 (1991): 3–12.

———. "The Courtly Dance Manuscripts from Fifteenth-Century Italy." Ph.D. diss., University of New South Wales, 1992.

———. "Dance and Identity in Fifteenth-Century Europe." In "The Partnership of Music and Dance: Essays in Musicology and Dance History," edited by Anne Buckley and Cynthia Cyrus. Unpublished manuscript.

———. "Dance and the Garden: Moving and Static Choreography in Renaissance Europe." *Renaissance Quarterly* 52, no. 3 (1999): 805–36.

———. "Dance in Early Tudor England: An Italian Connection?" *Early Music* 26, no. 2 (1998): 230–44.

———. "Dance Steps and Music in the Gresley Manuscript." *Historical Dance* 3, no. 6 (1999): 2–19.

———. "Disorder in Order: Improvisation in Italian Choreographed Dances of the Fifteenth and Sixteenth Centuries." In *Improvisation in the Arts of the Middle Ages and the Renaissance*, edited by Timothy J. McGee, pp. 145–69. Kalamazoo: The Medieval Institute, 2003.

———. "The Four *Misure* in Fifteenth-Century Italian Dance." In *Terpsichore, 1450–1900: Proceedings of the International Dance Conference, Ghent, April 2000*, edited by Barbara Ravelhofer, pp. 1–6. Ghent: Institute for Historical Dance Practice, 2000.

———. "National Characteristics in Fifteenth-Century Dance: An English Exemplar." In *Proceedings of the Society of Dance History Scholars Annual Conference, June 1998*, compiled by Linda J. Tomko, pp. 21–27. Society of Dance History Scholars, 1998.

———. "The Platonic Theory of Ethos in Fifteenth-Century Italian Court Dance." *Literature and Aesthetics* 3 (1993): 42–54.

Nocilli, Cecilia. "Dance in Naples: Relations between the Aragonese Court and the Neapolitan Barons (1442–1502)." In *Proceedings of the Society of Dance History Scholars Annual Conference, June 2002*, compiled by Stephanie Rieke, pp. 90–95. Society of Dance History Scholars, 2002.

Nowaczek, Jadwiga. "The Misery with the *Misure*—A Practical Approach." In *Terpsichore, 1450–1900: Proceedings of the International Dance Conference, Ghent, April 2000*, edited by Barbara Ravelhofer, pp. 7–8. Ghent: Institute for Historical Dance Practice, 2000.

Onians, John. "Alberti and ΦΙΛΑΡΕΤΗ: A Study in Their Sources." *Journal of the Warburg and Courtauld Institutes* 34 (1971): 96–114.

Owens, Jessie Ann, and Anthony M. Cummings, eds. *Music in Renaissance Cities and Courts: Studies in Honor of Lewis Lockwood*. Warren, Mich.: Harmonie Park Press, 1997.

Padovan, Maurizio. "Da Dante a Leonardo: La danza italiana attraverso le fonti storiche." *Danza italiana* 3 (1985): 5–37.

———. "La danza nelle corti italiane del xv secolo: Arte figurativa e fonti storiche." In *Mesura et arte del danzare*, edited by Patrizia Castelli, Maurizio Mingardi, and Maurizio Padovan, pp. 59–111. Pesaro: Pucelle, 1987.

———, ed. *La danza in europa fra Rinascimento e Barocco*. Rome: Associazione italiana per la musica e la danza antiche, 1995.

———, ed. *Guglielmo Ebreo da Pesaro e la danza nelle corti italiane del xv secolo*. Pisa: Pacini, 1990.

Page, Christopher. *The Owl and the Nightingale: Musical Life and Ideas in France, 1100–1300.* Berkeley: University of California Press, 1989.

———. *Voices and Instruments of the Middle Ages: Instrumental Practice and Songs in France, 1100–1300.* Berkeley: University of California Press, 1986.

Palisca, Claude V. *Humanism in Italian Renaissance Musical Thought.* New Haven: Yale University Press, 1985.

Palmieri, Matteo. *Vita civile.* Edited by Gino Belloni. Florence: Sansoni, 1982.

Parenti, Marco. *Lettere.* Edited by Maria Marrese. Florence: Olschki, 1996.

Payne, Alina A. *The Architectural Treatise in the Italian Renaissance: Architectural Invention, Ornament, and Literary Culture.* Cambridge: Cambridge University Press, 1999.

Percival, W. Keith. "Grammar and Rhetoric in the Renaissance." In *Renaissance Eloquence: Studies in the Theory and Practice of Renaissance Rhetoric,* edited by James J. Murphy, pp. 303–30. Berkeley: University of California Press, 1983.

Pisan, Christine de. *The Treasure of the City of Ladies, or, The Book of the Three Virtues.* Translated with an introduction by Sarah Lawson. London: Penguin, 1985.

Pius II, Pope (Aeneas Silvius Piccolomini). *Aeneae Silvii: De liberorum educatione.* Edited and translated by Joel Stanislaus Nelson. Washington, D.C.: Catholic University of America Press, 1940.

Platina (Bartolomeo Sacchi). "On True Nobility." In *Knowledge, Goodness, and Power: The Debate over Nobility among Quattrocento Italian Humanists,* edited and translated with an introduction by Albert Rabil Jr., pp. 269–98. Binghamton, N.Y.: Medieval and Renaissance Texts and Studies, 1991.

Plato. *Timaeus.* In *The Collected Dialogues of Plato, Including the Letters,* edited by Edith Hamilton and Huntington Cairns, pp. 1151–1211. Princeton: Princeton University Press, 1963.

Polk, Keith. "Foreign and Domestic in Italian Instrumental Music of the Fifteenth Century." In *Musica Franca: Essays in Honor of Frank A. D'Accone,* edited by Irene Alm, Alyson McLamore, and Colleen Reardon, pp. 323–32. Stuyvesant, N.Y.: Pendragon Press, 1996.

———. *German Instrumental Music of the Late Middle Ages: Players, Patrons, and Performance Practice.* Cambridge: Cambridge University Press, 1992.

Pontremoli, Alessandro, and Patrizia La Rocca. *Il ballare lombardo: Teoria e prassi coreutica nella festa di corte del xv secolo.* Milan: Vita e Pensiero, 1987.

———. *La danza a Venezia nel Rinascimento.* Vicenza: Neri Pozza, 1993.

Premoli, Beatrice. "Note iconografiche a proposito di alcune moresche del Rinascimento italiano." In *La moresca nell'area mediterranea,* edited by Roberto Lorenzetti, pp. 43–53. Bologna: Forni, 1991.

Prizer, William F. "Games of Venus: Secular Vocal Music in the Late Quattrocento and Early Cinquecento." *Journal of Musicology* 9, no. 1 (1991): 3–56.

Puppi, Lionello. "Nature and Artifice in the Sixteenth-Century Italian Garden." In *The History of Garden Design: The Western Tradition from the Renaissance to the Present Day,* edited by Monique Mosser and Georges Teyssot, pp. 47–58. London: Thames and Hudson, 1991.

———. "The Villa Garden of the Veneto from the Fifteenth to the Eighteenth Century." In *The Italian Garden,* edited by David R. Coffin, pp. 83–114. Washington, D.C.: Dumbarton Oaks, 1972.

Quintilian, Marcus Fabius. *The Institutio oratoria of Quintilian.* 4 vols. With an English translation by H. E. Butler. London: Heinemann, 1920–22.

Rabil, Albert, Jr., ed. *Renaissance Humanism: Foundations, Forms, and Legacy.* 3 vols. Philadelphia: University of Pennsylvania Press, 1988.

————, ed. and trans. *Knowledge, Goodness, and Power: The Debate over Nobility among Quattrocento Italian Humanists*. Binghamton, N.Y.: Medieval and Renaissance Texts and Studies, 1991.

Rebhorn, Wayne A., ed. and trans. *Renaissance Debates on Rhetoric*. Ithaca: Cornell University Press, 2000.

Robey, David. "Humanism and Education in the Early Quattrocento: The *De ingenuis moribus* of P. P. Vergerio." *Bibliothèque d'humanisme et renaissance* 42, no. 1 (1980): 27–58.

Rosenberg, Charles M. "The Use of Celebrations in Public and Semi-public Affairs in Fifteenth-Century Ferrara." In *Il teatro italiano del Rinascimento*, edited by Maristella de Panizza Lorch, pp. 521–36. Milan: Edizioni de Comunità, 1980.

Ross, James Bruce, and Mary Martin McLaughlin, eds. *The Portable Renaissance Reader*. New York: Viking Press, 1953.

Rossi, Vittorio. *Un ballo a Firenze nel 1459*. Bergamo: Istituto Italiano d'Arti Grafiche, 1895.

Ruiz, Teofilo F. "Elite and Popular Culture in Late Fifteenth-Century Castilian Festivals: The Case of Jaén." In *City and Spectacle in Medieval Europe*, edited by Barbara A. Hanawalt and Kathryn L. Reyerson, pp. 296–318. Minneapolis: University of Minnesota Press, 1994.

————. "Festivités, couleurs, et symboles du pouvoir en Castille au XVe siècle: Les célébrations de mai 1428." *Annales: Economies, sociétés, civilisations* 3 (1991): 521–46.

Ryder, Alan. *Alfonso the Magnanimous: King of Aragon, Naples, and Sicily, 1396–1458*. Oxford: Clarendon Press, 1990.

Rygg, Krystin. *Masked Mysteries Unmasked: Early Modern Music Theatre and Its Pyphagorean [sic] Subtext*. Hillsdale, N.Y.: Pendragon Press, 2000.

Rykwert, Joseph. "Theory as Rhetoric: Leon Battista Alberti in Theory and in Practice." In *Paper Palaces: The Rise of the Renaissance Architectural Treatise*, edited by Vaughan Hart with Peter Hicks, pp. 33–50. New Haven: Yale University Press, 1998.

Saalman, H. "Early Renaissance Architectural Theory and Practice in Antonio Filarete's *Trattato di architettura*." *Art Bulletin* 41 (1959): pp. 89–106.

Salmen, Walter. "The Muse Terpsichore in Pictures and Text from the 14th to 18th Centuries." *Music in Art* 23, nos. 1–2 (1998): 79–85.

Salutati, Colucio. "In Quest of Dante." In *The Three Crowns of Florence: Humanist Assessments of Dante, Petrarca, and Boccaccio*, edited and translated by David Thompson and Alan F. Nagel, pp. 14–15. New York: Harper and Row, 1972.

Schmitt, Jean-Claude. "The Ethics of Gesture." In *Fragments for a History of the Human Body*, edited by Michel Feher, Ramona Naddaff, and Nadia Tazi, vol. 2, pp. 128–47. New York: Zone, 1989.

Schroeder, Eunice. "The Stroke Comes Full Circle: ⊕ and ∢ in Writings on Music, ca. 1450–1540." *Musica disciplina* 36 (1982): 119–66.

S'ensuit l'art et l'instruction de bien dancer. Paris: Michel Toulouze, n.d. Facsimile edition, Geneva: Minkoff, 1985.

Seznec, Jean. *The Survival of the Pagan Gods: The Mythological Tradition and Its Place in Renaissance Humanism and Art*. Translated by Barbara F. Sessions. New York: Princeton University Press, 1953.

Smarr, Janet Levarie. "The Pyramid and the Circle: Ovid's 'Banquet of Sense.'" *Philological Quarterly* 63, no. 3 (1984): 369–86.

Smith, A. William. "Una fonte sconosciuta della danza italiana del quattrocento." In *Guglielmo Ebreo da Pesaro e la danza nelle corti italiane del xv secolo*, edited by Maurizio Padovan, pp. 71–84. Pisa: Pacini, 1990.

————. "References to Dance in Fifteenth-Century Italian *Sacre Rappresentazioni*." *Dance Research Journal* 23, no. 1 (1991): 17–24.

————, trans. *Fifteenth-Century Dance and Music: Twelve Transcribed Italian Treatises and Collections in the Tradition of Domencio da Piacenza*. Stuyvesant, N.Y.: Pendragon Press, 1995.

Smith, Christine. *Architecture in the Culture of Early Humanism: Ethics, Aesthetics, and Eloquence, 1400–1470*. New York: Oxford University Press, 1992.

Southern, Eileen. "A Prima Ballerina of the Fifteenth Century." In *Music and Context: Essays for John M. Ward*, edited by Anne Dhu Shapiro, pp. 183–97. Cambridge, Mass.: Department of Music, Harvard University, 1985.

Sparti, Barbara. "Antiquity as Inspiration in the Renaissance of Dance: The Classical Connection and Fifteenth-Century Italian Dance." *Dance Chronicle* 16, no. 3 (1993): 373–90.

————. "Breaking Down Barriers in the Study of Renaissance and Baroque Dance." *Dance Chronicle* 19, no. 3 (1996): 255–76.

————. "Dance Not Only as Text: Getting the Full(er) Picture of Dance in Renaissance and Baroque Italy (c. 1455–1650)." In *Proceedings of the 22nd Society of Dance History Scholars Annual Conference (10–13 June)*, compiled by Juliette Willis, pp. 195–206. Society of Dance History Scholars, 1999.

————. "Dancing Couples behind the Scenes: Recently Discovered Italian Illustrations, 1470–1550." *Imago Musicae* 13 (1996): 9–38.

————. "Improvisation and Embellishment in Popular and Art Dances in Fifteenth- and Sixteenth-Century Italy." In *Improvisation in the Arts of the Middle Ages and the Renaissance*, edited by Timothy J. McGee, pp. 117–44. Kalamazoo: The Medieval Institute, 2003.

————. Introduction to *De pratica seu arte tripudii: On the Practice or Art of Dancing*, by Guglielmo Ebreo da Pesaro, edited and translated by Barbara Sparti, pp. 3–72. Oxford: Clarendon Press, 1993.

————. "Jewish Dancing-Masters and 'Jewish Dance' in Renaissance Italy (Guglielmo Ebreo and beyond)." *Jewish Folklore and Ethnology Review* 20 (2000): 11–23.

————. "Rôti Bouilli: Take Two 'el gioioso fiorito.' " *Studi musicali* 24, no. 2 (1995): 231–61.

————. "Stile, espressione, e senso teatrale nelle danze italiane del '400." *Danza italiana* 3 (1985): 39–53.

————. "Would You Like to Dance This Frottola? Choreographic Concordances in Two Early Sixteenth-Century Tuscan Sources." *Musica disciplina* 50 (1996): 135–65.

Spencer, John R. Introduction to *Filarete's Treatise on Architecture*, by Filarete, translated by John R. Spencer, vol. 1, pp. xvii–xxxvii. New Haven: Yale University Press, 1965.

Stanley, Eric. "Dance, Dancers, and Dancing in Anglo-Saxon England." *Dance Research* 9, no. 2 (1991): 18–31.

Steintz, Kate. "The Voyage of Isabella D'Aragon from Naples to Milan, January 1489." *Bibliothèque d'humanisme et renaissance* 23 (1961): 17–32.

Stevens, John. *Words and Music in the Middle Ages: Song, Narrative, Dance, and Drama, 1050–1350*. Cambridge: Cambridge University Press, 1986.

Strong, Roy. *Art and Power: Renaissance Festivals, 1450–1650*. Woodbridge: The Boydell Press, 1984.

————. *The Renaissance Garden in England*. London: Thames and Hudson, 1979.

Strozzi, Alessandra. *The Selected Letters of Alessandra Strozzi*. Translated with an introduction by Heather Gregory. Berkeley: University of California Press, 1997.

Thesiger, Sarah. "The *Orchestra* of Sir John Davies and the Image of the Dance." *Journal of the Warburg and Courtauld Institutes* 36 (1973): 277–304.

Thompson, David, and Alan F. Nagel, eds. and trans. *The Three Crowns of Florence: Humanist Assessments of Dante, Petrarca, and Boccaccio.* New York: Harper and Row, 1972.

Tomasi, Lucia Tongiorgi. "Botanical Gardens of the Sixteenth and Seventeenth Centuries." In *The History of Garden Design: The Western Tradition from the Renaissance to the Present Day,* edited by Monique Mosser and Georges Teyssot, pp. 81–83. London: Thames and Hudson, 1991.

Trexler, Richard C. "Florentine Theatre, 1280–1500: A Checklist of Performances and Institutions." *Forum italicum* 14, no. 3 (1980): 454–75.

———. *Public Life in Renaissance Florence.* Ithaca: Cornell University Press, 1991.

———, ed. *The Libro Ceremoniale of the Florentine Republic,* by Francesco Filarete and Angelo Manfidi. Geneva: Librairie Droz, 1978.

Trinkaus, Charles. *The Scope of Renaissance Humanism.* Ann Arbor: University of Michigan Press, 1983.

van Eck, Caroline. "Architecture, Language, and Rhetoric in Alberti's *De re aedificatoria.*" In *Architecture and Language: Constructing Identity in European Architecture, c. 1000–c. 1650,* edited by Georgia Clarke and Paul Crossley, pp. 72–81. Cambridge: Cambridge University Press, 2000.

Venturi, Gianni. "The *Giardino Segreto* of the Renaissance." In *The History of Garden Design: The Western Tradition from the Renaissance to the Present Day,* edited by Monique Mosser and Georges Teyssot, pp. 88–90. London: Thames and Hudson, 1991.

———. "Scena e giardini a Ferrara." In *Il Rinascimento nelle corti padane: Società e cultura.* Bari: Di Donato, 1977, pp. 553–67.

Vergerio, Pier Paolo. "De ingenuis moribus." In *Educazione umanistica in Italia,* edited and translated by Eugenio Garin, pp. 69–119. 9th edition. Rome: Laterza, 1975.

Veronese, Alessandra. "Una *societas* ebraico-cristiano in *docendo tripudiare sonare ac cantare* nella Firenze del quattrocento." In *Guglielmo Ebreo da Pesaro e la danza nelle corti italiane del xv secolo,* edited by Maurizio Padovan, pp. 51–57. Pisa: Pacini, 1990.

Vigarello, Georges. "The Upward Training of the Body from the Age of Chivalry to Courtly Civility." In *Fragments for a History of the Human Body,* edited by Michel Feher, Ramona Naddaff, and Nadia Tazi, vol. 2, pp. 148–99. New York: Zone, 1989.

Volpi, Guglielmo. *Le feste di Firenze del 1459: Notizia di un poemetto del secolo xv.* Pistoia, 1902.

Ward, John O. *Ciceronian Rhetoric in Treatise, Scholion, and Commentary.* Turnhout, Belgium: Brepols, 1995.

———. "From Antiquity to the Renaissance: Glosses and Commentaries on Cicero's *Rhetorica.*" In *Medieval Eloquence: Studies in the Theory and Practice of Medieval Rhetoric,* edited by James J. Murphy, pp. 25–67. Berkeley: University of California Press, 1978.

———. "Renaissance Commentators on Ciceronian Rhetoric." In *Renaissance Eloquence: Studies in the Theory and Practice of Renaissance Rhetoric,* edited by James J. Murphy, pp. 126–73. Berkeley: University of California Press, 1983.

Watkins, Renée Neu, ed. and trans. *Humanism and Liberty: Writings on Freedom from Fifteenth-Century Florence.* Columbia: University of South Carolina Press, 1978.

Welch, Evelyn S. "Sight, Sound, and Ceremony in the Chapel of Galeazzo Maria Sforza." *Early Music History* 12 (1993): 151–90.

Westfall, Carroll William. *In This Most Perfect Paradise: Alberti, Nicholas V, and the Invention of Conscious Urban Planning in Rome, 1447–55.* University Park: Pennsylvania State University Press, 1974.

———. "Society, Beauty, and the Humanist Architect in Alberti's *De re aedficatoria.*" *Studies in the Renaissance* 16 (1969): 61–79.

White, Alison. "Boethius in the Medieval Quadrivium." In *Boethius: His Life, Thought, and Influence,* edited by Margaret Gibson, pp. 162–205. Oxford: Blackwell, 1981.

White, Hayden. *Tropics of Discourse: Essays in Cultural Criticism.* Baltimore: Johns Hopkins University Press, 1978.

Wilentz, Sean, ed. *Rites of Power: Symbolism, Ritual, and Politics since the Middle Ages.* Philadelphia: University of Pennsylvania Press, 1985.

Wilson, David R. "The Art of Transcription: A Discussion of the Issues in Transcribing Using Fifteenth-Century Italian Texts." In *On Common Ground: Proceedings of the Dolmetsch Historical Dance Society Conference, 24th February 1996,* edited by David Parsons, pp. 30–37. Salisbury, Wiltshire: Dolmetsch Historical Dance Society, 1996.

———. "The Development of the French Basse Danse." *Historical Dance* 2, no. 4 (1984–85): 5–12.

———. " 'Finita: et larifaccino unaltra uolta dachapo.' " *Historical Dance* 3, no. 2 (1993): 21–26.

———. " 'La Giloxia'/'Gelosia' As Described by Domencio and Guglielmo." *Historical Dance* 3, no. 1 (1992): 3–9.

———. *101 Italian Dances (c. 1450–c. 1510): A Critical Translation.* Cambridge: Early Dance Circle, 1999.

———. Review of *The 'Copia di M° Giorgio el del guideo di ballare basse danze e balletti' As Found in the New York Public Library,* by Andrea Francalanci. *Historical Dance* 3, no. 1 (1992): 32.

———. *The Steps Used in Court Dancing in Fifteenth-Century Italy.* Cambridge: Published by the author, 1992.

———. "Theory and Practice in 15th-Century French Basse Danse." *Historical Dance* 2, no. 3 (1983): 1–2.

Wilson, David R., and Véronique Daniels. "The Basse Dance Handbook." Unpublished manuscript.

Witt, Ronald G. "Civic Humanism and the Rebirth of the Ciceronian Oration." *Modern Language Quarterly* 51, no. 2 (1990): 167–84.

———. *In the Footsteps of the Ancients: The Origins of Humanism from Lovato to Bruni.* Leiden: E. J. Brill, 2000.

Wittkower, Rudolf. *Architectural Principles in the Age of Humanism.* 4th edition. London: Academy Editions, 1988.

Woods-Marsden, Joanna. *Renaissance Self-Portraiture: The Visual Construction of Identity and the Social Status of the Artist.* New Haven: Yale University Press, 1998.

Woodward, William Harrison. *Vittorino da Feltre and Other Humanist Educators.* New York: Bureau of Publications, Teachers College, Columbia University, 1963.

Yates, Frances A. *The Art of Memory.* 1966. Reprint, London: Pimlico, 1992.

Zambotti, Bernardino. *Diario Ferrarese dall'anno 1476 sino al 1504.* Edited by Giuseppe Pardi. In vol. 24, part 7 of *Rerum italicarum scriptores,* ed. Lodovico Antonio Muratori, revised by Giosue Carducci and Vittorio Fiorini (Bologna, 1928), pp. 1–501.

Index

Jennifer Nevile has a Ph.D. in musicology from the University of New South Wales. She has published many articles in early music, history, and dance journals, including *Early Music* and *Renaissance Quarterly*. She is currently an Honorary Research Fellow in the School of Music and Music Education at UNSW.